…erson or persons have for

made divers kinds of noises

by Mrs Ricketts att

…e notis that if any person

…uther or authers thereof

…hall Receive a reward

on the Conviction of the

…cerned in Makeing such Noises

…mplice or acomplices

…rdoned and be intitled to

…onviction of the offenders

Sainsbury   marclands

Sep^t 20th 1771

NELSON'S DEAR LORD

NELSON'S DEAR LORD

A Portrait of St. Vincent

BY

EVELYN BERCKMAN

LONDON
MACMILLAN & CO LTD
1962

MACMILLAN AND COMPANY LIMITED
St Martin's Street London WC 2
also Bombay Calcutta Madras Melbourne

THE MACMILLAN COMPANY OF CANADA LIMITED
Toronto

ST MARTIN'S PRESS INC
New York

PRINTED IN GREAT BRITAIN

FOR
RUPERT GUNNIS
A SMALL RETURN

ACKNOWLEDGMENTS

My most grateful thanks are due Lieutenant-Commander P. V. Kemp, Archivist of the Admiralty Library, who for four years has interested himself in my search for material and who — over another fourteen months — has read each chapter of this book as it was completed, saving me from such landlubber's errors as raise the smile, all too readily, among those versed in maritime language and affairs.

Mr. David Leggatt, Chief Librarian of Greenwich Central Library, has put me endlessly in his debt by his brilliant suggestion that I consult the Minute Books of the Directors of the Greenwich Royal Hospital. The sight of these was, for me, the first opening of a door on the real eighteenth century, and a first transfusion of life into a mass of material up to that time lifeless.

Mr. E. K. Timings, Assistant Keeper of the Round Room at the Public Record Office, along with tireless and generous assistance, has kept me in a state of awe at his power of conjuring up material from the obscurest corners of recorded history, in a building crammed to the roof with a thousand years of it. Incidentally he believes that the lawsuit between St. Vincent and Nelson has been consulted and read for the first time, so far as he knows.

As for other meetings and adventures, who could have foretold that the search for Baird would lead to Baird's silver watch ticking away on a mantel-piece only four miles distant, in the home of his great-great-nephew General Sir William MacArthur, himself a surgeon but a military not a naval one ? Or that Mary Ricketts, not to be traced in any catalogue, would materialize through a happy accident of recollection on the part of her great-great-grand-daughter-in-law, Mrs. Douglas Ramsay of London ?

With all my heart I thank these friends, and all others, for their help. Their knowledge and kindness have shed light on what otherwise would have been a hard and unillumined, perhaps an impossible, path.

Without Mr. Michael Robinson, Keeper of the Print Room at the National Maritime Museum, who indicated to me the whereabouts of pictures and miniatures not only in family or private hands but largely unknown, I could never have found the superb Stuart or Reynolds portraits or the Baird minia-ture. I offer Mr. Robinson my thanks, as also the owners of these treasures who permitted me to use them.

The unfinished Gilbert Stuart portrait has never before been published.

The likeness of Nelson — published in a book for the first time — is the 'lost' Abbott portrait, its whereabouts obscure for the past hundred and sixty years, until 1961, 'when it appeared at Christie's blackened and dirty. Bought by a West End dealer, cleaning and restoration revealed the treasure, a genuine Abbott (1760–1803)'.

Through the generous interest of the Reverend C. A. Harris, Vicar of St. Michael's at Stone, I was able to find Martha Lady St. Vincent at St. Peter's Church at Caverswall, whose Vicar, Mr. A. V. Yates, found for me the register with the entry of her burial. To these friends I offer my sense of their kindness and my gratitude.

The Cosway miniature of Mary Ricketts was run to earth through a newspaper advertisement, and the likeness of Henry Jervis comes from family souvenirs in the British Museum.

Note : In quoted passages, *Italics* are the original writer's, SMALL CAPITALS the author's ; round brackets the original writer's, matter in square brackets the author's.

CONTENTS

ILLUSTRATIONS

ILLUSTRATIONS

BEGINNINGS OF AN ADMIRAL

THE boy John was fitted so conspicuously and exclusively for the profession he followed that it seems natural to call him Admiral from the very beginning, as if he had been born into the world complete with gold lace, epaulets and Star of the Bath. His actual entrance — considerably less spectacular — was into the family of a barrister-at-law named Swynfen Jervis. This man, who had a various if undistinguished career, has retreated so far into the shadows that it is a little difficult to persuade him to come a few steps forward and allow himself to be scrutinized in detail. Yet this scrutiny might be worth enough to pay its own way, for two reasons: first because his nature impelled him to do his son a curious ill-turn which has been commended in print as 'wise' parental discipline. It remains to be seen whether his action should be denoted by such a term, or by one much less creditable ; whether, in fact, Swynfen were capable of wisdom or discipline for himself or others, or even of anything that can be dignified by the name of commonsense. The second reason is less immediate. Behind every great effect stand causes, rank upon rank, diminishing into distance always more and more remote until forgotten or untraceable — and it may be that in the person of this unknown lawyer, the father of John Jervis, we have one of the earliest contributing factors toward the career of Horatio Nelson, still not to be born for a quarter of a century.

'My father', John said when an old man, dictating in his breakfast parlour to Edward Brenton, who wanted to write a

life of him, 'had a very large family, with limited means.'
But why *very large family* ? Swynfen's progeny, on examination, breaks down into two sons and two daughters, four
children never having been regarded as a number extravagantly
rabbitlike in that or any other age. Perhaps John retained
some hazy impression that his father was saddled with other
dependents, but by later evidence quite the opposite is true,
and in any case Swynfen was the man to make short work of
relations, however near or necessitous, asking for financial
relief. So if the statement *very large family* may be taken with
reservations, the next phrase, *of limited means*, might also come
under question or attempted analysis.

What are limited means ? What is poverty ? Poverty,
now a word of endless inflections, in the eighteenth century
was pent within much stricter boundaries ; it meant simply
the man who had no bread and no shirt and no roof and who
was never likely to have them, a stratum of society far removed
from gentlefolk. John Jervis, when still a boy, had experience
of actual bare-boned poverty, hard as the decks he slept on —
but throughout his life he seems to have believed that his
plight was due to his father's lack of money. But by luck we
are able to take a closer look at Swynfen's finances than was
possible to John, three thousand miles away, and we are free
to entertain our own view of Swynfen's 'limited means'.
Nor does he seem the kind of man to have confided his income
— in money or its equivalent — even to his wife, since it will
appear that she used poor peoples' shifts in dressing her children, such as would ordinarily have offended the pride of a
woman of her class. During the hazards of shame and desti-
tution to which John's father abandoned him, the chances of
the boy's not surviving at all were at least even.

'He was solicitor and counsel to the Admiralty,' John
continues, still speaking to Brenton, 'and Treasurer of Greenwich Hospital.' But John left home for good when he was
twelve, so that any impression of his father's career must have
been conveyed to him by Swynfen himself, who evidently

made his association with the Admiralty and the Hospital sound successful and important. To find out just to what extent his account of himself accorded with the facts — how successful he really was, and how important — might also illumine the character of this man who invited shipwreck into his son's life and has been rather patted on the head for it than otherwise.

Swynfen's earliest law practice was in Staffordshire (where John was born in 1735), but even at that distance from London he had attracted the eye of exalted authority as early as 1745, when he was instrumental in catching one Mr. Morgan 'and the papers found upon him'. Morgan in other words was a spy, one of the floating fragments thrown up after the last, bloodiest effort to bring a Stuart back to the throne of England. No less a person than the Duke of Newcastle congratulates Swynfen for his part in the arrest, conveys to him direct the thanks of the King, then goes on to instruct Swynfen 'to talk to Mr. Morgan in such manner as may induce him to make a full discovery of everything he knows', and in the course of this beguilement Swynfen is to give Morgan to understand, but not directly, that he will escape punishment for his treason if he will turn in his confederates. Perhaps the Admiralty solicitorship was part of Swynfen's reward, for his service in this capacity begins at about the same time as the Newcastle letter, which is dated December 10th, 1745. The solicitorship being the first of the scanty biographical details offered by his son, let us look at its first.

CASE

A Lad 15 years of age having been lately kill'd on Board of His Majesties Ship the Devonshire by another Lad of the age of 13½.

Whether such Lad by reason of his tender years can be tried by a Court Martial.

Mr. Jervis's Opinion : *I conceive that an Infant tho' under 14 years of age may be tried in this case by a Court Martial, by virtue of the Ct^s (?) 13th & 14th, Chap. 49, if on the High Seas*

*or within the Jurysdixion of the Admiralty the Fact were committed,
but whether such Infant go guilty of Murder or not depends on circumstances and instances of Dyscretion at or after the Fact committed* [that is, whether the boy seemed to display responsibility before or after the murder] *as under the age of 14
an Infant is not presumed to have Dyscretion.*

Jervis's own dry voice and strange penmanship, hairy as
an armadillo, tiny, tight and contorted, full of involved capitals almost impossible to decipher ; a secretive handwriting,
one might say, and his opinion never so forthright that he
cannot retreat from it in case of need. From the pages that
passed under the eyes of this dry ingrown man, over two
hundred years ago, there glare forth for one moment, out of
an old darkness, violences of shipboard life Hogarthian in
their ferocity and ugliness.[1]   One of the earliest of these
opinions is dated from the Middle Temple, April 13th, 1749 ;
he is now established in London. But his residence is in
Greenwich, fifteen miles away on the river, and this is
important.

Returning to his Admiralty solicitorship, however, the
remarkable thing about it — the one remarkable thing — is
the scarceness of his name in its documents. English ships
sailed all the waters of the world and anchored in every port ;
the troubles and legal complications arising from this enormous
traffic were endless, and all these thousands of cases involving
ships and cargo had to be referred direct to the Courts of
Admiralty. Yet they gave Swynfen almost nothing to do ;
other solicitors' names appear on page after page of fat dockets,
while his is found not one time in twenty. Why was this ?
incapacity on his part ? the demands of his private practice ?
prejudice against him, aroused by his own personality ? Whatever the cause, he fades early from the scene, again sliding into
the shadows and baffling observation. This elusiveness we
will see duplicated so exactly later in his life that it may be

---

[1] For another of Swynfen's cases, see Appendix I.

ascribed to him, without unfairness, as a trait of his character. But to sum up : his last Admiralty opinion was dated August 4th, 1750, so he was with them only three years and they gave him next to no employment, a record one can hardly call brilliant.

So much for Swynfen's 'Admiralty solicitorship'. Next in order of examination might come the second biographical item supplied by his son John : his career as 'Treasurer of Greenwich Hospital'. It is in this capacity that he emerges much more clearly into the light, since — by fantastic luck — he left behind him a trail of actions and even characteristics singularly well-defined and singularly unattractive, a series of vital clues to himself. The people who impelled him to show his worst side so frequently were the Board of Directors of Greenwich Royal Hospital. Since his association with them lasted for nine years, it may not be irrelevant to consider them in some detail.

* * *

The Royal Hospital at Greenwich was founded in 1696 by private subscription, the deceased King Charles II having headed the list with a donation of £2000. An enormous gesture of humanity for a period in which destitute old age was abandoned to what end it might find in stray holes, alleys and almshouses, the Hospital was first and last meant to provide a home for the homeless, shelter for the shelterless, care and nursing for the disabled and helpless, remembrance for the forgotten. And if over the centuries its practice was sometimes under fire, yet there was never any question about the integrity of its first and original purpose — never more nobly stated than in a regulation Minute of a Directors' meeting of July 23rd, 1748 : 'As a great number of His Majesties ships will soon be paid off, and among the discharged seamen there will be probably a great number so worn out and past their labour as to be proper objects for the charity of Greenwich Hospital,' these men 'will have a RIGHT to be received into

B

the Hospital, and desiring the Directors to consider what part
of the Hospital can be immediately fitted up to receive them.'

To open one of the stiff shabby covers, broken from its
spine, of the big journals that contain the Directors' Minutes
of Greenwich Royal Hospital, is to swing the door wide on a
busy world long vanished, creating by its very nature one of
the worst pitfalls to the pursuer of a single thread named
Swynfen Jervis ; there is hardly a page but offers lures to decoy
the imagination down sidewindings and around corners. The
charmed eye is first taken with an entry dated October 3rd,
1747 : 'A Petition from Mr. Bridges the Bug-Killer was
read and rejected'. On this peremptory and cryptic note Mr.
Bridges vanishes with the shadow of misfortune over him,
and is no more seen — for the moment. Then on November
14th, 1747 : 'Order'd : that the Materials of the house called
the Naked Boy be advertised to be sold'. Vainly the mind
hovers about such a name for a house. Was it from a statue
or a frieze ? Was it the sign of an inn ? The Naked Boy will
remain mysterious while the Bug-Killer will be elucidated ;
all a matter of luck what one finds. The pages swarm with
doctors and apothecaries, agents, gardeners, nurses and truss-
makers and cooks, tradesmen who supplied the Hospital ;
clock-makers and masons pass in review, organ-builders and
organists. This stream of people, and the torrent of their
troubles and complications, inundated the Board of Directors
without let-up or relief.

The Board itself — kept up to a specified number when
death or resignation caused vacancies — met in theory every
'sennit', but in practice the Directors came together as often
as the welfare of the Hospital required, sometimes only
three days after the regular meeting. Their attendance varied ;
never fewer than eight were present, and never more than
sixteen, the larger number usually turning up when important money-matters were to be discussed, and their conduct of
the Hospital's affairs testifies eloquently as to the sort of men
they were : able, certainly ; thorough and patient, with a con-

sistent generosity of outlook. No detail was too large for them to scan, none was too niggling, petty or tiresome. They heard everybody's point of view before arriving at a decision, and their intention was single-minded and manifest — to give to each person as much justice and satisfaction as was humanly possible, regardless of the petitioner's rank in respect of goods or worldly position. Also — and this is important in view of later developments — they were energetic and, above all, prompt. Any business brought up at one meeting was almost certain to be disposed of at the next, and understandably ; it was their only means of insuring that they were not swamped by the ocean of detail that heaved about them on all sides.

The first of their preoccupations was, of course, the Pensioners themselves, the old salts who repaired in ever-increasing numbers to the Hospital as their last refuge upon earth, and considering that they had to be sick, hurt or enfeebled to qualify for admission, one can only marvel at their indestructible faculty for getting themselves in trouble. The free board, lodging, clothes and medical care they received apparently failed to content their souls, for the chief preoccupation of their days, their most feverish activity, seems to have been to regain the feeling of independence — or some small, dear crumb of it — by getting a few extra shillings in their pockets by all or any means. There was only one approved and orthodox means of attaining this end : by petitioning the Board for 'Money in lieu of Provisions'. The phrase appears over and over, plus innumerable reasons for asking, and the Board was invariably indulgent toward this request, granting it without question or argument except in cases of incorrigible offenders ; in sixteen years of Minutes there are no more than three or four refusals. But the Money in lieu of Provisions must have yielded an insignificant working capital, for the Pensioners displayed a desperate zeal and activity in their pursuit for more that led them into avenues of speculation by no means approved : 'Complaint being made to the Board that several of the Pensioners have sold their shoes ; Order'd, that Mr. Ridley [the solicitor] do prosecute the Persons who have bought the said Shoes', and after that a more ambitious variation on the same theme : 'The Board being informed that many of the Pensioners carry their Beer out of the Hospital and sell the same ; recommended, to reinforce the Minutes in the best manner possible, in order to prevent the said abuse for the future'. A slightly sceptical note seems to pervade that last, as if the Board well knew that Shoes were more easily disgorged by the Purchaser than Beer. A year later it is painfully evident that the extra-mural selling of Beer continues, and the Board shows it means business by putting teeth in the regulation : 'A ten-shilling fine for the first offense and expulsion for the second'. (From where would a Pensioner ever get ten shillings ?)

Quite frequently Pensioners managed to get outside the sheltering walls of the Hospital (did they find their security dull, those survivors of the turbulent lower-deck life ?) and on re-entering the world often stepped into quite remarkable degrees of hot water : 'Peter Richards the Pensioner in Marshalsea Prison for debt, prays to be allowed money in lieu of provisions.' Next in frequency after indebtedness was theft, but one brilliant spirit got himself jailed for receiving stolen goods ; really a lofty flight for an old man whose stay in the Hospital must have impaired his outside connections, and his arrival behind bars proves how triumphantly he had surmounted this disability.

There were also the general welfare and needs of the Pensioners, supervised by the Directors with unceasing vigilance : 'Two clean shirts a fortnight is very insufficient for keeping the Pensioners clean and wholesome ; Order'd, that they should be allowed two clean shirts a week . . .' as soon as that many shirts are available. Great outcry from the sick in the infirmary with regard to their provisions, and an order from the Board 'for a proper person to look after that affair and see Justice done.' Then a charge is made which, for an institution of this nature, is as serious as can be : 'Complaint being made to the Board, that the people in the Helpless Ward have not that care and attendance which is necessary ; the Physician is desired to enquire into the same.' Rapid action was taken on this one, the doctor reporting : 'An examination having been made into the complaints relating to abuses in the Helpless Ward, the same appeared to be without foundation,' and a great relief to the reader.

There was likewise the mass of detail, mountainous, in relation to supplying the vast institution with food and drink, heat and light, drugs, bedding and a thousand other necessities. 'The Hospital is very ill-served with tripe by its present contractor' ; there is a leak in the pipes occasioning the loss of seventy barrels of beer ; the last load of coal delivered has been found to be lightweight. The purveyors are ordered 'to explain that matter', but two meetings later the Board concludes resignedly 'that such differences frequently happen in the Coal Trade'. A parcel of beds and bedding 'never lain on' is coming up for disposal, 'which may be very well worth while to purchase for the Hospital ; Order'd, that the goods shall be inspected' — and so on and on, interminably.

Tripe, beer and coals might be voiceless, but those who supplied them were not, and every week the Board was assailed by an anvil chorus of tradespeople. 'A petition from Tristram Everest the Butcher, setting forth that he has been a loser for some time on the meat he has served into the Hospital, and praying relief' : the wool supplier is a loser by the cloth he sells them, and the Price of Indico is Up. The supplier of Candles wants more money (he gets it), and Mr. Skrymsher the Plumber represents the great rise on the price of lead ; Mr. Mosely who furnishes coats for the nurses 'cannot serve the same any longer unless the price be advanced'. Many a smile must have circulated around that gathering of stately men as they debated nightcaps and towelling, the virtues of one flannel as against another flannel for aching old limbs, and other domestic details to which they would be strangers in their own homes.

Nor can one forget that the army of inmates had to be served by an army of attendants, and the problems arising from staff are back-breaking after their accustomed manner : 'There is a great want of spare nurses' : Bowden the gardener is fired 'for his ill-behaviour and great insolence', and the Steward finds that the business of his office is getting so much beyond him that he must pray for an additional clerk, which is allowed. Now reappears an old friend, this time mentioned in more enlightening terms : 'A report relating to Mr. Bridges the Bug-Killer was read ; Order'd, that he do cleanse the ward over again, as he did last year ; the same not being cleared according to his contract' — which he did, not success-fully enough to win the Board's future affections, it seems, for some months later he woos them rather uneasily with fresh proposals 'for cleansing the Hospital of Buggs' [sic]. Alas for Bridges ; 'The Minutes were produced of his former unsatisfactory service', and thus overtaken by the Nemesis of his own shortcomings, he vanishes into outer darkness. Another concluding note, slightly sinister, reminds us that skulduggery flourishes everywhere, in places high and low : 'It is a common practise with Nurses of the Hospital, by irregular methods, to obtained Wills from sick and helpless patients' : this must be stopped.

Again, from the Pensioners themselves — that great anony-mous mass of the infirm and decrepit—came wayward, discon-certing flickers and flashes of individuality not yet extinguished, these running the scale from minor offences to the deeper shadings of accident and tragedy. 'Jeremiah Dykes a Pen-sioner having run away and stole several things from one Sam'l Russell' is pursued and brought back, the stolen articles are found on him and the Hospital will pay the costs of prosecuting him. Rarely — and pathetically — some of the Pensioners feel so restored by the Hospital's care that they think themselves able to resume the hard life of seamen, but the effort usually seems unsuccessful : 'Six Pensioners lately sent to serve at sea [and well fitted-out with clothes and a sea-chest at the Hospital's expense] were returned unservice-able' : pilfering fingers, of course, have stripped them of all their possessions.

Incidents more painful are not wanting, to remind the spectator that the whole condition of life, in the Hospital, is one of inevitable decline. 'George Jennet, a Lunatick Pensioner discharged from Bedlam as incurable' is on the Hospital's hands ; they are willing to maintain him elsewhere, but no one wants to be saddled with him. The matter is finally shuffled off onto the Steward, who must somehow find 'a private madhouse, but so that the costs do not exceed the whole cost of a Pensioner to the House'. The Board must have had discouraging reports on this attempt, for later on they merely instruct the Steward to place out another insane person 'on the best terms he can'. Then there was Peter Blundine 'run over by a cart', and the Board will pay for burying him and allow his wife money in lieu of provisions, up to the time of his death. Finally a last, brief prominence for another ancient, his curtain falling to an inexpensive tune : 'Thos. Jackson a Pensioner having hung himself, Mr. Maule has been at four shillings and sixpence expence for sending to the coroner, and fourpence for each member of the jury.'

The Hospital in its physical extent was an enormous property, and the upkeep and management of all this fell to the Board likewise. The water-engine at the brew-house is much decayed ; the granary, being so contiguous to the river, is infested very much with vermin ; the Hospital will sue the masons if they do not remove all their stone from the Hospital wharf in ten days. The Hospital coffee-house is turned into an alehouse 'contrary to intention and agreement : Order'd, that Mr. Hills must desist from selling beer and ale and not occupy it otherwise than merely as a coffeehouse'. By the way, Swynfen's son John, the future Admiral, attended the foundation's school, kept by a master whose name has variously appeared in print as Swindon and Swindell, but there he is in the Minutes, large as life — the Rev'd Swinden,

official schoolmaster at a salary of £44 a year, and now applying to have an additional twenty-foot strip of ground added to
his lease ; apparently he wanted to enlarge his playground.

And climaxing the mass of detail the Board carried on its
shoulders was the chief, heaviest responsibility — the administration of the Hospital's money. In theory this matter was
supervised by the Admiralty and there are isolated instances
of the Greenwich Directors being called on the carpet by their
superiors : in practice, the handling and disposition of important sums was in their hands — their scrupulous hands —
entirely. At each meeting the Treasurer's balance was read
out first, never less than eight thousand or more than thirty
thousand pounds, though when it became so unwieldy the
Board would direct its investment — in three per cent bank
annuities mostly, though the purchase of other property is
recorded. In addition they received rents and income on
mortgages and enjoyed Parliamentary grants, these last
sometimes slow and difficult of collection. And topping
the enormous golden heap was another revenue that flowed
sometimes in streams and sometimes in trickles but whose
sum-total was vast, a glittering lure on which the eyes of
seamen high and low were hungrily fixed — prize-money
from captured ships and cargo. This fascinating subject, to
be considered later, is here mentioned among the Board's
thousand preoccupations only to demonstrate that they brought
to the greatest details, as to the least, the same thoroughness
and patience, the same inexhaustible, unvarying fairness and
good will.

It was before this body of men that Swynfen Jervis made
his first appearance on November 4th, 1747.

*   *   *

He brought with him a warrant from the Lords of the
Admiralty appointing him one of the Board of Directors, and
Treasurer of Greenwich Hospital. Also he produced a second
warrant, appointing him Auditor of all accounts. Both were

read out loud by the clerk to the gathering and ordered 'to be entered into the Minute Book, and Mr. Jervis took his place at the Board accordingly'. The clerk's first entry misspells his name Swinfen. Some of his new colleagues may have known him more or less because of his solicitorship to the Admiralty during the last two years. They were to find out a good deal more about him. His first duty as Treasurer was routine — to pay the malt bill — and the company adjourned 'to Saturday sennit'.

He missed almost two months of meetings after that, rather inconsiderately one would think, though his name was read out at a meeting ten weeks after his first appearance : his advice on a mortgage was to be asked, also he was instructed to submit in three weeks an account of prize-money received by him.

There is no record that he submitted the report, but during his further absence an interesting Minute was noted in the books — interesting because it relates to something so largely forgotten that a present-day enquirer can be told, by official sources, that 'Jervis never lived at the Hospital'. So a slight thrill is permissible on finding evidence to the contrary, an entry dated February 16th, 1748 : the Directors ordered that 'the Steward do supply coals for airing the Auditor's apartment' — a first positive indication that quarters were being prepared for him. Another ten weeks were to pass before Mr. Jervis troubled to attend the body of which he was a particularly essential member, but on April 30th his name actually appears among those present, and it is hard to stifle the suspicion that he was there because he had something to ask for. 'A letter from Mr. Jervis the Auditor was read, desiring that as the General Court have been pleased to allow him an Apartment in the Hospital, the Board will be so good to recommend that he be made such allowance of coals, candles and other stores as they shall think proper ; resolved, to make him an allowance equal to what is allowed the Secretary.'

His absence is now partly explained ; he had been busy
moving his wife and children from London, where, by the
way, their residence had displeased a member of the family
whom Swynfen would rather not offend — more of him
later.   Note also the promptitude with which the Board
acted on his request for stores ; they will be less anxious to
oblige him later, when they have had more of a taste of him.

The grant of coals and candles apparently encouraged
Swynfen to turn up at the next meeting, where in any case
he had to exercise an important part of his functions : he
'laid before the Board an account of the Neptune, a French
prize, amounting to £405 : 10 : 10'.   The sum this time was
comparatively small, but with England incessantly at war
with France and Spain the capture of ships was frequent, and
the selling value of the ships themselves and their cargoes
sometimes enormous.   At this same meeting Swynfen also
submitted his regular Treasurer's account : a balance in his
hands of over thirty thousand pounds.

A little less than three weeks later events began to thicken,
and Swynfen to give evidence of those peculiar traits of
character that distinguished him.   The date was June 11th,
1748, which meant he had held his posts of Treasurer and
Auditor only four months, but even that early he had lost no
time in precipitating hostilities with another member of the
Board.   Behind the scenes a running fight must have been
going on for some time before evidence of it broke surface
into sight of the Directors, and into the sparse and uncom-
menting narrative of the Minutes.

First he exposed a complaint : he asked, with more or less
rancour (we are privileged to use a little imagination on such
details), for the surrender of certain documents which he
claimed related to his Treasurer's accounts, and which were
at present in the hands of the Secretary.   Obviously he had
been hard at work for some time trying to detach them from
their present custodian, and the Secretary was not giving way.
Secondly, in support of his complaint, 'he laid before the

Board a Paper containing some Propositions for the Opinion of the Board'. Then a slightly irregular note is sounded in the Minutes : the meeting was adjourned, with no word of when action was to be taken on Mr. Jervis's 'Paper' — and yet we have seen that it was the invariable custom of the Board to dispose of one meeting's affairs at the next, exceptions to this being so few they are hardly worth noting ; arrears of business were anathema to them. Yet in this case they are obviously delaying, as if they hoped not to be driven into taking official cognizance of Swynfen's grievance. By doing so — especially by supporting him — they must offend another official of longer tenure, an equally important and perhaps much-better-liked associate of theirs. Yet among themselves they knew evasion was useless, the matter would come to a head and have to be settled ; what the Minutes indicate by merest allusion must have been decided in private colloquies, stately gentlemen sounding each other in drawing-rooms by twos and threes, wigged heads laid together, low-voiced opinions passing about until they were agreed as to their procedure. The next meeting would plainly be important, but before it took place (as with all crucial meetings, public or semi-public) issues were clarified in advance and the stage completely set.

The date of the meeting rolled around, and — significantly — Mr. Treasurer was not present. It is hard to resist the picture of Jervis conducting a canvass of his own before the meeting, buttonholing individual Directors and putting his case to them, eagerly scanning impassive faces and trying to read in them their probable predisposition toward him, for or against. His reading was better than his writing in this case, for he seems to have gathered beforehand what would happen : that the day would go against him and he would receive, in the presence of the assembled Board, a snub which was in effect a cutting rebuke.

Therefore on June 22nd, 1748, only Jervis's empty chair received the Directors' decision, consisting of two parts.

First, as to his demand for the documents now in custody of the Secretary : his right to see them was conceded if they had any connection with his work as Treasurer, but once having examined them, he had to give them back ; 'the Board are of opinion that the said papers do continue to remain with the Secretary, AS THEY ALWAYS HAVE DONE'. The second part of the decision was rather worse — and not only worse but unprecedented, an exhibit in the Board's history very nearly unique. One sentence covers it, by its mere reticence eloquent. 'The Paper laid before the Directors by Mr. Jervis at their last meeting was read AND ORDER'D TO BE LAID ASIDE.' Only that, unremarkable perhaps at first glance, yet it is also true that in six hundred pages of Minutes, covering over ten years of meetings, there is no comparable incident. We have seen how grumblings, dissatisfactions and complaints battered them like an incessant surf, and no instance exists (at least over that period) of careless adjustment or summary dismissal ; with endless desire to do their best for people they would listen and listen until a way was found to satisfy as well as possible any complainant, high or low. In this solitary instance, however, we have a document quickly and silently huddled out of sight, with a careful absence of remark and a still more careful absence of description. And what could have been the nature of 'Mr. Jervis's Paper' so tantalizingly veiled from us by the discretion of the Minutes ? Guesswork is as limitless as unrespected, yet there seems a reasonable conclusion : only a personal attack of extraordinary and determined virulence could have pushed the Directors into the uncharacteristic tactic of hushing it up quickly, nor does it seem far-fetched to envisage Mr. Secretary — the one who would not give up his records — as the target for Jervis's abuse.

Whatever the truth of the matter, it is undeniable that Swynfen failed to turn up at the next twenty-three meetings ; from June 22nd to February 25th he did not appear even once, nor is there a single recorded instance of any excuse or apology, written or relayed by word of mouth, on his part. Yet his

continued absence must have constituted not only an intolerable inconvenience but also a major impediment to the whole
work of the Directors, since in any organization the treasurer's
office is perhaps the most essential, the keystone by which the
whole structure stands or falls. During his absence of seven
months the Board never ceased giving him orders and instructions and undoubtedly these were conveyed to Jervis,
but by whom ? No subordinate or delegate of his is so far
noted in the Minutes, to say nothing of the unsatisfactoriness
of orders given at second hand, especially orders so vital.
The Board's uneasiness at this state of affairs must have been
extreme, but no word of it seeps into the Minutes ; we are at
liberty to guess at the amount of comment among themselves.
Remember also that Swynfen, *living in the Hospital*, could
hardly have avoided casual encounters with other Directors
who lived there, such as the Governor and the Physician ; he
must have had a thousand opportunities for informal explanation if he wanted them. Was the memory of his rebuff still
rankling to such a point that he kept out of his colleagues'
way deliberately ? But whatever the fact, Mr. Treasurer
Jervis failed to grace all meetings for about seven months,
until almost with a shock we find him actually giving signs
of life in March 1749 — not in person, but in the form of a
letter.

'The Directors being informed that the Treasurer's State
of Health do's not permit him to attend the Board so constantly as could be wish'd for the good of the Hospital, which
they are very much concern'd at ; and therefore desire' that
he will appoint some regular substitute for the purpose of
receiving the Board's orders.

And now Swynfen's long absence is explained on the
simplest grounds possible — illness ; but considering the
nature of the temperament being revealed to us even in flying
and fragmentary glimpses, it is difficult to suppress a sceptical
twinge as to the nature of that illness. His long absence from
meetings seems to originate from the occasion of his rejected

letter.   Could his indisposition have stemmed from the same
cause ?   For to a man of that peculiar disposition — irritable
and jealous of his authority, tightly-knotted about the central
core of his own self-esteem — a public humiliation is the very
worst thing that can happen, a hurt more lingering than any
malady and more incurable ;   Swynfen is not the first man to
have been made sick by a blow to his vanity.

In any case, one Mr. James Gunman was named as Swynfen's regular delegate, and the complications ensuing on this
arrangement were not slow in lifting their heads — as soon
as the very next meeting.   Some important documents had
to be signed, and instantly a bank refused to accept Gunman's
unaccompanied signature as Treasurer of the Hospital ;   a
co-signer had to be found, and for this purpose a Mr. Wood
is hastily produced from thin air ;   he was certainly not a
Director.   And at the next meeting a major instance appears
— if any were needed — of the enormous responsibilities of
the Treasurer's office ;   a list was submitted to the Board of
captured ships (prizes) with names and addresses of the agents
who had sold them, and that list was *nine* pages long.   The
money-total which it represented may be imagined, and the
Treasurer was ordered 'to take all Necessary Measures, for
obtaining the Moneys due thereon'.

But actually to whom — in the prevailing ambiguity —
were these orders addressed ?   To Jervis, still titular Treasurer,
since he had never formally resigned ?   To Gunn, whose
signature was unacceptable to the bank ?   To the lately
materialized Wood, of no defined status ?   To add to the
general confusion Jervis turned up at the next meeting and
submitted his routine Treasurer's account, which makes everything perfectly clear ;   he was Treasurer and not Treasurer,
at one and the same time.   He proceeded to miss three out of
the next five meetings, and it was at one of these that another
occasion of utmost urgency arose, and instructions were
delivered to the hiatus which Mr. Jervis's corporeal presence
should have filled :   'The Treasurer is desir'd to furnish an

account of what agents he has appointed abroad' to take care
of the prize-money due the Hospital. Of course the instructions were relayed through some channel, for the list appeared
at the next meeting though Jervis did not : offered by Mr.
Wood, it listed the agents appointed by Jervis, 'what are their
Securities and in what Sums they are bound'. Nine more
meetings passed with no sign of him, though at the tenth
(Sept. 2nd, '49) we note passingly that the Directors now
issue their Treasurer's instructions to Mr. Wood, only a super-
numerary of no recognized position ; we are free to imagine
their exasperation at this state of affairs, but somehow they
let it drag on, perhaps from the usual tendency to avoid unpleasantness — the awkwardness of forcing the issue and oblig-
ing Jervis to discharge his duties more efficiently, or resign.

Now to review Swynfen's situation : he and his family
have long since been occupying the apartments provided by
the Hospital, as part of his pay. Just what these apartments
consisted of is no longer known, since even the memory of
his residence there has died out, but we know from the
Minutes that a disabled lieutenant was assigned five rooms,
and a high officer's accommodation must have been much
more extensive ; we even know he had a garden, for at one
meeting the Governor of the Hospital himself actually applied
to the Board for one, pointing out with plaintiveness 'that
all the other officers have gardens, and he has none'. (He
failed to get it.) But Swynfen now has his living quarters
free of charge, and he receives 'stores' — candles, coals and
oil, perhaps cleaning materials ; repairs to the fabric are paid
for by the Hospital, also redecoration. In a word he is well
dug-in and — presumably — is still drawing two salaries as
Auditor and Treasurer ; perhaps it is his reluctance to surrender these last that keeps him from taking a clear-cut line
of action and resigning as one or the other, but clarity of any
sort appears not to be his strong point.

Two more meetings passed before Mr. Treasurer-not-
Treasurer appeared again, but both those occasions were so

pressingly important as to compel his elusive presence. At
one he had to receive instructions 'that the Hospital Accounts
usually call'd for by Parliament be prepared', and at the next
the Steward presented his regular quarterly accounts to be
settled. And yet another urgent matter extorted his attendance
even a third time : the Book of Works and Repairs was up
before the Board for review and payment, and the bills
amounted to over £5000.

Now Swynfen has turned up three times running, but he
makes up for it promptly. The next eleven months may be
compressed ; the object of our pursuit attended nine out of
the next twenty-eight sessions. Once or twice Gunman was
there deputizing for him, but generally not. On October
27th, 1750, however, he comes to life with a bang — as usual
when he wanted something — and incidentally we note that
his style and title have changed, though he is still simultaneously
in and out of the treasurership.

'An application of Mr. Jervis the Auditor was read,
setting forth that all the Officers of the House are allow'd
Table-Money except himself and praying the Board's recommendation for the like Allowance ; Order'd, that the same
be laid before the next General Court for their consideration.'
In other words, they made him wait by passing the matter
on to another administrative body, nor is it strange that the
Directors were not inclined to overreach themselves on his
behalf ; if they considered that he had done little enough for
the Hospital, while pressing his claim to everything he could
get from it, they had a certain amount of reason on their side.
A search of the Minutes fails to reveal whether he got his
table-money or not, but very likely he did ; to refuse him
would have been impracticable, perhaps impossible. At any
rate (perhaps encouraged by the free nourishment) he begins
to show up at almost every other meeting over a six-month
period, and his name now appears in the *Directors Present* list
as Swynfen, so presumably he had corrected the clerk. Was
it from deliberate malice that that functionary promptly

Captain Sir John Jervis, at about the age of 47, wearing captain's undress uniform with the Star of the Bath

misspelled his name, after knowing it for three years, as 'Jarvis' ?

The green shimmer of the new spring hung about Greenwich in the next month, and perhaps as a seasonal manifestation Swynfen lifted his voice again, moving the Board that a room of his 'which is now floored with Stone, be floored with Deal', which was done for him. Around the same time may be spotted another faint landmark in his uneven passage as Treasurer ; Gunman, his former deputy, has long since vanished and the dim figure of Wood is being mentioned in his stead. Yet Mr. Gunman bursts into unforeseen prominence shortly after, presenting his warrant as Director and — unexpectedly — Treasurer. Had the Board become desperate and forced through the nomination, trying to end once and for all the impossible situation in which, at meeting after meeting, they issued vital instructions to an empty chair, or to a substitute of dubious competence ? A rather curious entry seems to give weight to the conjecture, for the Directors approved, at one fell swoop, three sums totalling £614 for 'Treasurer's Deputies'. They were the men to protest vociferously at the least suspicion of unnecessary charges, yet here they are, passing these very considerable sums without a murmur. Were they exclusively fees for Swynfen's 'deputies' — in which case he had been an expensive proposition for the Hospital — or had the Board been obliged to spend some of this money on having arrears of Treasurer's work brought up to date ?

Whatever the fact, Mr. Gunman soon becomes vocal on his own account, and Swynfen himself begins attending rather more frequently — perhaps to keep a baleful eye on his successor ? For Gunman was not too slow in making claims for this and that ; after being in office less than seven months he represented to the Board 'that he has had considerable Trouble and some Expence on account of the Unclaimed Share of Prizes, and desiring to have some allowance made him by way of Poundage.' This might have added up to quite an attractive

c

little percentage, and it must have killed Swynfen, now only
Mr. Auditor, not to have thought of it first. Nor could his
vanity have been soothed to get an order, at that very same
meeting, to lay his accounts before the Clerk of the Cheque
before presenting them to the Board ; had there been such
inaccuracies in his figures that a preliminary vetting of them
was now in order ? A continuing trouble and confusion are
still sensed in the financial department, but it took another
few months to come into the open and demonstrate that the
new Treasurer was being swamped by the complexities of
his job : 'The Treasurer is desired to acquaint the Board why
the sixth and ninth articles of his Instructions have not been
comply'd with and to lay before them his reasons for the
same'. Nor did Swynfen lose any time in sniping at his
foundering supplanter ; in March '53 he is protesting in open
meeting that the latest Treasurer's reports have not been
delivered to him, and next meeting Wood retaliates by
charging Swynfen with holding out on certain fees to which
he considers himself entitled. What hidden antagonisms
simmered continuously below the surface are not now discoverable, but at intervals they heaved up from below, leaving
pock-marks as in lava.

In the winter of '53 Swynfen, asking for something else,
unveils a further angle of his domestic economy. He himself was modestly not present, but 'a letter from Mr. Jervis
the Auditor was read, requesting a settled allowance in lieu
of all Fees ; the Board adjourned the further consideration
thereof to this day three weeks'. A longish interval for this
particular body to impose, but obviously they took their time
in acceding to any request of Swynfen's, and why not ? His
record of service was not such as to endear him to his associates.
But good as their word and within the stipulated time the
Directors 'took into consideration Mr. Jervis's application for
an additional salary in lieu of all fees, for which he now
receives, salary included, the sum of £124 yearly, out of which
he is obliged to pay £34, leaving him £90. And in regard

[considering] the Auditor is an Officer of rank and the Office
an Office of great trust and consequence to the Hospital : the
Directors therefore propose a salary of £100 per annum — '
and his departmental expenses to be borne by the Hospital.
Eminently fair ; and in the postscript lies, perhaps, the true
value of what he received.   One hundred pounds per annum
was no mean income in those days when a poor gentleman,
on the evidence of Mr. Peregrine Langton,[1] could make a
decent showing for fifty ; but besides the hundred pounds
his free board and lodging, heat and light — for his family
of six — surely were worth another hundred or two.   His
servants included a coachman, and this in the exact period
when he was refusing his son John the meagrest, most elemen-
tary assistance.   Not that he got his hundred pounds all that
easily, for the Board repented at the very next meeting
('reconsidered', they put it) and passed on their proposals to
another body, the General Court.   This instance of retreating
from their word is also unheard of and unduplicated in ten
years of Minutes, but it seems to have been Swynfen's specific
talent to extort uncharacteristic behaviour from anyone.
Probably they had been fed up with him for a long time.   On
the other hand it is probable that he got the salary arrangement
he was asking for, or his objections must have been recorded
in the Minutes.

In another four months the office of Treasurer has defeated
the new incumbent, who vanishes soundlessly, and in May
'55 one Charles Saunders 'presented his patent in place of
James Gunman'.   Be sure that Swynfen, on the sidelines, is
waiting for him to make the first false step ; he had it in for
any successor of his.   At present, all he can do is continue
sniping sporadically at the late Treasurer, Gunman ; he is
dissatisfied with some lists of his and states he cannot pass
them as they are incomplete ; eight months later he is still
complaining.   But in late January '56 he certifies that Gunman's accounts are settled and signed at last and presents the

[1] In Boswell's *Johnson*.

bills for his fees, and the Board 'order'd, that the same be allowed him' — to the tune of £275 : 3 : 6, not a bad addition to his yearly hundred and his keep.

Presumably encouraged by this sweetener, he establishes a phenomenal record of attendance, actually being present at nine out of the next ten meetings, and at the eleventh the Directors have a most important job to entrust to him ; by this time they should have known better. For it seems that the accumulated records of the Hospital were by now so voluminous as to be getting out of hand, and the Board orders 'all deeds and writings belonging to the Hospital be delivered to Mr. Jervis, and the Board recommended him to employ proper persons to put the same in order, and to report the expence thereof when completed'. Superfluous, that last injunction, but Swynfen received the fearsome mass and set to work, for ten weeks later he put in his bill for £22 : 4 : 0, his expenses so far for the Record Room.

Ten days later he attended the meeting of August 14th, 1756, and — from that day vanishes from the Board of Greenwich Royal Hospital as if a trap-door had opened under him. None of the usual forms attend his departure — no resignation, no advance notice, no remark ; an unexplained void gapes where Mr. Auditor has been. Yet almost a year later the Board is ordering 'that the safe in Mr. Jervis's apartment be allowed', so though he has given up his job for all practical purposes, he has by no means given up the dwelling and other appurtenances of the job, and almost simultaneously the Directors discover that he has bungled the cataloguing commission, according to his usual custom. Attempting to straighten it out, they order Mr. Everest the solicitor 'to sort, methodize and index' the contents of the Record Room. Meanwhile no one wants the responsibility of keeping its keys, originally to have been in the custody of Jervis ; the Lieutenant-Governor has just begged off, so that Mr. Everest, protesting, is finally landed with them. Other bits and pieces of Mr. Auditor's unfinished business continued to haunt the

Board so late as 1760, when two Directors are prevailed on (very unwillingly) to mediate in a long-drawn-out tax row between the Hospital and the parish that Swynfen was supposed to handle.

One more oddity or deviation — again unique — attends the fading-out of Mr. Auditor Jervis. When any resident officer of the Hospital, high or low, quit his job and consequently his habitation on the premises, it was a matter of cast-iron routine to go through it room by room with an inventory and check the contents. There are a dozen such references in the Minutes, and no missing articles, however trifling, escaped the official eye. But with Swynfen it was otherwise. Everyone's departure was recorded, but not his ; everyone's apartment was inventoried, but not his. Difficult, irregular and obscure from first to last, he shuffles forever from the Minute Books, having been a centre of discord during the nine years of his incumbency, and leaving behind him a legacy of messes and unresolved situations for others to straighten out. This appears the sum-total of his career as 'Treasurer of Greenwich Hospital' : obviously his son John heard a quite different story.

By now anyone might be excused for forming his own opinion of Swynfen, and it is amusing to have it confirmed by a little discovery made *after* the above material was gathered, a letter dated 1745. And the voice is not that of an outsider but of Swynfen's own father, speaking from that fatally-full knowledge of character that marks family conversation. 'I wish you would leave off complaining for it is really disagreeable to me', he cheeps acidly. 'I have been at a very considerable expence. I would have been willing to bear half the expence of Jacky's being called to the bar, but that, I understand by his letter this day, is not likely to be at present ; that disappointment gives no unhappiness to Your loving Father.' One lawyer in the family is enough, he seems to be saying.

By the way, this letter seems to deal a death-blow to the

coachman story, a Jervis legend as inevitable in its way as
Washington's cherry-tree.   According to this, John was
destined for the Bar ; one day in 1747 his father's coachman
says to him, 'O don't be a lawyer, Master Jacky, all lawyers
are rogues'.   And presto, Jacky's decision is taken ; he will not
be a lawyer.   He himself in old age repeated this tale of his
boyhood, so of course it happened, and equally of course, by
then, it had assumed in his mind a disproportionate weight,
for his grandfather knew two years earlier that he would
never be a barrister.   But the coachman's remark may have
clinched a decision that was taking form slowly in the boy's
mind, his words touching off the ultimate flare, like fire to a
long fuse.   And the fact that his father was a lawyer had —
perhaps — something to do with it . . . ?

Now, in any case, we have at least a partial picture of
the Swynfen who pitchforked his younger son 'wisely' into
potential disaster for want of the most trifling help.   But by
the evidence of the Minutes and the attitude of his own father,
Swynfen never did anything wise in his life.   Also by now we
can risk a guess at his income — not actually in figures, but
from the number of its sources and his style of living.   With
his Greenwich job went a hundred pounds a year plus sizeable
fees, his house, household supplies, table expenses and part
of his children's education.   His Admiralty solicitorship was
worth a small sum.   There was his private law practice,
chiefly, it seems, on the Northern Assizes.   He had to travel
far to attend them, so it must have been worth his while.
Finally, there was family money in the background ; his
father's letters exercise that prerogative of interference possible
only to a parent of means.   'One thing indeed is disagreeable
to me, I mean my Daughter's [Mrs. Swynfen's] keeping so
large a family in town at greater expence than you can well
bear, for what good end I know not.   I wish that may be
amended, for while I am willing to lay a good foundation for
you to build upon for your family, I am not willing your wife
should waste it before it comes into your hands.'   More evi-

dence of two extremes between which Swynfen vacillated —
foolish extravagance and foolish penny-pinching. Evident,
also, is his father's scant respect for his judgment.

And what of Swynfen's excuse to the Board for slighted
duties — ill-health ? No mention of his illness is discoverable
in family correspondence of the period, and the Jervises were
all writers of long letters full of family news ; sickness was a
thing they dwelt upon in detail. Perhaps, if he were really
sick, frustrated ambition was at the root of his malady — a
man touchy, thorny, assiduous in invoking dislike ; a man
who loved and longed for power and position, who regarded
these with reverential awe (once he wept bitterly because the
family great man, Sir Thomas Parker, was unable to dine
with him) and yet whose capacities and temperament forbade
his ever attaining them.

Now to go a step further and consider that aspect of
Swynfen's behaviour that had to do not with accounts and
figures but with the welfare of the living creature who was
his second son John. And if it be asked, 'What sort of man
was it who could do such a thing ?' perhaps the foregoing
story has enabled us to say, in part, what sort of man he was.

*　　　*　　　*

Some time in 1748, after the conversation with the coachman, John, aged thirteen, ran away from school and hid
aboard a ship docked at Woolwich.[1] For three days he stood
the misery of cold, hunger, the bedless state, the eternal damp
of the hold and stink of the bilges, an episode — except for
the last two items — strangely prophetic of another that was
coming towards him at no great remove of time. Then he
crawled out and came home.

The household was in commotion and his mother dis-
tracted, of course, and it seems that his sister Mary spoke to
him severely, or 'warmly', as he puts it. This is Mary's first

[1] His own account of it. See Brenton's *Life of Earl St. Vincent*, vol. i,
pp. 16-19.

appearance in the long important rôle she was to play in his
life, a rôle that only ended some seventy-six years later. But
at the moment her young energetic voice had not its accustomed influence with him, and his mother's method of
meeting the crisis — by weeping — likewise left him unmoved.
He would be a sailor, and that was the end of it. Swynfen
was away on the Northern Circuit, and Mrs. Swynfen could
not pick up a phone or send a wire to the effect that Jacky
was behaving dreadfully. Wringing her hands, she appealed
to her brother — not the Baron of the Exchequer, Thomas,
but a lesser light named John. Big John argued with little
John, also to no purpose. When it appeared that the boy's
intention was fixed, the grown-ups seem to have capitulated
rather rapidly. No direct naval connections existed in the
family, apparently, so the next thing to do was find someone
to make the necessary introductions. A relay of friendly
ladies passed the word along, and almost in no time Jacky
received a note, asking him to call early next day on Commodore George Townshend, who as commander-in-chief
was going out to Jamaica in the *Gloucester*.

Uncle John accompanied, on this important occasion, a
small figure enduring all the child's acute sense of being made
ridiculous, in a coat 'made for me to grow up to' with sleeves
engulfing its hands and skirts touching the ground. The fresh
morning chill saw the two of them presenting themselves
promptly at a small house in a small fashionable street off
Berkeley Square. The Commodore was all too evidently
not awake ; they waited a considerable time before an uncouth
figure in dressing-gown and night-cap, with eyes hardly open,
lurched downstairs. In a voice hoarse and rusty with its first
usage of the day, he asked John how soon he would be ready
to join his ship. John said, 'Directly.' 'Go tomorrow,'
said the Commodore, plainly in no mood to spin out the
interview. 'I will give you a letter to the first lieutenant.'
In this way the Admiral was launched on his career, with no
fuss at all. The oddest circumstance about it is that all this

seems to have been done without notifying or consulting
Swynfen, far away in Staffordshire. Was his wife too apprehensive to tell him ? or did she know he would hardly care
one way or the other ? The answer, buried in one of those
multitudinous seams of family relationship, appears lost
forever.

In any case young John (Jacky no more, even to his sister)
was shortly being received aboard the *Gloucester* by the first
lieutenant. It appears that that officer was no improvement
on his Commodore — in fact the reverse.

'I have too much respect for my readers,' shudders
Brenton, who had the story from Jervis's own lips, 'to describe
the scene ; suffice it to say, that in point of gross immorality
and vice, it outdid anything described by Smollett in his
Roderick Random.' But the scene to which he alludes so
darkly is, in that day and age, easy to reconstruct. The ship
was in dock, the captain and Commodore absent ; drunken-
ness was nothing, and the presence of women aboard, even
during the voyage, was checked only according to the individual attitude or caprice of the captain. The chances are that
John had to locate the lieutenant in his quarters, and that
the tableau revealed by the opening door was of sprawling
rowdiness, gross befuddlement and idiotic hilarity, nakedness
probably. The picture hit him hard and stayed with him all
his life, for though he was tough there was no coarseness in
him. Brenton even believes that it kept him, thenceforward,
on the straight and narrow, but it is permissible to differ from
Brenton in thinking that anyone so level-headed as John
Jervis would ever sacrifice his career to imbecile escapades of
the moment. Not that his nature exhibited the slightest
Puritanic taint — the opposite, actually ; but he possessed
first and last the inbuilt balance-wheel of strong characters,
with whom the avoidance of extremes is a fundamental
instinct.

Now the Admiral is on his way ; the *Gloucester* has sailed,
Midshipman Jervis aboard with his total capital in his pocket

— 'my father gave me twenty pounds at starting' — and we
will sail also in a quick detour around his early training, and
towards an event in his life some two or three years distant.
This, apart from his purely professional preparation, is one of
the most important things that ever happened to him, and the
impelling force behind it was Swynfen, his destructive hand
no less potent at three-thousand-mile range than among the
Greenwich Board of Directors, much nearer home.

*   *   *

The date was about 1751 ; John had been on ships stationed
in the West Indies since '48.   During those three years his
financial resources consisted of his father's twenty pounds,
and his pay-tickets.   These require a word of explanation.
On joining a ship, a seaman immediately received a
ticket good for two months' pay.   Every six months he was
supposed to receive tickets sufficient to bring his wages owing
up to date, and undoubtedly he did get them as promptly as they
could be issued him in ports more or less distant from home.
But the snag was, that these tickets could be cashed *only* at
the Navy Pay-Office in London.   This rule had occasional
exceptions, in that a pay-ship might visit craft in foreign ports
with actual currency for their officers and crews, but such
occurrences were too rare to be counted on.   Therefore a
seaman with only remote prospects of getting home could
amass a number of pay-tickets and yet be penniless — unless
he took the quick, easy way out by disposing of his tickets
for what they would fetch.   Money-lenders with facilities
for cashing them at their full value would always buy them,
provided the owner would take a discount or loss on them of
about twenty-five per cent.   Especially to a younger man,
not yet believing in such a thing as the future, the chance to
exchange his little wad of these objects — pocket-softened
and taking on a valueless look over the months and years —
for the convincing feel of cash in hand must have been
irresistible.

This custom of selling tickets was probably universal among most ranks, John not excepted. With his few shillings of pay and with his father's twenty pounds vanished (he had made it last for three years, and the reluctance and anxiety with which he had doled out his pence may be imagined) he must have been driven to the wall by poverty, or he would not have ventured to do what he did — draw upon his father for another twenty pounds. An interval elapsed, and the thunderbolt fell. The bill came back protested.

All disaster is relative, and the scale of this disaster, in a penniless boy's life, was epic. And he never forgot it ; in his oldest old age, speaking of it, his voice would change, his emphasis grow harsh. A peculiar shame always attaches to the dishonoured cheque, and into exactly what miserable impasses of humiliation, explanation and apology this one threw him he never said, so the story cannot now be found. But the degree of catastrophe can be gauged by the means which he took to meet it, involving the most drastic reversal and rearrangement of his accustomed life.

In the first place, he left his mess at once, and the mess was the foundation-stone of the Navy's social structure. A man ate with his equals — officers with officers and similarly down through the ranks — and the care taken to insure his being compatible with every other man in the mess was not only vigilant but ruthless ; if one man persisted in disliking another the disliked one was out, and there are cruel stories of men barred from all messes, eating furtively alone or huddling with other pariahs in unwilling companionship. But an officers' mess (and midshipmen were officers under instruction) involved its members in certain obligations, such as their share of whatever table luxuries they could afford — wine mostly, indispensable in helping to wash down the vile food and lend to the barren repast some faint tinge of conviviality. But whatever the expenses incidental to a man's position, he had to be ready at all times to keep up his end. Then not only the mess was involved, but the matter of appearance ; in all ports there were public and private social affairs at which visiting ships' officers were a great feature, eagerly invited and entertained, and then as now a person had to be neat and smart and clean, by his turnout reflecting credit on the service and ship to which he had the honour to belong. It is reasonable to conjecture that the greatest drain on John's resources, at this time, arose from the matter of clothing. In the years between thirteen and sixteen, daily hard work and exercise were turning his body from a boy's to the man's frame familiar to us in all portraits of Jervis — the formidable shoulders and deep chest and straight heavy legs that gave him the planted stance of an oak ; how long ago had the horrid dragging coat foisted on him by his mother been outgrown ? During shore leave, too, a growing boy, a bottomless pit on legs, would see the native vendors with trays of sweet fresh fruit, after the months of ship's diet, stale and mouldy and wormy ; with what compulsion the hoarded coppers would be charmed out of his pocket against his will, during jaunts ashore with his friends, a roving band with young eager eyes for everything, and money for nothing or next to nothing. Now, at one stroke he was out of everything — the mess, the company of his natural associates, participation in their pleasures after duty ; down upon him moved his season of penance for his moments of indulgence, for all those bananas and mangoes he had had no right to buy.

Having taken the long step down from the social level to which he was born, his next act was to attack the weight of his obligation, the twenty pounds that hung on him like a millstone. Whatever a boy of sixteen would have had in the way of possessions had to be disposed of ; we know he sold his bedding, also any extra clothes or shoes he happened to have. He might own a pistol or a dirk by now, and certainly these would go. His instruments of navigation and other professional equipment he must hang onto at all costs. When he had scraped these resources bare, he could even raise a microscopic amount of actual cash by bringing into play the recognized and permissible game of juggling pay-tickets, and his method of doing it was as follows :

Any seaman in good standing had the right to apply for transfer to another ship, provided the captain of the other ship wanted him and would supply a man from his own crew to replace him. On transfer to the new ship, he got his pay-ticket for service in the old, less what he owed the purser for slops, tobacco and so forth. Then, on joining the new, he immediately received, likewise, his ticket worth two months' pay. With these double earnings he could amass quite a lot of tickets, only providing that enough captains were willing to have him and willing to exchange men of their own for him. That he was able to change ship so frequently speaks volumes for his reputation, young as he was ; he was already known as a good man to have aboard. The tickets he accumulated went the way of many tickets, with a difference. His plight, far worse than that of the ordinary hard-up seaman, must have been common shipboard gossip. In a small port the news would percolate to other ears, including the money-lenders'. They would know all about the straits he was in and how to take fullest advantage of him ; others they would cheat of the quarter of a ticket's value, young Jervis they would cheat of nearly half. He had no choice but to take what they offered, of course.

It took him three years to work off his debt, and very likely our reconstruction of that period might be more emotional than his, since he was no complainer and no self-pitier. He would become very clever at finding snug places on deck, at night, for his mattress ; we know he had one because later he ripped the ticking off it and made himself a pair of trousers, which sounds like the end of the mattress. After that we can picture the tropic night in heat or rain and the young figure curled up wherever sacking or canvas offered him a pillow. He made and washed his own clothes and cobbled their pieces together when they showed a disposition to part company, and developed a skill above the ordinary at

barter with the natives, extolling the virtues of a piece of salt
pork saved from his meal in exchange for fresh fruit or vegetables. But the worst of his plight must have been the unbroken isolation — the lonely figure in garments of his own
manufacture, seeing his former companions depart for merry-
makings ashore, furbished and polished to their highest gloss,
and they would see him too ; he could not be eternally
slinking out of their sight, nor would he try. What his
thoughts were at that time, and his feelings, could not have
been different from those of any other boy, especially the boy
that he was — spirited, affectionate and full of fun, with the
social warmth and magnetism that he retained to the very
end of his days.

Now, in the new life that had suddenly cut him off from
everything familiar and pleasant he had ever known, his one
concern was survival, and with all his tenacity and resolution
he braced himself to survive. He had to have some refuge
for his thoughts, and this he provided for himself by sewing
together the letters from his sister Mary and re-reading them
in his times of recreation. But the only whole garment left
in his threadbare existence was work, and this he pulled
around himself with the intentness of a man in a freezing wind,
trying not to leave one seam open to the blast of adversity.
It was in this period that he laid the foundation of his enormous
professional familiarity with the last nail, splinter of wood and
stitch of canvas that went to make up a ship ; no part of her
was secret from him, down through her darkest holds to her
bilges and her ballast. From the first he had been lucky in
his instructors, 'very clever fellows', the first lieutenant and
the ship's master Mr. Williamson, and his chief companion
in his present situation seems to have been an old quarter-
master named Drysdale, who gave him the additional lessons
in navigation that brought his skill to top pitch at an unusually
early age, and this skill he continued to sharpen and enlarge
by volunteering for every species of duty in small boats.

On exactly what decks he laid himself down at night,

during his wanderings from ship to ship, is perhaps a matter too obscure now to trace. His misfortune is supposed to have come on him while he was serving on the *Ferret* sloop, but his name is not on *Ferret*'s Wages Book during her five years on the West Indian station between 1748–53. Some accounts seem to spell her captain's name as Scroope when it was in fact Carr Scrope (his own signature in the Wages Book) so perhaps the detail of John's being aboard is also doubtful.

As to the approval and even applause accorded Swynfen for his action in stopping the cheque, these are based on the salutary uses of adversity and on the assumption that all adversity is equally valuable as a builder of character. No theory could be more fallacious. Any living creature undergoes adversity and any character is shapeless without it, but there are degrees of adversity from which the spirit fails to recover equilibrium ; which leave behind them fatal impairments of the elasticity called hope or confidence. This is especially true if the trial is not only sudden but disproportionate to one's years and experience. A boy of sixteen is not supposed to have great reserves of character and determination to draw on, and if the long-extended rigour had worn him down into discouragement, sullenness or self-distrust, no one could have blamed him. If it had driven him to disreputable companionship or worse, no one could have blamed him. That he survived not only intact but with heightened qualities is entirely due to himself, and no thanks to his father. He was somehow never downcast, only grim, intent on repaying the money and healing his shame. To do this he had to become a different person in the twinkling of an eye, and the power of transition was found in no outside source, but all within himself.

It should be said at once that John appeared to hold no grudge whatever against his father for the long-lasting injury ; parents were not yet the fashionable scapegoat for everything. Five years later the two men were on friendly and even affectionate terms, which is merely a further testimony to the largeness of John's nature. His letters to Swynfen may be suspiciously brief, but it is only fair to say that he wrote even to Mary in this manner when overwhelmed with business.

In any case, alone and unhelped, John Jervis had bought himself free of his predicament by the time he was nineteen, through the happy accident of being much more extraordinary than anyone could have foreseen. And somewhere on the long hard road he had picked up the thing that ever after would be his peculiar distinguishing mark, his own unique stamp and seal of character. Driven back on himself for so many years, he had apparently lost the need felt by most people for approval, for the buttressing applause or concurrence of others. At nineteen he was still midshipman Jervis but at the same time, mysteriously, he was also the future Admiral Lord St. Vincent, with a formidable power of making up his own mind without reference to others. From that time the fulcrum of his judgment in the enormous decisions he would have to make when literally England's whole future hung in the balance, rested — for once and all, for better for worse — within himself.

Captain Sir John Jervis, M.P., at about the age of 55, in court dress

II

MORE BEGINNINGS OF AN ADMIRAL

THE stages by which one young seaman arose, more important to him than to this type of narrative, will be enumerated as quickly as possible. No one should be surprised to hear that the semi-pariah of the West Indian station passed 'a rigid examination for lieutenant, with great credit', his sister Mary reports proudly. He was twenty-four by now, and even that early was giving evidence of his ability to attract to himself the confidence and affection of remarkable people, such as General Wolfe — with whom, by the way, he had gone to school at Greenwich. He was Wolfe's professional collaborator also during the siege of Quebec ; it was the ship he commanded, the *Porcupine*, that took up her station in the channel under heavy fire, to cover the landing of the English troops.

Wolfe is long-vanished but a shimmer still marks the place where he stood, the luminescence of high courage, capacity and extraordinary power to evoke love. Moved by who knows what premonition on the night before his death, he entrusted to Jervis his will, some notebooks, and a miniature of his fiancée, Katherine Lowther, that she had given him. Around this miniature has grown an attractive legend : that Jervis, at Wolfe's request, called upon Katherine on his first arrival in London and put the miniature into her hands, as coming from Wolfe. The story apparently derives from the first life of Jervis ever written, the *Memoir*[1] by Tucker. Now Tucker — no writer but an accountant and commission agent, who produced the sort of book that might be expected of an amateur — seems to have heard this version as a sort of family

---

[1] Tucker gathered the material ; after his death, his son put it together.

tradition, and repeated it without enquiring into its accuracy. What really happened was, that Wolfe consigned the articles to Jervis to be delivered to his mother ; the miniature could not have been taken to Katherine immediately because Wolfe's will directed that it be 'set in jewels to the value of £500' before being returned to her. Mrs. Wolfe carried out her son's wishes handsomely, for the jeweller's bill came to more than five hundred. These facts unfortunately deal the death-blow to the series of appealing tableaux conjured up by the Tucker account : the stately drawing-room, the young naval officer bringing the miniature, the lovely girl holding out both hands for the heartbreaking present, and so forth. As a matter of fact Jervis, in executing the commission, had no direct encounter even with the dead hero's mother ; he gave the things to an aide-de-camp named Bell, who made the actual delivery to Mrs. Wolfe.

Wolfe's schoolmate, by now, was at home on many seas in the age-old grapple among England, France and Spain for trade and territorial expansion. Three years earlier he had commanded his first ship *Experiment* during the illness of her captain and at the moment was acting commander of the *Porcupine*, though not titular captain. Only one year later, at twenty-five, he was Post-Captain of the *Gosport*, the magic word *post* differentiating his status from any he had ever had previously. For the mere fact of commanding a ship did not confer captain's rank ; commanders and even lieutenants filled the position of captains on smaller ships, like John himself in *Experiment*. But the word 'post' before 'captain' meant your appointment to a rated ship, so classed because of her larger size and number of guns ; it meant that you were a proper, undeniable, formally-recognized captain, and attaining this position meant that an officer had leaped the gap between indefinite and definite rank, once and for all.

The next stage after that towards a higher position was slow in coming, and once having appeared through John's sheer merit — the most laborious and uncertain ladder that then could be — the others followed with a deliberation even more relentless and heart-breaking. At forty-seven he fought and took the immense *Pégase* off Brest, the French ship suffering frightfully in numbers dead and general damage, Jervis's hardly at all. For this victory the Order of the Bath was at once conferred on him and probably he had its star embroidered on all his uniforms, as was then the custom. About a month later he heard he was to be knighted, and the one to write him the good news was Lord Keppel, to whom he stood in the peculiar relationship which will next appear. This is 1782, and he is now Captain Sir John Jervis. Thirteen years must go by, and during them he is walking up the steps of promotion — rear-admiral, vice-admiral, then Admiral Sir John Jervis. In July 1795 he is sixty years old and on the threshold of the most brilliant and resounding part of his career. At this point we make a full stop and go back sixteen years, when there occurred the first incident that brought John into the public eye in the sense of making him newsworthy.

This was his appearance, in 1779, as witness in a spectacular court-martial. Spectacular because it is not every day that one British admiral brings against another British admiral the charge of criminal cowardice ; specifically, of trying to avoid combat with an enemy fleet. But such was the charge that Admiral Sir Hugh Palliser brought against Admiral Lord Keppel, and John, holding in Keppel's fleet his most important command so far — captain of the eighty-gun *Foudroyant* — was during the whole trial under heavy fire by the prosecuting officers and by Keppel himself, who cross-examined in his own defence. The cold print of the stenographic report barely conveys, at this date, the furious undertow of resentment and ill-feeling that must have run beneath the whole course and conduct of the trial. For Palliser, hating Keppel and known to be jealous of him, was suspected of having published anonymous pamphlets against him as well as having

written him anonymous letters previous to the trial. Moreover, though under Keppel's command in the fleet, Palliser
was a Lord of the Admiralty and Keppel was not, so the junior
officer was in the paradoxical position of having enough influence to bring his senior to trial. The decision to subject
Keppel to a court-martial produced an uproar in the service
and a number of naval captains petitioned the King against
it, but Palliser was apparently able to override these demonstrations and put Keppel in the pillory.

A trial on so major a charge can never lose all interest, nor
can the higher lights of its testimony — so many of them
emanating from Captain Jervis that it may be said in effect that
he dominates the trial, although Keppel's cross-examinations
on his own behalf are extremely impressive.

'Did I use my utmost endeavours as an officer', he
questioned Jervis, 'to bring them [the French fleet] to action ?'

'You used the most unremitting endeavours', Jervis
declared unqualifiedly, and with similar definiteness sustaining
the ruthless interrogation at whose end Keppel must lose his
life if found guilty, he demonstrated that he was absolutely
unshakable when standing on professional ground. Perhaps
it was this impressive assurance that saved him from rough
handling by the examiners when he preferred not to give an
opinion as distinct from evidence, although another witness
of much higher rank was badly mauled for precisely the same
refusal ; perhaps he already seemed a man whom none — not
even his superiors — could trample over rough-shod with
impunity. With his logbook in his hand, and permitted to
refresh his memory by referring to it, he could account for
every moment of his during the battle, for every signal made
and every slightest shift of wind. And little by little, from his
and others' testimony and with the lethal inevitableness of a
worm eating its way out of concealment, creeps the shattering
truth : the engagement had failed to take place because
Palliser's ships, contrary to order, were too far away to respond
to Keppel's signal to attack until it was too late. The trial

blew up in the face of Palliser, who had invited his own disaster, and John's evidence had been a principal factor in the vindication of his chief. In his captain's full-dress uniform, worn for the trial, he must have been a splendid figure, probably with an attractive speaking voice ; his laugh is mentioned as attractive, a tremendous peal — in moments of uncontrollable amusement — fit to open cracks in the ceiling. His greatest flaw in this period of good looks, a friend remembered long after, was his straight lank hair, but he covered it with a wig 'tied up in ribbons and called a Ramillies wig'.

To strangers and to the public at large he must have seemed the very image of a successful man, but he had had bad luck as well as good ; his career had included important commands but also he had been on the beach for four years, with not a single job ; part of this blank period he filled in by going as a paid passenger — at a cheap fare probably — in a merchant ship to Cronstadt. During this voyage his unresting specialist's eye discovered the haphazard quality of the vessel's pilotage. 'All the charts are wrong', was the comforting conclusion he came to, and having brought along his own chart, he marked and corrected it minutely ; if ever he had to serve in these waters, he would be prepared. Then work was available once more and he returned to the Navy, this time to serve uninterruptedly up to the day of his retirement.

Before going on to detail some of the higher adventures and brighter lights in his life as a seaman, an overall survey of what he had become by early middle-age might be illuminating. For now his character was set ; not in an authoritarian or arrogant sense, but as being deeply-marked in a pattern that was his alone, and which he retained to the end of his life. And its chief outlines, many of them, were not only admirable but uncommon in high-ranking naval officers of his day as being far in advance of the times, and prophetic of the fact that he would be the man behind the Navy's break with its past in all its romantic picturesque splendour and its dark concomitant horrors of disease and suffering, criminal corruption and waste.

First of all he had acquired the most minute and extraordinary knowledge of the men under him, which means he had taken the trouble to acquire it. This degree of interest of a superior in his subordinates is the exact opposite of the usual eighteenth-century attitude, and not easy to duplicate in any of his contemporaries, whether Army or Navy. Jervis knew the common seaman, the warrant officers and ranking officers, upside-down and inside-out. He knew how they behaved, and he knew the conditions on land and sea that impelled them to this behaviour. He was enormously concerned for their welfare and fought for them all with equal vigour and tenacity, in the service and out of it. 'I never yet have forsaken any man who served well under me', was how he expressed his article of faith at one time, and at another he was claiming relief for the family of 'a poor seaman who died in my service, and whose protector I therefore am'. His seamen's needs were in his mind always and everywhere, not excepting such exalted spheres as the Royal drawing-rooms. 'The King told me Vinegar sweetened with Honey was the most sovereign remedy for influenza.'

On those members of his shipboard population who were officers, he was much harder than on the men — this was also uncharacteristic of his time — demanding more of them in proportion to their superior advantages and education. 'Officers with families ashore', runs one of his orders, 'must remember that their men have no such resources, only the lowest brothels, and must not leave them to their own devices.' *Do not be in too much of a hurry to abandon them*, he is saying in other words, *merely because you have somewhere to go, for they have nowhere*. With similar intent he commands later, 'Officers must not manufacture pretexts to go ashore, such as shortage of water or docking for minor repairs', always trying to protect his lowest ranks, poor foolish children who rushed upon their shoreward fate and reeled back to the ship bilked of every penny and deathly sick, poisoned with bad liquor or the other dire infection. Inserted in the Wages Book, after each shore-leave, are long lists of men treated by the surgeon and charged accordingly.[1]

These were a few of the problems that pressed on him without intermission, but his care — endearingly — went far above and beyond daily routine toward a less tangible, but loftier, ambition for all ranks under his command ; he wished always to increase and uplift in them the sense of their own dignity. This intention of his was perhaps never formulated in words even to himself, but his every action in regard to his men points like an arrow to the same objective. 'Whenever anyone addressed him, even the lowest seaman, he would take off his hat and stand bareheaded.' And this was no mere gesture, but a spontaneous and natural outgrowth of his profound respect for every man, high or low, who was an honest member of that working unit called the ship's company. The fact of his taking off his hat was perhaps unimportant, but the attitude that it expressed was not unimportant. The ordinary seaman, a creature semi-illiterate, scarred and buffeted afloat and swindled and buffeted ashore — what feelings were aroused in him to see an admiral uncovering to receive his communication, what confused gratification or appeasement, what obscure raising of himself above his ordinary plane, if only for a moment? Instinctively he would realize his superior's sincere wish to do him honour, and surely the realization could not be harmful. And the chief who uncovered before his men expected every officer under him to do the same, and the importance he attached to this courtesy is evinced by the many irritable allusions, in his Order-books, to its slighting or scamping. 'The hat to be removed entirely from the head, and not merely tipped backward one or two inches.' Deficiency of manners had no more chance of escaping his eye than did, say, abuses of authority ; no less

[1] These lists are headed 'Venereal Cures' : were real cures possible in that day ?

than ashore, he was vigilant to protect his men from mis-
treatment aboard ship. For instance, he noted that 'punishments more frequently occurred with the evening duties',
after the officers had messed together in the wardroom ; 'the
natural inference was that by the freer circulation of the glass
on such occasions, some of the party too often became heated
and irritable'. Knowing this, he was likely to look long,
hard and with disfavour on severities inflicted late in the day,
and above all he objected to captains dining too frequently
with wardroom or gunroom officers, for these occasions
were apt to generate quarrels, and the anger so induced was
too often taken out on the men. Jervis himself — it was
well known — never punished after the serving of the
allowance of grog.

All this was by no means leniency but reasonableness,
and reasonableness was only one stone in the masonry of
another trait that towered out of his character : his absolute
and rigid sense of justice. He hated unfairness and favouritism
with a mortal hatred, and would one day make his hatred
the instrument of another break with a tradition at least four
centuries old in army, navy, law and church, and it would
take a bold man to prod the great sleepy Moloch, sated and
universally worshipped. Back-to-the-wall circumstances arising from stark necessity hammered him into a terrible figure
of discipline — whom no one need fear to approach, para-
doxically, but the insubordinate, the shirker or the gambler ;
on this trinity he had no mercy, his aversion to gambling
being another concept foreign to the time in which he lived.
Gambling was not only the very best form in the very highest
circles, but the non-gambler was considered a milksop or
eccentric, in fact hardly a gentleman. Yet his contempt for it
was stubborn, as little affected by the contemporary attitude
as his other opinions ; to his last moment his likes and dislikes
would be peculiarly, individually and unchangeably his own.

Last of all, surmounting the edifice of character upraised
through decades of hardest labour and bare-fisted experience,

his most pre-eminent quality flashed out like a spire catching the light — his power to assess and to estimate character and ability, to know exactly what he was looking at, and how best to make use of it. 'One of His Captains', otherwise anonymous, put it more formally : 'He was a man endowed with a talent of penetrating and distinguishing the true characters of men, and employing them on the service best suited to their abilities ; DEPENDING ENTIRELY ON HIMSELF' for his final decision in these matters. By his middle fifties the straight vigorous carriage of his youth had changed to the one that appears more or less in all his later portraits, showing how habitual and characteristic it was : his broad shoulders now perceptibly hunched and thickened at the back of the neck, his head carried low and thrust forward like a charging bull's, his glance coming up at you from under the heavy tufted brows. His eyes show large and of a very clear blue, and like all blue eyes they could chill with dislike or be warm with amusement or affection. His glance is penetrating and comprehensive ; out of the canvas he still sums you up with appraisal not unkind but only cool, detached and fatally accurate.

This in scantiest contour, mental and physical, is Jervis at fifty-three. He had reached a distinguished eminence in his profession and knew that the workings of seniority would bring him in due course to other honours, but perhaps he himself felt that he had made port ; that the most active part of his seaman's career was behind him, and from this point nothing much could happen to him. If he thought so he was wrong, because from this point everything happened to him. He was ready for greatness, and ready too for the meeting — one is tempted to call it The Meeting — with a naval captain then of no great prominence, a man of nearly forty who, feeling himself thwarted and held back by unappreciative superiors, was beginning to fret at his restraints with discontent and bitterness more and more vocal : a short, slight, rather frail man named Horatio Nelson.

III

THE ADMIRAL AND THE SOFT JOB

STUPID, senseless or reprehensible as the moral patterns of an age may appear to following generations, yet they seem beyond argument ; like the colour of eyes or hair, they must be accepted for what they are. But if they limit criticism they permit unlimited discussion and inspection ; we are privileged to look as long as we want at the special aspect of Jervis's time, called patronage.

This curious phenomenon, which dominated every gradation of every social class, in turn owed its power to another conception that fastened upon the whole known world its pitiless grip of steel, rigid and immovable — the idea of rank. The mere idea of superior status so worked on men's minds as to produce emotions hardly conceivable ; so tremendous the sense of position above one's own that courtiers burst into genuine tears at a royal mark of favour, the lord's underling and the squire's villager were similarly overwhelmed by any condescension from above, the lower clergy truckled painfully to the higher clergy, the apprentice was reverential toward his master, and so on down the line.

All the civilized world acquiesced in this arrangement ; governments combined to uphold it. It followed like clockwork that people should skim the cream from literally everything in sight, according as their social position gave them more or less power to do so. It also followed that no outsider had a chance of breaking in. The net result of this many-fingered grasp on all the things worth having was called patronage.

The machinery of patronage was simple : someone higher

up, for various reasons, gave something to someone lower down. The something might be a title, a wife, an income, an appointment, sinecure, job or apprenticeship. Along with this procedure there might operate, also, a system of purchase. A man could buy himself an heiress to marry ; he could buy regimental rank or, according to his pocket, he could buy the regiment itself. Once having bought it, the regiment was literally his to dispose of as he liked — not to a foreign power certainly, but he was free to re-sell his command at the best profit he could get, with very likely a little horse-dealing on the side, and no one dreamed of questioning his right to do so. The Navy, it is true, made no practice of selling commissions to the unqualified — perhaps because the spectacle of an in-experienced man commanding a ship in a storm would be too outright an embarrassment ; also they had their cargoes to think of, a consideration with which the Army was unencumbered. But it had its own systems of favouritism, scores of them, including such irregularities as the 'name-on-books' trick — that is, entering the name of a very young child on the ship's books as one of its complement, every month that his name stayed there counting toward the necessary six years of experience before the Admiralty would give him a commission. Someone sufficiently influential had to get the child registered, that was all, and in like manner people moved into governorships, bishoprics and all manner of livings, according as the name of some patron stretched over them like an umbrella to ward off the inclemencies of exposure and penalty. Older than Adam all this, and merely offered as a contrast to Jervis's stand on the subject of job-giving and advancement : that these should depend, not on a young man's patron or the eminence of his family connections, but on the single basis of ability — of merit. If this sounds merely the dullest commonsense, we have only to recall the universal practice of the age — with its long fingers immovably clenched on every profession and every trade — to realize how revo-lutionary and how daring was Jervis's whole approach to the vast problem of rewarding and handling men. And to keep him in his proper frame of time, remember that he had attended parties given by Catherine the Great and toured the France of Louis XVI, even though his life reached into the nineteenth century. To give his ideas and his acts their full weight, one might put it this way : with no precedent to guide him, he laid the axe of his courage and integrity to the roots of entrenched privilege.

Jervis stayed ashore long enough in his forties to do two things : get married, and become an M.P. The Parliamentary episode happened to him and should be recorded, but it means less, perhaps, than any other professional period of his life. His temperament was active and administrative, not oratorical ; still, having considerable facility of expression and hard commonsense, he did the things one would expect him to do — spoke up for neglected and pensionless seamen and kicked the supports from under a proposed naval project upraised on a foundation of well-camouflaged graft. He did not originate or sponsor large remedial measures because the patterns of correction did not yet work that way. Social reform, a rickety foundling, was not likely to find a cradle in the Lords or Commons ; social conscience, necessarily the foundling's father, was a Johnny-come-lately and operated through isolated persons ahead of their time. For instance, Elizabeth Fry was upset over the fate of women in prisons and did something about it, but such manifestations were individual and unofficial, and though on the increase were rare enough. Therefore, Jervis's chief value as a reformer was not parliamentary, but resolves itself rather into the matter of his association with, and attitude toward, the men he commanded ; a thing personal to him but momentous, since in his high place his example was conspicuous and he had the power to impose his methods as standard practice — not forgetting, also, that his life was interwoven with tens of thousands of other lives.

In order to appreciate the novelty and originality of his

position, one has only to contrast it with the view that other
naval and military figures, before and indeed after him, took
of their lower ranks.   No need to labour or exaggerate the
issue of inhumanity since inhumanity exhibits an endless
variety of shapes, but it might be said that the first inhumanity
that high commanders practised toward the rank and file
was a large, excluding obliviousness.   Wellington's opinion
of it, 'the scum of the earth' : his allusion to a passing soldier
as 'that article' (and Wellington was Jervis's contemporary)
illustrates the point accurately enough, for the common
soldier or seaman was just that, an article.   The article was
there to render obedience, and for no other reason.   If it
balked or rebelled, it was stamped into the ground.   For
efficiency's sake one would maintain it in as good condition
as possible, but if not, it hardly mattered ; no one would be
called to account for thousands of men unnecessarily dead.
If the supply of the article ran out it must be replenished,
never mind how or from where.   As for its having separate
identity or individuality, such a likelihood had probably never
occurred to the majority of gentlemen in posts of authority.
This is not to say that individual close relationships did not
exist between admirals and lower seamen down to the very
humblest, because scores of references in letters prove the
opposite.   Every high commander had favourite officers and
crew members, transferring them to every ship where he
hoisted his flag so as to keep them always with him.   He
wanted them to share his good fortune, and was often touchingly concerned lest his bad fortune — his reverses or disgrace
— should harm their prospects of advancement.   This was
admirable but its significance and scope were limited ; in the
last analysis it was merely the attitude of the grand seigneur,
whose concern for his dependants was bound up less with
them than with the matter of his own personal pride and
consequence.

Jervis's attitude toward the man under him — of whatever
rank — was so bound up with the man's inner well-being, as

well as the outer, that there is no comparison. His view of the man was essentially one : he saw him in relation to his work, and how he must be treated in order to give his best to that work. Not by good feeding or stabling only, but by the much more powerful means of appealing to a man's sense of his own importance. Jervis's respect for the job was so intense, his appreciation of the man who did it well so constant and so conspicuous, that it ended by instilling into the man a new conception of himself : that his own dignity and the dignity of his job were inseparable, and ill-performance of the one must mean damage to the other. This pride or responsibility, call it what one will, is the fountain of all achievement and the backbone of all discipline. Not the discipline of cowing or suppression, but the discipline springing inexhaustibly from the wells of a man's respect for himself. This is not the highest conception of man perhaps, but it towers above the conception of man as a well-treated dependent, and it is with this interpretation of discipline that Jervis's name should be forever associated. Invariably, when he wanted to stiffen a man's performance, he began by bolstering his self-esteem.

Jervis's concern for his subordinates, high and low, never slept and never wearied. The expression of this concern varied, of course, according to the man he had to deal with, but what did not vary was his knowledge of their individual circumstances, enormous in extent and often surprising in the details he found out, or that were confided to him in some moment of misery. This alone should shatter the idea of him as a granite-and-lead embodiment of authority whom everyone was afraid to approach. Unfortunate people were never afraid of him, and undeserved misfortune opened his door faster than anything else.

For a quick survey of the methods by which he got from his men the utmost that was in them, we might begin with the highest ranks under his command and work downward.

On behalf of the officer class of his Fleet — admirals,

captains, commanders and six classes of lieutenants — he
wanted, first and foremost, promotion. A man who was able
had the right to prompt recognition of his ability, he argued ;
reward too-long-delayed or not forthcoming at all ate out
the substance of his hope and withered his good intentions.
From Jervis's dispatch-books and private letters all during his
professional life one can draw examples, literally by the hundred, of how he hammered at the Admiralty early and late
over their dilatory or indifferent response to this vital question.
Promote, promote, promote, ran the burden of his song :
your present rate of promotion is too slow : if promotion
continues so sluggish and so languid, what incentive will
ambitious young men have to join the Navy ? And his
official communications on this score were varied with any
number of icy personal letters, expressing surprise that the
advancement of deserving officers had been held up, for no
good reason that he could see. Up and down the ladder of
rank swept his gaze, giving to each man's achievements the
same degree of scrutiny, evaluation and support. 'I declare I
have never experienced greater alacrity and desire to carry
orders into prompt execution, than in Admiral Curtis —
Captain Poulson's whole conduct under my command shows
him to be an officer who never makes difficulties, and is very
fit to be employed in a much higher station than he now fills
— Lieutenant Mottley's indefatigable labour, industry and
ability are such that I beg leave to recommend him, in the
strongest terms, for promotion to the rank of commander —
for two seamen who saved the *Alcmene's* dispatches from the
French' he asks, and gets, an annual pension of twenty pounds.
Skill and resource and alertness, courage and endurance, these
were the things he appreciated, and he was determined they
should be productive — not only of his approval, but of
practical benefits to the men who deserved them by working
so hard and so well.

Postponing for a later moment his view and his treatment
of the Marines (a contingent particularly dear to his heart),

the next large body of men with whom he was in close and constant contact were the shipboard and dockyard artisans. These were the shipwrights, master-caulkers and plain caulkers, smiths and above all the carpenters, whose reports on ships make such good reading and use such lovely language as : 'Extreme good ; whoever built her, did her a deal of justice'. But the same reports also demonstrate with what terrifying, incredible speed a ship in tight and brilliant trim, at the highest peak of maintenance and efficiency, could be reduced to a mass of trembling wood and flapping canvas rags — and this not by the shocks of war but merely by the wear and tear of sea and weather. Only yesterday, or almost, she triumphed through wind and waves, a terror to the enemy ; today, the carpenters report her as so crazy and so ruinous that she must be dealt with in an English dockyard, only they doubt whether she can survive the voyage to get her there. The importance of these experts could hardly be exaggerated, since in the last resort it depended on them whether a ship were seaworthy or not, and Jervis was fully aware of it. Hence his analytical eye fell upon them quite as piercingly as upon his officers ; he would do anything to keep or help a shipwright whom he knew to be especially valuable.

Once, in particular, he wrote direct to the Secretary of the Admiralty, Evan Nepean, over the predicament of a boatswain in Gibraltar dockyard. Before doing this he must have had a long talk with the man, probably taking a good deal of time in order to draw out of him the tale of his daily miseries and his suicidal mood, and if the letter is not actually unique one may safely call it unusual as coming from an Earl and Commander-in-Chief managing, at the same time, a large-scale war. The man is unable to live on his wages, Jervis reports, the cost of living at Gibraltar being so high, 'with meat (and very bad too) at three reals the pound, and everything else proportionately dear, insomuch the poor man is necessarily in debt [Jervis hated people unnecessarily in debt] and under great oppression of spirits.' This hopeless state of mind was a matter of utmost concern to Jervis, because 'I have been witness to his masting of three ships, using poor equipment, without damaging a shilling's worth of material or hurting a man's finger'. Such master-craftsmanship must not be lost to the King's Navy, he urges ; the Admiralty must do *something* 'to rescue this useful and meritorious officer from the despondency he is in'. Knowing by this time a little about Jervis and his practical approach to distress of any kind, it is safe to say that he probably put his hand in his pocket and gave the man enough to clear his worst debts, while waiting to see what authority would do for him. A little extra spark of affection for the Admiral kindled in at least one person, not so much because he knew what the carpenter had to pay for meat, but because he knew the meat to be not worth the money.

These were the people — officers, seamen and workmen — who came most directly into relationship with Jervis in the sense that he could stir up or retard their chances of advancement, give jobs to them or take jobs away. This, in theory at least, was a simple procedure for him, since their definite qualifications made them readily classifiable. But his genius for assessment went further and concerned itself with the man apparently valueless because not so easily classified, the odd man out whose abilities did not leap to the eye but required a little patient consideration and digging. For instance, there was a young Lieutenant Stevens whose health had cracked just enough, under the climate, to make him unequal to heavy duty. This must have meant the end of his naval career and the waste of his long years preparing for it, a moment of blackest realization for anyone. But Jervis took time, at a most terrifyingly crucial point of the war, to write to the Admiralty about him. The Transport Board ought to find a job for the young man, he suggested, because 'he appears to have a head of arrangement'. This was the more penetrating of Jervis in that indexing and cataloguing were almost unpractised and their value scarcely understood, and

E

numerous other of his letters stand witness to how many, many times he tried to discern, or to imagine, what the misfit could do — and the misfit had no place in the eighteenth century ; its wheels went over him without mercy.

There was another case out of the common run, but much more light-hearted. A Lieutenant Prescott wanted to resign his commission and go home. Jervis nosed about discreetly and discovered the reason : his grandfather had died and left him some money, and the dashing youth — Jervis knew him to be dashing — was dying to get to London and spend it. The idea did not appeal to the Admiral because Prescott was clever and capable — 'he has it in him to make a good officer' — so he wrote the Admiralty, suggesting that the application to resign be rejected. 'This may be the means of rescuing a young man from the jaws of destruction', Jervis intones piously, with perhaps a small grin underlying the piety at the thought of the gay young blade done out of his binge, all unknowing of the doer. But the incident not only illustrates the alarming extent of his information about his men, but his deep personal interest in them and his readiness to take trouble over them, for the Prescott letter was written when he himself was at the lowest physical ebb, just one month before illness drove him home from his command.

Late in his career, Jervis had a long, searing experience with large-scale mutiny. The story will appear in its proper context and is here mentioned only to illumine both his rock-like firmness and his resilience. Mutiny is perhaps the bitterest pill that any naval commander has to swallow ; more bitter than defeat, for defeat can be honourable, but in mutiny there is no honour or other balm, only the confirmation in the commander's own eyes of his failure — his failure as an officer and as a man. One of Jervis's admirals at the time (for the trouble broke out simultaneously in a number of ships) was rocked from top to bottom by the cataclysm. He was charming and intelligent, unusually humane as the times went, and had so treated his crew that they presented 'an uncommon appearance of happiness and good understanding, and a uniform, ready and chearful obedience to every command'.   And now they turned on him ; beneath the smiles black treachery had been brewing all the time, and the bitterness of the letter he wrote Jervis is not to be described.   Never, never trust a ship's company again, runs the burden of his disillusionment ; no matter how contented and well-disciplined they seem to be, put no faith in them but have them watched always, like dangerous animals.

Take, by contrast, Jervis's position at the same time.   The mutiny was more of a blow to him than to anyone, since it endangered the whole campaign for which he was responsible, and if anyone had a reason for reversing a lifelong attitude and turning vindictive and misanthropic, it was he.   Instead, his behaviour was exactly the opposite.   It happened that at this period he had ordered commanders of all ranks in his Fleet — himself included — to turn in the most detailed and comprehensive report on the state of their individual ships, nineteen in all, and these reports are fascinating not only as presenting, each one, a little teeming world of many compartments enclosed in a wooden shell and topped by sails, but as unconsciously revealing the qualities of the men who had prepared them.   The reports were filled in on identical printed forms, so that there is a resemblance among them — but also a difference, and what a difference !   Every commander touches, of course, on the state of his crews ; the sick, the well, the discipline, clothing in adequate repair or not, the mention of fresh meat and vegetables given when these are available, and so forth.   Then they pass on to the matter of supplies and equipment, and somehow the impression is given that much more exactitude, care and interest have been expended on these than on descriptions of the ship's company, as if the writers were incomparably more concerned about commodities than about men.

With Jervis it was different.   In contrast to the colourless wording of the other reports, his interest in his subject warms

the official forms and crams them full of life. Not that he
scanted the subject of stores either, for it was not his way
to overlook anything. 'Provisions for three months good in
kind, except the biscuit which appears to be old. Fresh meat
cut up fairly in the presence of four witnesses, OFFICERS AND
OTHERS NOT ALLOWED CHOICE PIECES OR PREFERENCE OF ANY
KIND'. This recalled a bad old practice when officers got the
meat and the crew got gristle and strings. 'Onions, oranges
and lemons distributed equally, with a reserve for the sick.'
This, an echo of the times — very recent — of scurvy. 'Water,
105 tons. Cloathing well-attended to, beds regularly aired.
The ship's company in high health and a very good company,
boys of the second class very stout.'

Now he passes to the state of the sick. 'A number of
persons on the sick list, fever, flux, accidents, rheumatism,
colds, but chiefly ulcers among the quota men.' Here his
individual touch breaks through. 'Several of these are
nuisances.' But when he talks of the surgeon and his achievements, his pen begins to sing. 'The sick berth admirably
arranged, fresh provisions constantly given, and the patients
treated with the utmost tenderness, skill and humanity.'

Then he proceeds to individual crew-members, com-
menting doubtfully but with strict fairness, 'The Gunner
infirm, but appears to have a good moral character.' The
Master, though, is a different story. 'Take him all in all, the
best I ever served with.' The state of his Marines bucks him
up, too. 'The best detachment I ever saw.' Again and again,
as if compelled, he has to break away from stores and ordnance
and revert to a subject much nearer his heart ; mutiny cannot
so embitter him as to dim the glow of his pride in his darlings,
his ships' companies. Not that partiality ever blinded him,
either, for only a year later he is contemplating a body of
Austrian Marines and noting moodily, 'Very fine, and far
superior to our own.'

Again, disturbing notes in his dispatches remind us of an
aspect of mutiny mostly overlooked or forgotten — its after-

math. Mutiny was a destroying angel that passed over a ship and scored deep marks not only in crew but officers, and pitiful cases like these were left on Jervis's hands to cope with as best he might. In one ship a steady stream of desertions 'proceeded entirely from the weakness of the commander, and will show how much fitter Captain Ellison is for Greenwich Hospital than to be placed on the *Marlborough* after the mutiny; his nerves are shook to imbecility'; also there was another poor man, an officer of Marines: 'His mind is deranged; it would be an act of humanity to contrive his retirement on full pay.'

Along with Jervis's system of giving jobs to the able, not the well-connected, went a constant assessment of individual qualifications in terms whose precision was rare in that day and age, and it is fascinating to see with what exactitude of shading he distinguished among every degree of capacity, never with the slightest tendency — it would seem — to overrate or under-rate. For instance, from two ships of his Fleet he expects no service whatever, since 'their Captains are good sort of men, but totally unfit for stations in these times of difficulty'. Note, however, that his disappointment in these officers cannot mislead him into total disparagement. 'The Captain of this ship [*Warrior*] though a man of talent, is so unsuited for duty of this kind that here he is lost.' Also he places responsibility squarely where it belongs. '*Warrior*, mainly through the incompetence of her officers, has thrown away two sets of topmasts and three jib booms.' Sometimes, when judgment had to be too harsh to allow of mitigation, he would avoid identifying an officer by name. 'This ship (it is with pain I say it) is in very feeble and improper hands.' Unexpected people sometimes drew his fire, such as a parson whose conduct he called 'shuffling, and he is unworthy to fill the office of chaplain in any of H.M.'s ships'. Also, when necessary, he did not hesitate to fling a whole contingent into outer darkness. 'For the most part, the lieutenants who have come to me from cutters and luggers are helpless animals.'

Now for a class not yet mentioned, which came directly under Jervis's notice and — indirectly — his influence and management : the midshipmen. These might have been included in the officer category since they were potential officers, but there is something so appealing about these young boys that they attract special attention, all the more since theirs was the layer of shipboard society most openly created by the practice of patronage. That is to say, the candidate for midshipman had to have his nominator, just as Jervis had his long ago, and it was a reasonably iron-clad principle that the more highly-titled the proposer, the better chance his protégé had of getting on a ship. Not where Jervis was concerned, however ; if he had any leanings toward favouritism it was on behalf of this special class, and invariably his influence was thrown not to the boy with the most aristocratic recommendation, but to sons of old sea-officers or their widows. In such cases, also, preference usually went to those in the poorest circumstances, and Jervis made no secret of his position but stated it openly, again and again : that if they owed a duty anywhere, they owed it to old Navy men or their families, and few got past this barrier of his convictions on the strength of a patron, however exalted.

These careers in the bud, on Jervis's ships, were under his eye from the first since it was he who forwarded their passing certificates to the Admiralty, but of direct contact with them he probably had little. However — as with everything on his ships — he knew all about them, and the stray glimpses and gleams we get of his treatment of them add up to something consistent and infinitely attractive. He spared young hearts. When he wrote to warn his favourite sister Mary, whose sons were in training on his flagship, that her boys must not be better-dressed than the other boys : when he warned his nephew Henry that he must not wear his new jacket because the other boys' jackets were not new : was he remembering himself standing shamed before his first patroness in the wretched coat with skirts trailing on the ground and

sleeves falling down over his hands ? When he insisted, even
exaggeratedly, on such elaborate formality and courtesy
among his men, was he remembering Commodore Townshend frowzy with sleep half-falling downstairs in his bedgown,
and Townshend's lieutenant with the smells of debauch coming
off his disordered clothes, both reminding him, by their
manner of reception, just how much of a nobody he was ?
Perhaps the great Earl of St. Vincent, Commander-in-Chief
and Knight Grand Cross of the Order of the Bath, had never
climbed so high that he lost sight of an odd-looking boy in
breeches botched up from mattress-ticking, standing lonely
and watching, from the deserted deck, his former companions
piling into the launch to go ashore. Perhaps the young midshipman, exiled from the pleasures, friendship and mess of his
kind, munching solitary meals in stray corners and sleeping
on the bare deck, stayed with him all his life.

Whether or not this is so, a peculiar gentleness marked
his dealings with the youngest officers, a peculiar readiness to
find extenuating circumstances for them if he could, as for
one young fool : 'While the defence set up by Lieutenant
Harris does not amount to a complete justification of his conduct, it tends to a mitigation of censure. The fact is, his only
notion was the idle one of having a last fling with an old
messmate.' But none of them need expect special favours,
more than anyone else, for Jervis had only one yardstick.
Through the years there grew up around him a body of sea-
officers famous for a skill almost legendary, based on the
soundness of their training. They called themselves 'St.
Vincent's School', and every single one of them had advanced
according to how Jervis's measuring-rod rated their capacities
as higher or lower, and for no other reason.

These were the principles that guided him when he chose
the 'Band of Brothers' that surrounded Nelson at the Nile.
They were the principles that guided him when he chose the
man whom they surrounded.

IV

THE ADMIRAL AND THE DOCKYARDS

TWENTY years after Jervis had gone to his grave, a young man married a girl who happened to be Queen of England. The young man had remarkable abilities extended and developed by far-reaching education, and began his married life with hopes of being his wife's helpmeet and collaborator in a sense not only personal but official. At once, however, he was undeceived. Even if Victoria had been inclined to let him participate in her political existence she could hardly have done so ; of that sacrosanct territory which comprised the power and the functions of her queenship, she was not the most jealous guardian by any means.

This being the case, her husband, disappointed of the larger theatre of activity, looked about him for occupation nearer at hand. From the first the royal couple had been inconvenienced by fantastic discomforts and inconveniences at whichever of their seats they happened to be residing at the time, and Albert turned his attention to a detailed examination of the royal households. He was not long in discovering that the various inefficiencies under which the Queen and he had been suffering were only the outward manifestation of something going on beneath the surface — which, when he dug it out, proved to be a root-system of dishonesties, graft and flagrant perquisites — a growth unbelievably intricate and enormous, undisturbed for many years, richly manured by greed and screened off from sight behind a thick interwoven hedge of self-interest. This might be no surprise, seeing that the hundreds of upper and lower servants inside the royal establishments, and the hundreds of tradesmen outside, formed a combination of opportunities too powerful for human nature to resist. What was surprising, though, was the attitude of nearly all these profiteers, once caught red-handed in their poses of peculation. Their outcries filled the air, of course, but far from betokening shame or repentance, their tone was of high and genuine moral indignation ; the indignation of those barefacedly robbed of benefits to which they had a just and undoubted right. The ancient abuse, over the years, had taken on the patina of ancient privilege — respectable ancient privilege — and the emotion of those deprived of it was sincere and simple outrage, mixed with accusations of cheese-paring unworthy of royal palaces and references to stingy minor royalties and German ones at that.

Now if an inexperienced young man like Albert could turn up skulduggery on such a scale at Windsor and Buckingham Palace, what might an experienced old one like Jervis [1] exhume if he bent an inquisitor's eye upon an establishment so enormous as a dockyard, with its hundreds of workmen and its mountains of stores and supplies ? And multiply this dockyard by six, in an age when periodic checks and scrutiny were not yet a matter of routine, and who shall say what the systematic investigator might find if he, like Jervis, were profoundly experienced in every detail that had to do with a ship?

The smell that wafted off the King's six dockyards — more and more contemptuous of the nostrils it offended — was nothing new ; for years there had been comments and enquiries from those who suspected the worst, and latterly there had been a certain amount of pressure on the Admiralty to lay the whole affair open as with a surgeon's scalpel and see what went on inside. The trouble was that the pressure was sporadic and uneven, and its indecision was matched by certain qualities in the then First Lord, Earl Spencer. Spencer was a man of undoubted conscience who took his responsibilities tremendously to heart ; at news of the Nile victory

---

[1] By the time of the Admiralty investigation he had become Lord St. Vincent, but for the sake of clarity he will be called Jervis until a later chapter.

he tumbled to the floor in a faint, proof of how cruelly and deeply the tensions of his job had cut into him. He had no wish to neglect or evade anything, but apparently he was a sensitive man, devoted to science, art and books, and certain activities were not his line of country. Or perhaps he felt within himself that unnerving lack of practical knowledge which keeps a man from taking full and effective grasp of a situation. At any rate, faced with the prospect of turning the dockyards inside-out and its unpredictable consequences of uproar and hostility, it seems that he simply lost courage. Better not disturb the unknown bloated shape that lay heavily on the yards for fear of seeing its real outlines and daring its enraged claws, reaching to what heights and depths nobody knew ; in his reluctance to stir up the gorged incubus Spencer had plenty of company, and for the whole duration of his time as First Lord it appears that he adopted a set policy of averting his eyes and preferring to know nothing. Consequently the yards went along as they had done for scores of years, with the scandal becoming always more brazen, more openly derisive of disguise or law alike. Remedy would have to wait upon a peculiar combination — of a decisive event to push matters to a show-down, and of a decisive man who would take command once the battle was joined, and who would be perfectly unmoved by its bedlam of yells and screams and abuse, its hatred and menaces. The man appeared when Jervis became First Lord of the Admiralty in February 1801. The event, in February, snapped at the heels of his installation. The man and the event collided, and the explosion followed.

Strikes are usually called to coincide with some period when the inconveniences they cause are hardest to bear, as for instance, holidays. But England's worry at the moment was not holidays but merely survival, for still the Napoleonic war went on and on, the nightmare riding its tidal-wave crest of huge armies, navies, force, might, conjured up endlessly out of distance and draining its opponents of endurance, money and blood. Many-branched, hostilities had now moved north ; a fleet was preparing in the dockyards for a Baltic campaign and the need for this fleet was desperate, in tune with the country's chronic state of desperation.

It was at this precise moment that a body of delegates, representing all six dockyards, converged upon London and the Admiralty with a demand for increased wages. The amount of the increase asked was just one hundred per cent, or doubled wages. They brought with them a prepared statement referring to increased costs of living. The average wage of the dockyard worker was, at that time, about one hundred pounds annually. To understand whether this figure was adequate or inadequate, a glance at current costs of living is necessary, and — more informative still — at current conceptions of what constituted a fair income. Because contemporary notions of a man's financial position in the world, though not based on exact figures, somehow turn out in the end more or less well-grounded ; in like manner the early nineteenth-century idea of poor, fair or good income may be taken as a measurement rough and general, yet as one not misleading ; not exact in the sense of decimal points, but practical. For those people who then moved about and worked and worried, who paid rent, food, clothes and amusements, incidental expenses and taxes, knew the impact and demands of life as encountered daily, not as derived from tabulated figures. They had the handling of money and they knew money's worth ; they knew what money would buy.

Always bearing in mind that the point under discussion is a comfortable livelihood by workman's standards, not gentry's — which was something else again — we might start with the fact that modern experts whose subject is money say that a hundred pounds, in 1801, must be multiplied by ten to approximate its present-day value. Some even say by twenty ; strike a medium and say by fifteen. In that case the dockyard worker's wage was £1500 annually, an income not despised even now by the educated professional classes with children in public schools and certain social appearances to keep up, considerations with which the dockyard workman was not burdened. Furthermore, in addition to his regular wages he enjoyed continual overtime, based on a system of deliberately putting unskilled workmen with skilled ones for the express purpose of holding back the progress of the working unit as a whole and stringing out the job as long as possible ; this practice of mixing weak and strong grades of labour was called 'shoaling', from which all the gang (as they were called) benefited. So did the Quarterman or Foreman, whose function it was to estimate the work done and keep a record of what the men had earned, and since his own wage was based on a percentage of these estimated wages, it is fairly certain he would take care not to be a loser by the process. What this 'earned' overtime amounted to has never been found out ; the practice was too widespread and too well protected 'by the connivance of the various boards and commissions supposed to check and control expenditure', for they were getting their rake-off too. Sheridan, in the Commons, reckoned the total wastage at three million pounds per annum, of which fraudulent wages might be fifty per cent, say a million and a half of public money a year. Multiply by fifteen once more for present-day equivalents.

The dockyard labourer, some claim, was under a disadvantage compared to the country labourer, who always had a garden and a pig to eke out his livelihood. But how do we know the dockyard man had none ? All the surroundings of London, at that time, were predominantly rural. And even if the shipbuilding artisan were gardenless and pigless, there were the perquisites he received from the yard. Wood from sawed planks, of which the wastage was enormous ; other fuel or its equivalents, even some furniture ; all these might make up the deficiency.

Then comes the question of what the weekly wage would buy. For lack of power to transform ourselves into the dockyard labourer's wife with her basket in hand, knowing just how far her money would go and how fast it seemed to disappear, we must fall back on contemporary records. And by luck there exist detailed lists giving the prices of everything and not in other localities but — amazingly — in the very neighbourhood of the dockyards themselves ; in a word, a bird's-eye view of *local* costs of living, as felt in the dockyard worker's pocket. The following figures are drawn from the accounts of Plymouth, Haslar, East Stonehouse and Greenwich Royal Hospitals. Since these institutions bought in large quantities at a reduced rate, all prices quoted have been advanced by fifty per cent, which seems to bring them in line with contemporary household accounts and local allusions. For the sake of fairness we shall base ourselves on the very highest prices, not the lowest.

Between 1801-5, beef was ninepence a pound, and mutton about tenpence. Potatoes were a penny a pound, oatmeal a penny halfpenny. A pound of cheese was elevenpence, of butter eighteen pence. Bread was fivepence a pound, milk eightpence a gallon. Sixpence would buy enough fish to give a large family two meals. Beer was fourpence a quart. 'The Best wheaten flour' sold for two and threepence the sack. Greens cost so next-to-nothing that it is difficult to calculate, say three farthings the pound.

As for other kinds of household commodities, which once bought would last for years : a bed could be had for seventeen shillings, a blanket for thirteen shillings, a feather pillow for five and threepence. Men's shoes were nine shillings the pair, boys' shoes six. Cloth was all prices ; good woollen could be had for four and five shillings a yard, good cottons for much less.

Then the very important item of rent : a house let for seven pounds thirteen a year, but the dockyard labourer would be more likely to occupy a cottage. Cottages let for one pound a year. 'A cottage and ground' let for two pounds ten, and cottage rentals are recorded of five

shillings a year. For that matter a house could be rented for
five pounds annually, a rate not beyond the pocket of a man
earning a hundred a year. Fuel was very important, too ;
coal was expensive, but with the abundance of free wood from
the dockyards their workers were not at the mercy of seasonal
high prices. Does all this make a wage of one hundred pounds
a year seem adequate ? When people called dockyard wages
'enormous', were they justified ? Again, a matter of opinion
or of greater knowledge of the period. But from the mouths
of dockyard employees we will learn whether the yard
artisan's pay was regarded as great or small, and we will also
see that this pay of about one pound eighteen shillings a week
topped current wages of labour — and skilled labour too —
by nearly twelve shillings a week.

Now, with perhaps a slight picture of conditions in mind,
we might go back to rejoin the dockyard delegates, about
one hundred and fifty of them, milling about at the doors of
the Admiralty — or in its entrance-hall, rather, for report
credits them with getting that far. Onlookers also say they
appeared sure of themselves. Well they might, with their
knowledge of the country's extremity, of all the dockyards
united behind them, and the threat they brought with them,
unspoken but implicit — stoppage of all work on the Baltic
fleet. Having left what they called their petition, which might
rather be termed an ultimatum, they withdrew, announcing
their intention to return after an interval (unstated) for the
Admiralty's reply.

Fast action was demanded in this moment, and Jervis was
never the man to let grass grow under his feet. His carriage
appeared in a hurry and he posted off to a meeting of the
Cabinet, specially called. He found it in a condition of funk,
wringing its hands, or at least friends of his did not hesitate
to come out later on and say so in print. If this body of
intimidated gentlemen implored him not to anger the workmen by opposing their demands, at this desperate moment of
national crisis, they must have used much the same arguments

as Canning some months later : that such opposition, during wartime, 'would serve but to irritate useful artificers and drive them from the public service'. Stuff like this had no interest for Jervis ; his single session with the Cabinet over, he drove back to the Admiralty and gave some orders.

Shortly after his arrival, the delegates reappeared. Again they succeeded in penetrating as far as the entrance-hall. Here they found a reception-committee sufficiently potent to turn them all into the street, at the same time informing them that they were thrown out of their dockyard jobs. Apparently the group, for all its size, was so stunned by these unexpected measures 'that no resistance was made, or disturbance of any kind'. In passing, it may be noted that its collective aspect, once the Admiralty doors had been slammed in its face, was not that of men unjustly repulsed after reasonable demands, but the sheepish, furtive one of people who have knowingly tried to over-reach themselves and failed. 'We waited six weeks too long', seems to have been their summing-up of the situation as they departed, and they were right ; they should have struck while they still had the more amenable Spencer to deal with, not a formidable man like Jervis. The formidable man now conducted some searing interviews with those responsible for dockyard performance. In consequence, work on the Baltic squadron was rushed through and it sailed as scheduled.

But the squadron's departure was by no means the end of the affair, only its beginning. The threatened strike and the delegation had given Jervis precisely the handle he wanted, and he lost little time in laying hold of it. He and all the other Lords of Admiralty set out for a tour of all six yards (Plymouth, Portsmouth, Chatham, Sheerness, Woolwich, Deptford) late in August 1802. By their order they were accompanied by the Comptroller and three other members of the Navy Board. As this was the body responsible for naval contracts and supplies, and since no considerable crookedness could have existed without their collusion, they could not have had much fun in being compelled to go along and have their noses rubbed in their own deficiencies.

The inspection took about a month, the Lords giving an average of four or five days to each dockyard. These surveys of their very brevity had to be superficial, but what they uncovered was more than reason enough for setting up a large-scale machinery of investigation, or, as it was called more staidly, 'Revision'. A Commission of five headed it, with committees under them. As for the size of the job they had taken on : the mere overhaul, detail by detail, and the accumulation of sufficient testimonies, took three years. It was the first investigation in history of dimensions so vast, methods so drastic, and results so effective and permanent — launched by the man who could be by turns courtliest eighteenth century, or most ruthless twentieth.

By now the muck-raking process is a stale old story, but what keeps its fascination in this case is the testimony itself — the stenographic evidence taken down by the Commission. Before them passed the most wonderful procession of paymasters, surveyors, clerks, foremen (or quartermen), carpenters, rope-makers, coopers, horse-masters and still humbler dockyard workers, all testifying under oath and preserving to us the authentic accent of the individual speaker. One by one they ran the gauntlet of the ruthless questioning — the shamefaced, the frightened, the excuser, the defiant or the merely ignorant and careless (these a majority) and more rarely the brazen, the scoundrelly or the downright inhumane. And never, since the beginning of the world, had arisen such a chorus of *I don't know, I can't say, I can't remember*, the blight of this mass-amnesia falling equally on baronets and labourers. Yet, on the credit side, the parade offered enough honest and responsible workmen-witnesses to redeem it from a total shame, and even — very rarely — the spectacle of a touching integrity. Old Mr. Ffinch, for example, a clerk of long, long service, was just due for retirement but postponed it on hearing of the Commission's imminent visit, 'because', he explained with tremulous dignity, 'I did not wish it to seem that I shrank from the inquiry.'

The structure laid bare by these months of inquisition resembled a tall old house rotten from its foundations and stuffed to bursting on each floor with every specimen of knavery, swindling and falsehood known since the beginning of time. The abuses fell under three main heads : Wages, Timber and Stores. Under each of these heads, bits of testimony build up a picture of what was going on in Denmark.

WAGES

Examination of Mr. Peng, Clerk of the Cheque (Paymaster's Office) of Plymouth Yard

Q. Is there any printed or written code of instructions in your office, under which you act ?

A. I never saw any, but understand there are some in the office dated prior to 1700.

Q. Who makes out the paybooks of the yard ?

A. The clerks in my office.

Q. Are the paybooks sent to the Navy Board for examination, prior to being paid ?

A. Never.

Examination of Joseph Tuck, Master Shipwright

Q. Who reports on the amount of work performed ?

A. The quartermen or foremen.

Q. Are the quartermen interested in the amount of work performed ?

A. Yes, for their own rate of pay is governed by the earnings of their gangs.

Q. Can they write ?

A. They all can write, but some of them write very badly.

Q. Are they capable of keeping accounts ?

A. As far as I know.

Q. How do they ascertain that men have done enough work to entitle them to double wages ?

A. I cannot say.

F

Q. Are there any classes of workmen who make out the bills for their own work ?
A. Yes, the cooper, locksmith and plumber.
Q. Does anyone superintend the work they do, or check their bills ?
A. No.

Examination of John Ancell, Shipwright

Q. Do you sign certificates that certain work has been done ?
A. Yes.
Q. What steps do you take to ascertain that the work has actually been performed ?
A. None.
Q. Does anyone examine the amount of work done, for which the bill was made out ?
A. No one.

Examination of Samuel Jones, Foreman of Shipwrights

Q. Do the job bills contain a true statement of persons employed on the work ?
A. No.
Q. Is the record of employment thereby rendered fallacious ?
A. Yes, it is fallacious. (*Then Samuel snatches at a straw.*) To a certain degree.

Testimony on employment might follow, as being closely related to wages.

Examination of John Penfold, Master Ropemaker of Plymouth Yard

Q. What amount of time are ropemakers obliged to remain in the yard ?
A. They are not obliged to remain any number of hours, but leave it when their day's work is finished.
Q. How long does it take them to do a day's work ?
A. Layers can do a day's work in three hours, spinners in three or four hours, and parters in two and a half hours.

Examination of George Smith, Clerk of Woolwich Yard

Q. Are workmen always checked when absent?

A. Not always.

Q. When absent and not checked, had they the same rate of pay as other men?

A. Yes.

Q. Have any men entered as absent, been taken from the absent lists?

A. Yes, I have occasionally indulged the men by taking them from the absent lists.

Q. When a man reports he is sick, does the surgeon visit him to see that he is so?

A. No, he does not.

The above is mild, however, compared with the discovery that horses were carried on the paybooks under fictitious names, and men were there, too, who had been dead for as long as three years. The nearly-dead were also well represented, for many workers 'were in the wane of their strength and life; the yards were literally made asylums for worn-out workmen. The lame and the blind drew the same wages as the best artificers.' Some men got themselves registered in as many as five distinct gangs working the same hours, and drew pay from all five. 'Every scruple, every fear, every restraint had been spunged away': the men correctly estimated the laxity and incompetence of their overseers, the Navy Board. For a fireworks ending to the subject of wages, we might take the case of the *Amaranth*, a smallish ship sent to Woolwich yard for repairs; afterwards she was sold for three thousand pounds. The bill for repairing her, however, had come to thirteen thousand, yet a ship of her class could be built, new, for twelve hundred pounds. On discovery of these interesting facts, the Commission put Edward Jesson, master shipwright of Plymouth Yard, on the griddle.

Q. Can you account for the charge of £13,600 for repairing the
Amaranth ?

A. I cannot account for it.

TIMBER

The importance of timber in the day of the all-wooden
ship is a point that hardly needs to be laboured.   On its very
first glance into the yards, the Commission found several
line-of-battle ships — the biggest and most important class —
which had been decaying in the slips for ten or twelve years
for want of timber to complete them.   Yet, by standing order,
the Navy Board was supposed to keep a permanent reserve
of seventy-thousand loads of timber, and to submit a yearly
account of it to the Admiralty.   When St. Vincent took
office as First Lord and looked into this supply, he found
twenty-eight thousand loads only, 'of which a great proportion was rotten, defective or unserviceable', and also found
that the account had not been submitted for the past seven
years.   This brings us to the question of supply, and some
quaint doings in connection with it.

Contractors proposed timber in lots to the Navy Board
while the trees were still standing.   On receipt of this proposal,
an expert from the yards went to examine them.   Those he
approved he marked and numbered, then filed his list at the
yard.   The trees, when felled and sent to the yard, were supposed to be examined to see whether their marks and numbers
corresponded with the expert's — or, in a word, to see
whether the yard was getting what it had bought.   Yet this
vital procedure was mostly neglected or omitted for a period
of sixteen years.   Worse, the Navy Board had ignored their
own expert who reported 554 trees in Sherwood Forest fit
for the Navy in 1797 ; these trees were not even felled until
1802.   Ships rotted away in the yards for lack of timber to
finish them, and forests rotted away 'because the ax was
refused to them'.   Meanwhile the Navy Board paid out
£35,000 to private timber merchants while ignoring their

own supplies of free timber from the King's forests. They also awarded an enormous contract for oak grown in Holstein marshes and demonstrably inferior to English oak, on the strength of samples ten inches long.

Examination of Thomas Jenner, Master Mast-maker

Q. Were the masts received on commission or those on contract most defective or sappy ?

A. They were equally defective and equally sappy.

Q. Were they accepted into the yard, whether defective or not ?

A. Yes.

Q. Is there now in the yard any considerable quantity of timber which has suffered for want of being timely used ?

A. Yes, there are logs which have been in the yard twelve years.

Deliberate mishandling of timber was another dark alley, but a little illumination is needed to understand its turns and twists. The great point in building wooden ships, it seems, was to choose trees whose original size matched the size of the ship for which they were intended. Lacking this natural affinity of dimension — if the tree were too large to begin with — it had to be trimmed down to size. This trimming process weakened the wood, so that the ship, from the very first stages of her construction, was less seaworthy than she ought to have been. Once aware of this fact, we are better able to understand a contemporary comment : 'In the yards we see the noblest oak of the forest, worthy to have formed the ribs of the proudest three-decker of Great Britain, sawed and hacked and chipped to make the floor of a sloop', and another : that the shipwrights deliberately 'build and repair small vessels with timbers of the highest classes'. The final exhibit in this display is perhaps the ultimate treachery, for it involves the basic, initial preparation of the wood.

Examination of James Jagoe, Shipwright of Plymouth Yard

Q. Do you believe that much timber has been spoiled in the King's yards, for want of skill and judgment ?

A. Certainly ; it was the practice until last year to employ young men from the Mould Loft in the conversion of timber, who were totally unacquainted with it.

CONTRACTS

now enter the scene. These were supposed to be advertised publicly and awarded to the lowest bidder. In reality, contracts lay in the gift of the Minister to the Crown, forming part of his regular apparatus of patronage. He gave them out at his good pleasure, mostly to the same tight little body of people — a closed circle. Such contracts had been held by the same family for as much as a century, descending from generation to generation 'like college leases', as one bystander put it. Occasionally, of course, there were hitches in this well-oiled system ; something would pop to the surface too flagrant and too outrageous to be easily suppressed. Then the Navy Board had to do something to preserve appearances, and they did. They took a contract away from one crooked purveyor, and gave it back to him again at double the price.

STORES [1]

consisted of leather, candles, copper sheets, nails, bolts, blocks, pump-gear, tallow in casks and other supplies — of which the most important by far were sails and cordage. Sails were manufactured by classes numbered from One to Seven. Number One, the class of principal sails — 'on which the very life of a ship depends in a storm' — were supposedly woven to take the heaviest punishment. The other classes diminished

[1] Thefts from the stores were astronomical. For want of space this must pass with a mere mention.

in sturdiness from number to number down to Seven, for use in dead calms or in the very lightest, gentlest airs.

'Upon the strength and sufficiency of the canvas delivered into the King's yards, it is evident that the safety of the Royal Navy depends', says a pamphleteer of 1802, with no fear of contradiction.   Seven years before, while fighting the most crucial campaign of his life, Jervis had roared repeatedly about the poor quality of sails with which he was being supplied. Little satisfaction he got : the Navy Board answered smoothly that they tested all canvas before it was bought, and their tests were such as to guarantee its adequacy.   Now that he was First Lord instead of a mere harassed commander-in-chief, Jervis must have had an extra pleasure in making them eat their words.   Their vaunted tests came under review : these consisted of applying weights to the canvas.   But strange to say they were not applied longways or sideways (to warp and weft) but in some other fashion.   The upshot was that the warp in the Number One heavy sail turned out to be no stronger than the warp in Number Seven, the thinnest and lightest.   Small wonder that Jervis's fleet had found its sails going to pieces again and again, sometimes under conditions that meant the end of the vessel and all aboard her.

'Now for the ROPES,' exclaims our pamphleteer quoted above, 'the last hope of a ship for riding out a storm, when her sails have burst under pressure of wind.'   Some very odd experiences with ropes had fallen to Jervis's lot during the same campaign ; aside from their tendency to snap under strain, his eagle eye had noted something else about them, and he ordered a general examination and measurement of cable in his fleet.   It all proved to be short of its purchased length.   He protested to the Navy Board, which supplied an explanation : the cable must have shrunk in coiling.   Jervis was not without a retort concerning this ability of cordage to shrink : he pointed out that it seemed to come and go, according to circumstance.   But all this had been years before he became First Lord ; then all he could do was to go in fear of his men dying in a welter of wreckage and sea-water, victims of far-away murderers who had fashioned their ships from rotten wood, rotten canvas and rotten rope.

* * *

In the dockyard farce, there were even some of the cast of characters who got up on the stand and gave each other the lie direct, as in the fruity case of John Head, master-cooper of Plymouth Yard, and his bright young assistant, Gilbert Hearder. Beer is the first chapter of this story — sixty-four casks of it bearing the King's mark, all stolen from the brewery of Plymouth Hospital. Officers searched for it and ran it to earth in a private brewery at Plymouth. So large a theft reeked of inside connivance, and somehow Gilbert knew too much about it. Just then the Commission's advent was rumoured, and Gilbert was invited by his master to take a holiday with all expenses paid. He was charmed to accept, naturally, and removed himself to a distance. The threat of the investigation seemed to pass, and he returned. Then the Commission materialized, without warning. Gilbert had no time to get away again ; they hooked him and put him on the stand.

Q. How long did you stay away from the dockyard ?
A. Between two and three months.
Q. Why did you leave the dockyard ?
A. Because I had mentioned the business. [Of the casks.]
Q. Did Mr. Head, your master, know where you had gone ?
A. Yes.
Q. Did Mr. Head or anyone else pay you anything for your support, during your absence ?
A. Mr. Head did not, but he told me to send to Thomas Warne [a publican] and he would give me twenty shillings a week.
Q. Did you send to Thomas Warne, and did you receive anything in consequence ?
A. Yes, I received a pound a week during the time I was absent.

Q. When you returned to the yard, did you receive anything from Mr. Head ?

A. He gave me ten pounds, and advanced my wages from nineteen shillings a week to twenty-six shillings.

John Head now shuffles into the limelight.

Q. Did you allow Gilbert Hearder anything for his support while he was absent ?

A. No, I did not.

Q. What wages did you pay him when he came back ?

A. A guinea a week and no more.

Q. Will you swear you did not pay him twenty-six shillings a week ?

A. I never paid him twenty-six shillings a week in my life.

Q. Will you swear you did not give him ten pounds after his return ?

A. I really cannot say ; I might give him ten pounds.

Q. Why ?

A. Thankful to have him back to work ; I could not get a man to work for me.

Q. Did you tell him to write Thomas Warne for money while he was absent ?

A. I do not know that I did.

Q. Will you swear you did not tell him so ?

A. I cannot charge my memory with it.

These were labouring men, but there were higher officials like Joseph Martyr, solicitor of Greenwich Royal Hospital, who when asked, 'Are you required to produce any vouchers for your disbursements ?' replied with indignation, 'Certainly not.' And just as today we have the spectacle of American criminals grinning the knowledge of their immunity and invoking the Fifth Amendment[1] under questioning, so we have eighteenth-century examples claiming protection with the identical formula, proving that if love is eternal, so is dishonesty. Sir John Turner, a former Receiver of Greenwich Hospital, is now on the stand.

[1] I decline to answer on the grounds that it may incriminate or degrade me.

Q. Did you gain any profit or advantage in resigning your office of Receiver ?

A. That is a question which I certainly object to.

Q. Upon what grounds do you object ?

A. Because it may possibly (though I do not admit that it will) tend to criminate myself.

Sir John wanted to have it both ways.

Now, from a dockyard employee's own mouth, comes evidence of what constituted high pay. Some wages accounts belonging to one quarter were carried forward into the next. Why was this done ? the Commission asked, and the clerk under examination replied, 'Because the earnings of the men appeared to be very great, seven and fivepence a day.' So a dockyard clerk found the current wage of dockyard labourers enormous. It seems conclusive.

*   *   *

REMEDIES

for this jungle of abuses were also jungle-like in aspect but simple in essence, for they grew from one central fact : that the business of all naval departments had enormously increased, and the bumbling, hit-or-miss methods of the past were completely inadequate to cope with it any longer. Sweeping and drastic changes had to be made, and this was done by the increase of personnel and by the iron-clad definition of the functions of separate offices and of the persons comprising them. All departments were put under committees whose duty it was to administer them, and to do nothing else. Officials found themselves hedged about with minute directives, contractors with penalties and restrictions which would make it extremely hard for them to turn a dishonest penny in future.

The impact of all this on Jervis himself may not be exaggerated but neither should it be minimized. Certainly he was subjected only to verbal, not physical assault, yet there is

no pleasure in standing under a foul Niagara of insults, male-
dictions and threats.   One jackass arose in Parliament and
offered 'to prove Jervis the greatest enemy the country ever
had' ;   a pamphlet came out stating that he had tried to suppress its publication by the offer of £3000 of public money,
and a newsrag, the *True Briton*, backed it up with similar libels.
Jervis sued them both, jailing the pamphleteer and smashing
the *True Briton*, but the atmosphere of hatred and lawsuits is
unsettling to most people and he, like everyone else, must
have felt the strain.   About this time he began his collection
of anonymous letters, still to be seen in the British Museum ;
one telling him he ought to be hanged, in which about six
attempts to spell 'inconceivable' end with a frantic blot like a
shriek, seems to have been his pet.   More wounding demonstrations he would have to weather by means known only to
himself, and in any case he was out of the First Lordship, his
party (Whig) having fallen by then, together with all its
incumbents in high office.   But he had had the courage to
uncover what no one else would touch, and what he had
begun went on steadily to its conclusion, which was in effect
the creation of the modern British Navy ;   he had forced
open its ancient picturesque fastnesses and let in the nineteenth
century.

Still, the affair yields one last vestige of eighteenth-century
jumble, paradox and delicious no-sense.   Jervis's great defender in the Commons was Sheridan, who in upholding him
eloquently had pointed out with virtuous horror the annual
total of waste and peculation in the King's yards.   But a Law
Court docket of the period exhibits the name, on page after
page, of none other than our friend Richard Brinsley Sheridan,
invariably being sued for sums from two hundred to seven
thousand six hundred pounds.   Because this superb wit,
orator, playwright and boon companion had one frightening
kink in his nature ;   he thought it really funny to swindle
tradespeople, and the bigger the swindle the funnier he found
it.   Jervis knew this of him, of course — all London did —

and one wonders how he felt about being championed by a man whose life exhibited every feature of slick, genial scoundrelism that he himself hated most. Yet Sheridan came out with scorching brilliance on the subject of Jervis's successor, who had probably never been on a ship in his life except as a passenger. 'That stupid, dull, insignificant Jervis is dismissed,' he declaimed, 'to make room for that old, gallant, experienced, tried seaman, Lord Melville.' Uproar in the House, and Canning struggling to make heard, in the din, his stuffy and lame reply. But this very same Lord Melville had been Treasurer of the Navy long ago, and when questioned on some of his past transactions had declined to answer. And on what grounds ? 'That it may tend to criminate me.'

And from all that mass of bygones, one more fragment of something undisclosed whisks past us with its small fillip of mystery, before vanishing forever into darkness. Jervis's name looks out unexpectedly from a docket of Admiralty Court cases ; he has received an anonymous letter and orders them to try and find out, at once, who wrote it — yet we have seen how he saved anonymous letters, rather cherishing the more scurrilous and vituperative. In the present instance the Admiralty put one of its solicitors on the trail, a man named Robert Bicknell. Bicknell prowled about, asking questions in a good many places, and came back with an odd story : the Navy Board had been receiving similar letters for five years past and had made every effort to find out the writer, without success. There, for lack of other leads, the matter had to rest.

But who was the man that could upset the Navy Board to such an extent and remain hidden ?

And what could he have written that disturbed Jervis enough to want him found so badly ?

V

THE ADMIRAL AND THE SCURVY

SEA-GOERS of Jervis's day and before tell how a ship driving along under full sail created a humming sound caused by the passage of the wind through her rigging, a many-voiced chord or drone of fuller or lesser volume that never ceased so long as she was in motion. And to this toneless music of her own making passed the dream, a flying, leaning tower of cloud, a vision that through the ages seduced men's hearts from the land and brought to their lips such words as

> Whither, O splendid ship, thy white sails crowding,
> Leaning against the bosom of the urgent West?

Of all that overwhelming impression, perhaps the chief one was purity — the sense of an unearthly purity eternally washed and guarded by sun, by boundless airs and waters.

But the impression was a lie, the virginal immaculate look a gross deception. Beneath the nobility of masts and sails were decks ; below decks were the holds, and below the holds, the bilges. The tall white goddess hid in her belly dark hells of wretchedness, unimaginable horrors and nightmares of helpless affliction and disease rampant. Death, the latter attendant on this state, was a mere incident by comparison and could only be welcomed as a deliverance.

Centuries before Jervis the relationship between food and health was perceived if not precisely known, and out of this unformulated knowledge comes an accusing voice from the past, the cry of a common seaman sufficiently articulate and literate to address to the House of Commons, in 1700, a pamphlet on 'victualling — the lowest and most corrupt office of the Navy. Where goods are bought by favour, the quality is not considered ; by this means we are supplied with Bread made of undue mixtures, as horse-beans, pease, rye, barley, nay, damaged pease, to the advantage of buyer and seller, but God knows very little to the advantage of the poor Sailors who dy'd by thousands in the West Indies. 'Tis true we Tarrs only, feel the effects of this management ; we only, at present, are gut-founder'd and poisoned.'

'We were fed with putrid beef, rusty pork and bread swarming with maggots.' Smollett's professional accents, forty years later, take up the poor seaman's tale. 'There was not an old empty pork tub or beef barrel that was not converted to hold water. So little pains was taken to cleanse these vessels first, that the water was corrupted and stank so abominably that a man was fain to stop his nose with one hand while lifting a drink of water with the other.' The human mechanism, so fed, reacts as might be expected. Nature's retort to this diet of filth was various in kind but one in result ; the men were laid low by fevers, ulcers, diarrhoea, insanity — and scurvy. The word survives today chiefly as a jocular term of disparagement, having lost all other meaning, most of all the meaning of the scourge for which the word stood as a symbol. Hard to imagine the terror with which it was once invested ; hard to realize that its advent, in a ship's company, could stop the heart of its commander with fear.

What was scurvy ? How did a man with scurvy look ? How did a man with scurvy feel ? What was the effect of scurvy on his performance as a seaman ? A great many descriptions are available from sensible laymen, and sharp-eyed medical description has been present in all ages and civilizations. Best of all, we can draw on eighteenth-century physicians who had attained considerable technics within the limitations that bound them, who had great powers of giving relief in many cases, who met the creeping, devouring shipboard ghoul hand to hand, and who finally exorcised it.

'Discoloured spots all over the man's person, swelled legs,

putrid gums, teeth loose, and above all an extraordinary
heaviness of the whole body', this heaviness developing into
a tendency 'to swoon after the least exertion, or even after
the least motion'.   The dismayed narrator in this case is
Admiral Lord Anson, who had good reason for his dismay ;
out of the hundreds of his whole ship's complement, only
six were fit for foremast duty. 'Surely the most singular and
unaccountable disease of any that affects the human body',
continues his perplexed and horrified voice. 'Its symptoms
inconstant and innumerable.'

'The scurvy made dreadful ravages.'   This is a non-
medical military man speaking in 1780 of scurvy, the land
variety, which 'differed in no respect', he noted, 'from that
usually contracted by sailors in long voyages. Men who were
hale and hearty before and equal to any fatigue, supported
themselves to their posts on crutches, and even so were hardly
able to move along.'   Broken bones, healed and united for
years, came apart in scurvy patients ; 'old sores and wounds
opened anew' : the general structure of the bone itself
crumbled away.

'Dejection of spirits, a difficulty of breathing, faces
strangely bloated and sallow,' chimes in a third voice, and
this one belongs to the great Dr. Lind, who in 1753 wrote the
first extensive work dealing with the problem, the *Treatise
on Scurvy*.   'Also this disease produces fevers, pleurisies, the
jaundice and violent rheumatic pains.'   Here he puts his finger
on four classic symptoms of all starvation diseases — terrible
pains in the joints, oedema (bloating), mental depression and
facial aspect of acute anxiety. 'Spungy flesh which bled at
the least touch', Lind continues.   'The men cried out when
turned abed.'   Any touch, on any part of the body, was un-
bearably painful.   Also there were those, apparently less
affected, who suddenly dropped dead while walking on deck ;
or a man not yet up might have been speaking in a strong
cheerful voice not three seconds before, start to get out of his
hammock — and simply die then and there, from the effort

of putting his legs to the floor. In a word, the man rotted alive where he stood, and there was no halting the strange plague that struck him down by the thousand and the ten thousand, in single ships or in fleets. Post-mortems were part of the desperate effort to penetrate the secret of scurvy, and a clicking or grating sound from the cadaver, as it was hoisted to the operating-table, told the surgeon in advance what he would find — that the entire bony frame had come apart at the joints.

Not the least painful part of the spectacle was the despair and bewilderment of ships' commanders, impotently beating their heads against the stone wall of the enigma. 'Why is this happening?' they cry. 'The men get plenty to eat and plenty to drink. We catch fresh fish every day. Why is this? why, why why?' Remedies by the hundred were anxiously tried and discussed. Dutch ships had less scurvy than the English, it was noted, and this was attributed to the daily ration of spruce beer. Preparations of spruce, accordingly, had quite a run for a time. So had vinegar, while various acids of grassy, vegetable or metallic derivation also had their disciples. And after all the trial, the effort and the hopes, the waiting with bated breath for results, one single fact stared them in the face. Nothing helped. Not one remedy, of all the remedies that had been tried, helped at all.

The strange thing is that knowledge of scurvy prevention had existed from 1593. Even more astonishing is the fact that the East India Company, from 1600 on, issued a regular daily ration of lemon-juice to its crews, and that the *Surgeon's Mate* by Woodall, published in 1617, prescribed 'the juyce of Lemmons, or in want thereof the juyce of Limes, Oranges and Citrons' as a 'precious medicine' against scurvy. Therefore, since positive knowledge of the cure had existed for two hundred years, why was the British Navy eaten alive with scurvy at the dawn of the nineteenth century? Perhaps through one of those inconsistencies impossible to explain, perhaps by the mystery of knowledge that goes underground

Admiral John Jervis, Earl of St. Vincent, wearing the robes of his Order

during the centuries and must be laboriously re-exhumed, such as the sterilization of operating-instruments, a procedure used by Roman surgeons over two thousand years ago, then somehow passing into oblivion and being discovered again after a lapse of eighteen hundred years.

In any case the tiny emergences (or re-emergences) of light, ray by uncertain ray, are thrilling, as dawns must always be thrilling even when not guaranteed pristine. Medical men of the eighteenth century seemed to know nothing of the earlier enlightenment ; in darkness they had to grope unaided, in darkness seek for the first, uncertain footholds.

'I have great reason to believe,' says a long-ago ship's doctor, 'that lives were absolutely preserved by a lemon squeezed into six or eight ounces of water and given twice a day.' But he seems dubious, apologetic almost, as if the simplicity of the remedy put it somehow beyond the bounds of belief. 'Two others [with scurvy] had each two oranges and one lemon given them every day. These they eat with greediness, upon an empty stomach.' This greed of the scurvy-ridden for citrus fruit has been recorded by other doctors of the eighteenth century ; gradually their voices take on more and more certainty. 'The most sudden and good effects were perceived from the use of oranges and lemons ; one of those who had taken them, being at the end of six days fit for duty.' 'As to oranges and lemons,' another voice swells the chorus, 'I have always found them an infallible cure IN EVERY STAGE OF THE DISEASE,' and by now the evidence is incontrovertible : 'The only cure is fresh lemons and oranges, given liberally ; or when they cannot be procured, the preserved juice.' The speed of the cure was also astounding : 'Almost instantaneous ; in a few days men who had been considered as dying, left their beds.' And most moving of all, perhaps, is to hear the first halting approaches to something still hidden from them and still to be hidden for two hundred years : 'FRESH VEGETABLE MATTER IMPARTS A SOME-THING TO THE BODY, WHICH FORTIFIES IT AGAINST DISEASE'.

G

Poignant echoes across the centuries, reminding us of how hard they had to work to arrive at what is commonplace to us, and of how much we owe them of our power to diagnose glibly, 'Total deficiency of vitamin C'.

Jervis, in his importance to the health of the fleet, is not here suggested as a medical discoverer. By the time he had begun promoting large-scale remedial measures, the cure for scurvy was known if not applied. But he had had a lifelong experience with sickness aboard and its inroads on manpower ; a line-of-battle ship with too many of her crew laid low must suffer in her performance. Scurvy was a great enemy of the seaman, but there existed yet a greater. The number one killer from time immemorial was typhus, and whether they called it 'ship's fever', 'jail fever' or 'camp fever' it was in all cases one and the same, a louse-borne disease luxuriantly flourishing aboard ship and encouraged by overcrowding, dirty bedding and physical uncleanliness. As to the less attractive habits of his seamen Jervis, of course — as with everything aboard his ships — had little to learn. 'The *Centaur* has been afflicted with a nasty infectious ship's fever, chiefly owing to the filthy practice of clothing the people in woollens, which are never washed or aired from the time they are first put on until they rot off.' And unwashed bodies clad in vile rags were only a little part of what he had to encounter, once he had the power to do something drastic about health on shipboard. But the story of his achievements in this direction is so much the story of the powerful medical instrument he found in his hand when he most needed it, that a digression must be made for the sake of Dr. Andrew Baird.

Exactly when Jervis first set eye on him must be taken on trust ; perhaps Baird has left an account of it somewhere. What we know is that Baird entered the Navy in 1781 as an assistant surgeon, so that he was an experienced man of fourteen years' service by the time Jervis became Commander-in-Chief in the Mediterranean in 1795. Eighteen or nineteen big ships were concentrated there, each with its own physician ; what singled Baird out for Jervis's notice, among all his fellow-doctors, also seems unknown. The chances are that his official reports first struck Jervis through some special quality of thoroughness, commonsense, ability and devotion. These were the traits that attracted him like a magnet, and he would make it a point to meet their possessor personally. We have already seen and will see again his fine selective nose for smelling out extra performance, and it served him as well with ships' doctors as ships' officers. The chief trouble with naval physicians of the period seems to have been that once they acquired a little private practice they tended to favour it to the detriment of their shipboard or institutional patients, but here in Baird, Jervis had found a man who only wanted to work himself to death for the good of the fleet.

The further steps of their intimacy are also obscure, but in 1799 Jervis appointed Baird as surgeon of his own ship, the *Ville de Paris*. This was the year when Jervis's health was breaking down now at this point, now at that, like a worn-out fabric that begins to give all over, yet it was essential that he stick to his job as long as humanly possible. Baird patched him up and kept him going. How much comfort it was to Jervis and how hard he leaned on Baird we will never know — the dour-faced, skilful man always at his elbow, vigilant to note impending trouble and to head it off whenever possible. But when Jervis's health broke decisively and compelled his return to England Baird went with him, which must indicate the seaman's absolute confidence in the doctor. Nor was the expression of that absolute confidence very long delayed.

Next year, 1800, was to offer the high and heartening spectacle of two experts pooling their resources for one of the best objectives that could be, the reduction of human suffering. Jervis had just been appointed to the command of the Channel Fleet, and it seems remarkable that this fleet, although in its home anchorage, was so full of scurvy that there seemed a fair chance of its being unable to put to sea, yet these were part of the fleet that Nelson was supposed to use in his next campaign. Here was Jervis's chance to move as he liked to move, and he drove for the heart of the abuse like a thunderbolt. Undoubtedly, for this Channel show of 1800, he and Baird had had a full-dress rehearsal during the Mediterranean campaign, 1795-9, where lemons and 'bed-clothes regularly air'd' appear frequently in the official correspondence and where an exceptionally high standard of health prevailed, a thing that never happened by accident. At any rate, here they were together, a perfect team by now, with abilities happily and peculiarly identical. For Baird was not essentially a medical discoverer so much as a skilled practitioner and administrator ; one of his gifts was for putting other men's discoveries into regular use among ships' companies, who left to their own devices would neglect known means of relief, exactly like the modern factory worker who leaves off his goggles or safety-helmet because the use of them is too much trouble.

Upon his tottering fleet, therefore, Jervis unleashed Baird like a bloodhound, and the bloodhound responded in a manner that showed how much the quarry was after its own heart. Baird explored every inch of every ship belonging to the Channel Fleet. He poked into wretched bunks and turned over piles of verminous rags used as casual sleeping-places ; he descended into holds forever sealed from air and sun, their walls creeping with damp from frequent washings, where in this year-round wet vapour men lay sleeping and breathing ; he looked with special minuteness — on Jervis's instructions — into 'the state of clothing and cleanliness of the men's persons'. Then he reported back to Jervis, and together they embarked on an occupation especially congenial to both their temperaments — of tearing up an old wrong by the roots.

First, they attacked the holds and sleeping-quarters reeking with damp, hotbeds of a dozen miserable complaints. Baird installed small stoves below decks and kept them constantly burning until the sodden holds and orlops were dried out. An earlier naval doctor had introduced the use of hot sand for scrubbing, instead of water, and Baird revived this practice. The use of stoves aboard was dangerous, but apparently he suggested or imposed such precautions that not one ship's fire was reported. Then the vile sleeping-bunks were torn out and replaced with 'comfortable berths for the sick and the well'. Even to these first measures the response was magical. The *Namur* had a third of her crew down with ship's fever. With the drying of the holds and reform of sleeping-quarters the fever vanished and the ship's standard of health rocketed upward and remained up. About this time Jervis became interested in soaps specially made for use in salt water and sent sample cases of one gross to each ship's commander, with strict injunctions to try them out and report on their efficiency. He went extensively into the question of ventilation, a thing hardly known in that day and regarded either as a madman's whim or an eccentric's foible ; he put down rigid rules on bathing and shaving.

And behind all this activity was Baird, Baird in an open boat all day and every day in all weathers, being rowed from ship to ship, tirelessly tramping miles of decks and holds, nailing minutest deficiencies in the beam of his trained medical observation and bringing back the results to lay before his chief. In this manner Jervis's own piercing eye received the additional faculty of being enabled to see through a doctor's eye, and really he must have enjoyed himself at this time because he was tremendously interested in health, symptoms and medicine. Actually, his massive correspondence with Baird from 1801–23 shows that he was an amateur doctor at heart, and if he had been trained as a physician must have made an extraordinary one. Now, with what he got from Baird and what he himself could contribute, he boiled down a thousand notes and observations into a regular system for the preservation of health at sea, and invented regular forms for the use of ships' doctors, and so special a thing could hardly have been evolved without Baird at his elbow all the time, helping him transform theory into practice.

The mere thought of printed forms is enough to induce the asphyxia of dullness, yet it works out, in the end, quite differently. To open one of the big folded dockets so frequently interleaved with Jervis's regular dispatches ; to see at a glance the number of sick men and their ailments, along with the surgeon's remarks ; all this is to have a picture of current medical practice at sea, along with a vivid idea of the afflictions more common to seamen. Inevitably, Baird would have some pungent things to say about the care of the sick and wounded aboard ship, and wherever he appeared the sickbays began to be provided, equipped and managed as never before.

Incidentally, one innovation for which Jervis and Baird were at least partly responsible was the regular instead of occasional issue of lemon juice ; after the first six weeks of a voyage, lemon juice was to be given to all crew members by standing order. Knowing the highly perishable nature of citrus juices, one may wonder about the means of preservation. Three are mentioned, the first by adding five or ten gallons of brandy to every sixty gallons of lemon juice ; the second, by adding sugar ; the third, by putting the juice in a vessel and standing it in boiling water until reduced to the consistency of oil, then bottling it *hot* — with particular directions to leave no air space between the liquid and the cork — which anticipates the discovery of modern preserving methods by a hundred years ; 'and by this means', says the doctor who gives the recipe, 'the qualities of twelve dozen lemons, or twelve dozen oranges, may be preserved in a quart bottle'.

For most of what was done Jervis, who never beat about the bush, gave Baird the credit. True, it was his authority behind Baird that enabled him to be so effective an agent, but the agent had a rare and individual power and his superior came out and said so in a variety of ways : 'Many measures

were suggested by yourself, so as to shut out those diseases
which in previous times occasioned such shocking mortality
among seamen. Infectious ulcer was subdued by your skill,
and is still prevented by the treatment and precautions which
you first adopted and recommended. Nor can I forget your
zeal and cheerfulness as you performed your duties as Physician
to the Fleet in a manner which I never saw equalled, and this
without the slightest additional emolument.' For he had
offered Baird extra pay in this period, and Baird had refused
it.

And what must he and Jervis have felt when the Channel
Fleet returned to port after being at sea one hundred and
twenty-one days — an unprecedented record — with only
sixteen sick men out of twenty-four sail of the line, '*although
the crews had not had a single fresh meal for the period stated*'.
It was a moment of confirmation and triumph, a moment
when a fledgling theory mounts up on powerful shining
wings, and Jervis gave it all to Baird in a voice like a trumpet :
'I ASSERT WITHOUT FEAR OF CONTRADICTION, THAT THE HEALTH
OF THE CREWS OF THE BRITISH NAVY HAS RECEIVED GREATER
BENEFIT BY YOUR SKILL AND EXERTIONS, THAN FROM THE
PRACTICE OF ALL YOUR PREDECESSORS.' And the ordinary
uninformed person is tempted to call this conclusive, or at
least to feel that Jervis's right to his opinion was better
founded than most.

These things done, Jervis unleashed Baird on the hospitals.
This formed part of the naval investigation then going on —
all of it happening together, in 1802 ; Jervis never had on
his hands one assignment sufficient to kill an ordinary man, he
always had three or four. In the case of hospitals and prison-
ship hospitals, he knew he could do no better than expose
them to Baird's gimlet eye, nor was he disappointed. The
five institutions that appear in the reports were at Deal, Plymouth, Portsmouth, East Stonehouse and Greenwich ; also,
there was a hospital ship called *Le Caton*. All were large, all
overcrowded and for years had been without supervision,

regular or irregular. All of them, when Baird began churning up the ooze, revealed the usual presence of leeches willing to batten on the helpless. Revelations began small and mounted upward.

Examination of Mrs. Mary Bevans, Matron
(Stonehouse Hospital)

Q. Have you reason to believe that necessaries prescribed for the patients have been appropriated by other persons ?

'I know nothing of it myself', she answered, discreet and close-mouthed in proper professional fashion. Then in the same breath she added, 'But I have been told by two nurses that Mr. Fuge [Surgeon] used to insert in his prescriptions wine and spices, which were not given to the patients but carried to Mr. Fuge's house.' This is the merest sample of the fascinating Mr. Fuge ; he was capable of much more spectacular heights. Nor was he unique, for other officials simply looted the hospital's wine, chocolate, cocoa and sugar on written or verbal request, and invariably the dispenser would comply ; it was not his business to irritate his superiors with flagrant displays of honesty. There were others, too, who could equal if not surpass Mr. Fuge's performance. At Deal the chiefs of all departments — the governor, agent, surgeon, dispenser and matron — lived at a distance from the hospital. The agent really ran the place or let it run itself, his chief interest being in two contracts he held there, for milk and vegetables. The matron's two bonny daughters appeared on the hospital payroll without the formality of ever appearing at the hospital ; the principal turn, however, offered Mr. Fuge in a starring rôle worthy of his talents despite the fact that he remained, from beginning to end, modestly withdrawn in the wings.

Examination of Captain Richard Cryke, R.N.
(Governor of East Stonehouse Hospital)

Q. Do you know of any patient refusing to have his limbs amputated by any of the surgical staff?

A. About five years ago there were two men who refused to let Mr. Fuge the surgeon amputate them, but were willing that Mr. Hammick [Fuge's assistant] should operate ; saying that they had no prejudice against Mr. Fuge, but had conceived a partiality for Mr. Hammick.

The Captain's nervous accents are those of one either trying to gloss over a nasty situation or disclaim knowledge of it, for the next examination — of Mr. Hammick — brings out a quite different story.

Q. Have you known any instances of physicians of the Hospital neglecting their duty to attend private patients ?

A. I recollect one case where an amputation was about to be done ; we were all assembled and the patient ready, when suddenly the operation was put off, Mr. Fuge the surgeon having been called away to a patient in Stonehouse.

Q. Have you known any patients refuse to be operated on by any of the surgical staff ?

A. Yes, two men in one day said they would rather die than allow Mr. Fuge to operate on them, and begged that I might be allowed to do it. They were left that night, and noon of the following day Mr. Fuge sent for me and said I might do what I pleased.

But things were not so simple for Mr. Hammick ; in both patients had appeared the thing they called 'mortification' and that we call gangrene.

'I went to the Governor,' he continued, 'and stated that the men were so much reduced that there was danger in the amputation. The Governor begged, for the sake of humanity, that I would operate on them. I did so, and the men recovered.'

That Mr. Fuge had resigned from the Hospital some time ago and thus escaped the Commission would appear to be one of the luckier events in his life.

A man fails to come to life through his work as he does through his own words, and Baird is so extraordinary a man that one would like to know more about him. Those of his family now living can tell us that he was born at Donemana, County Tyrone, and qualified in medicine at Aberdeen University. But in his personal guise he remains hidden, and this obscurity is not accidental but deliberate, something intended by himself and over the years consistently carried out. He had an odd phobia about having his letters preserved, and his life and all his habits point to a planned self-effacement. There do survive one or two first-hand stories about him which seem to indicate that, although too authoritarian and rigid a superior, his ordinary manner was unassuming, but effective for all that. A sea-officer tells how, when a midshipman, he had an accident to his knee bad enough to confine him to his hammock. As soon as it became evident that his recovery would be a long-drawn-out affair, the ship's doctor became anxious to transfer him to a naval hospital, and it was perfectly evident that he was doing this at the instigation of the captain, who preferred not to have disabled men aboard if he could help it. But the injured boy had no mind to be sent ashore ; he felt that his eviction from the ship meant the end of his sea-going career and resisted all efforts to get rid of him. While the unequal contest was going on, Jervis somehow got wind of it and sent Baird over to investigate. This solitary contact with the doctor so impressed the midshipman that his spare account of it, many years later, remains vivid. Baird came aboard without formalities of any sort, informing the captain that he was there unofficially and as a medical man only. He looked at the knee, then turned his head very slightly toward the surgeon and said in the quietest voice, 'I am astonished how you can want to put him off the ship.' That was all ; he had made no show of authority, given no orders, but then and there all talk of sending the midshipman ashore ceased.

Yet by a happy accident — of his having given evidence before the Naval Commission — the living voice of this concealed man is present to us, briefly.

Q. Are there persons in the Hospital who from age, infirmity or other circumstances, are incapable of performing their duties ?

A. Yes, the first physician, the first assistant to the dispenser, the butler and the cook.

Baird, like Jervis, went straight to the point, and like Jervis's his eye overlooked no one, high or low. And now, ushered in with his words, a dawn of modern medical practice.

Q. Where are operations performed in Plymouth Hospital ?

A. In one particular ward where an operating-table is placed.

Q. Would it be advantageous to have a room separately used for that purpose ?

A. Yes ; I recommended the idea to the Admiralty, and a separate operating-room is now in preparation.

An innovation — and an improvement over having operations without anaesthetic done in an open ward, in full sight and hearing of other patients. Baird is also present in the Revised Directions to physicians of naval hospitals, where again he helps initiate, or anticipate, modern methods. 'On admission of any patient, a correct history of his case to be taken,' and kept up to date until his discharge. 'Every patient on reception into the hospital, to be bathed in a tub with warm water and soap before he be put to bed' — that is, if he can stand it ; otherwise the nurse must 'gently' bathe him in bed. After that, 'his person to be kept clean' and his bed-wear to be changed every four days or oftener. 'When any patient be discharged, his bed and bedding to be made perfectly sweet and clean before any other patient be put into it ;

and in case of infection, they are to be fumigated with sulphur.'
The keeping of the patient's chart and the insistence on cleanliness were formulated in a day when the word 'hospital' was still a synonym for terrifying filth, suffering and neglect, as shown in Daumier's contemporary sketch of a live hospital patient in bed with a dead one. Baird's influence also appears in the revised code of Regulations, which raised qualifications and tightened performance, and where expensive drugs and fancy stores ceased to be kept in an open chest which the unscrupulous could plunder at will.

But over and above this administrative talent, Baird must have been a true healer. 'You saved his life . . . you saved her life', Jervis's letters say to him, over and over again, and there seems little question as to which — between his official rank as Commissioner and Inspector of Hospitals, or healer — Baird would rather be. His medical observation was minute, brilliant and unorthodox, in a day when the doctor had to find his own way in countless emergencies, where no precedent or mass of collected opinion stood to guide him. For example, he had noted, in a hospital for war casualties, that the healing-rate of wounds was slow and unsatisfactory, and that this condition seemed to prevail all over the hospital. Looking into the daily routine of patients' care, he found that the men disliked their daily dose of lemon juice and were bribed to take it by the inducement of two tablespoonsful of sugar. Taking the trouble to approach each man in turn, very gently and persuasively (he could be persuasive with the sick but not with the well) Baird got them to agree to one tablespoonful instead of two. At once the suppurative tendency of the wounds subsided and healing was stepped up. Yet what did the early eighteen hundreds know of excessive sugar as a promoter of acid reactions, inflammations and lowered resistance ? Very little surely, or not as an accepted fact. By trial and error men discovered the effect of food on their own systems and governed themselves accordingly, but this was about the limit of dietetic knowledge. Jervis when unwell, for instance, stopped using wine and butter and lived on lean meat, and his special curse rested on 'made' dishes — current term for food composed of mixed-up leftovers, covered with sauce and cooked a second time. Baird's own ideas on diet could not have gone much beyond Jervis's, but he divined many things that were still unknown.

'I beg to call your attention to the efforts of Dr. Baird,' Jervis wrote the Admiralty, later on, 'in correcting enormities of every description in all the naval hospitals and depôts for Prisoners of War ashore and afloat, with a purity and integrity I have no words to express.' He sent this letter when trying to get, for his doctor and old friend, full pay on retirement, for the last thing that seemed to interest Baird was his own welfare or even his own comfort. He lodged here and there, casually, often at Jervis's town house in Mortimer Street or sometimes in rented rooms ; Jervis's two homes were his nearest approach to a home of his own. Mostly he was on the move in his capacity of Inspector of Naval Hospitals, and kept in touch with Jervis from every point where these existed or where hospital ships were anchored. But apparently his chief payment consisted of the sight of people getting well, and what he and Jervis had done together was completely at one with the aim of the whole naval investigation — reduction of the odds against men who had to live at sea the greater part of their lives.

'Purity and integrity' : again Jervis had put his finger on the mainsprings of a man's essential nature. He must have been aware of his luck in having such a weapon as Baird ready to his hand just when he needed one, and aware, too, that such luck is not to be expected twice in a man's lifetime. It was against all chances, therefore, that on a winter's day of 1795 there should walk into the cabin of his flagship another unique human weapon — a weapon as effective as Baird at his most potent, but of quite a different calibre.

VI

THE ADMIRAL AND THE FIERY FURNACE

THE world seems periodically afflicted by the madness of individuals whose special obsession is total conquest and total domination. Or this dark angel may be not a man but a theory or doctrine, powered by many fanatics instead of one. But whether the pestilence rages under the labels of Alexander, Attilla or Hitler, or prowls under the more amorphous titles of communism or fascism, it brings in its train identical consequences — the same destruction of peace and common-sense, the same waste and distortion of lives.

The name of this devouring force, in Jervis's time, is familiar to us all. The rushing scarlet stream of the French Revolution had cooled and scummed into the corruption of the Directorate — a governing body of five criminals whose equivalents can only be found among Hitler's crew — and the indecencies of the Directorate let power fall into the greedy outspread hands, waiting below, of Napoleon. Into his career this phenomenon packed an amount of ruin, spolia-tion and dust of marching armies to have done him credit if he had had a century in which to accomplish it, instead of a comparatively few years. His subjugations, plunderings and intimidations included Italy, Spain, Germany, Austria and all the small independent kingdoms and principalities still bordering the Mediterranean, such as Naples ; the ambition that ate his entrails scourged him to Egypt and as far as Russia.

Americans can hardly appreciate the menacing closeness of this fearful neighbour. Napoleon was separated from Britain only by a few miles of navigable water, and the

English coast boiled with amateur activity in the shape of watch-fires piled high and ready to be lit in case of an alarm, volunteers setting up all-night vigils and local militia drilling feverishly. A good many intelligent, aristocratic and culti-vated people were amused by all this commotion. They were wrong : the threat was terribly real. Napoleon was considering and sifting plan after plan to cross the Channel and invade England, and if he failed to do so it was from no weakening of intention, only from bad luck. He himself, in after years, put a name to this persistent and recurring bad luck, and what was it — to be sure — but the English Navy. For these were England's two chief bulwarks against the loom-ing and ever-present Napoleonic menace : Wellington's army by land, Jervis's fleet by sea.

Jervis was pitchforked into the boiling Mediterranean mess just when Napoleon's mere name was demonstrating its greatest power to crush and overawe. Already the tramp of his armies was reinforced and expedited by the legend of his invincibility ; people, cities and countries, paralysed, simply gave up. Resistance hardly existed, or hid underground, and in any case, seen or unseen, was completely impotent. Swiftly, relentlessly, with single-minded purpose, Napoleon was crowding the English out of the Mediterranean. By threats or shows of armed force he was compelling port after port to declare itself closed to his most-hated enemy, making it impossible for their ships to victual and water, forcing damaged ones to be sent back long inconvenient distances to find an anchorage where they could lie up for repairs. Eng-land's centuries-old Mediterranean trade was, of course, killed. Also, for centuries she had depended on the Mediterranean for certain naval supplies that were absolutely indispensable, and one by one these sources were cut off. Italy, for example, refused to sell her any more rope. Never mind, said Jervis stoutly, we can get rope from Sardinia — while admitting that Sardinian cordage was not nearly as good as the Italian.

One hour's reading of Jervis's Mediterranean dispatches,

1795-9, is enough to show what the man was up against, and presents the picture of a job so staggeringly complex that the head swims merely in trying to define it. All Jervis had to do was keep an eye on the Spanish and French fleets in whatever ports they happened to be, prevent them from joining forces if possible and inform himself constantly as to their purpose and destinations if they left port. He had to protect English shipping as far as he was able, while being on the alert to harass and capture enemy shipping. He had to maintain relations with those Mediterranean powers not yet cowed into toeing the Napoleonic chalk-line, encouraging or flattering them to continue neutral toward England, or at least not actively hostile ; and some incidents of this nerve-racking and perpetual egg-dance were very funny, though perhaps Jervis did not appreciate them at the time. Outbreaks of plague in some ports were an anxiety — he had to be careful not to sail in where it was raging — and still another distracting element was the situation of English families, hundreds of them, now resident in Mediterranean towns and resorts ; as the hatred of their nation rose and swelled about them Jervis had to be ready with ships standing by to receive these people — and their property, for most Britons then living abroad were very rich — and somehow take care of them and get them back to England, and the fact that many of them were ladies did not make his task any simpler. Beyond all this, the war situation had spun a dense network of blockade and counter-blockade ; Jervis plugged the ports friendly to Napoleon wherever possible, and the enemy plugged the ports friendly to England. For instance, Captain Miller was blockading Trieste and Commodore Nelson was blockading Leghorn, but Jervis might be forced to take ships away from these commanders and send them on some other mission ; the thousand volcanic situations that ringed him about were ready to erupt at a moment's notice, and their craters assumed different shapes and had different boiling-points from day to day.

Admiral Lord Nelson, against the background of Santa Cruz where he lost his arm. The bows on the sleeve cover the opening through which the wound could be dressed without removing the coat.

Nor had he perfect freedom for the one thing natural to his temperament — action — for every move of his, every decision, had to be reported to the Admiralty. He was swamped, buried beneath a merciless avalanche of paper-work, and to get this cleared away before his ordinary work-ing day began he rose regularly between 2 and 4 a.m., these horrible hours seeming by now to have settled into a life-long habit. In endless streams the letters flowed from him, twenty or more a day sometimes, some of them of great length and complexity and dealing with a thousand matters the most diverse, large and small — his stationing of ships, the war situation, supplies, blockades, promotions, courts-martial, punishments, individual problems — all considered with the same unhurrying calm, without superfluous words yet never scamping any detail or aspect of the whole. One small unofficial matter that engaged his whole-hearted scrutiny, among all the enormous issues clamouring for his attention, was 'a very disgraceful transaction come to my knowledge from a request made by a Mark Linington on his death-bed'. Jervis then encloses proof that Mark had put nine guineas for safe keeping into the hands of Lieutenant Corner of the *Victory*, and that he was unable to recover it on application ; his dying entreaty had been that the money be recovered and sent to his family. The uproar and commotion Jervis raised over this incident is evidenced by the amount of space it takes up in his dispatch-book. Under a dozen subordinates he lit the hot fire of his wrath, demanding the fullest explana-tion of how such a thing could happen. Their long and exhaustive (and defensive) reports demonstrate his outrage at the breach of trust, his grim determination to get to the very bottom of the affair, his relentless pursuit of Corner ; more words were expended over the dead sailor's nine guineas than over Portugal's offer of millions in ships and assistance.

And — above and beyond, surmounting all other con-siderations — he had somehow to corner the Spanish and

H

French fleets and compel them to battle ; only by forcing
a showdown could he supply a decisive answer, yes or no,
as to whether England could break through Napoleon's
stranglehold on the Mediterranean. Moreover, Jervis, himself alone, was sole judge of when his fleet would be strong
enough to risk the encounter, and in this desperate calculation
there was no room for mistakes — no margin at all for error.

And what of the instrument with which Jervis had to
work all these miracles — his Fleet ? Surely the Admiralty
had strengthened him, in this crucial pass, with their utmost
resources of men, supplies and fighting ships in top condition ?
The true story may be read in Jervis's dispatches of the period,
and a more frightening picture never existed of a man with
his back to the wall defending himself against all comers,
with the wall crumbling behind him and his weapons rotting
apart in his very hands.

'The *Tarleton* is in such wretched condition that I tremble
for Lord Proby, his officers and crew. The mainmast of the
Egmont having failed in the spindle, was reported by three of
the most skilful ships' carpenters to be in danger of going
over at the first gale of wind.' The mention focusses our
eyes on these three skilful men, supremely important aboard.
On these experts Jervis depended when an exact estimate
('survey' they called it then) of a ship's condition was necessary, and all too often their reports make reading dismal
beyond words. '*Poulette* : Her decks, waterways, spirketting,
bottom between wind and water, and lower masts, are much
decayed, together with an entire want of sails and cordage ;
the said Sloop cannot with safety undertake a passage back to
England. *Belotte* : Altogether in such a crazy and infirm
state, as to be totally incapable of a passage back to England.'

And after a fight at sea, of course, the tale is even more
ruinous : '*Windsor Castle* : Thirty shot in the shell, several
of which near the water-line ; channels, deadeyes and chain-
plates damaged by shot. Topsides, wales and necks want
caulking. Quarters very leaky in wake of galleries. The

copper on the bottom in a very bad state and very foul, the butts and seams in a dangerous state, the O chain totally defective and work'd out, and when at sea under a press of wind blowing fresh, it requires the hand pumps to keep the ship free, she makes from 6 to 12 inches water each hour.' All this enormous overhaul was demanded by just one ship. Furthermore, if these were the tidings of comfort and joy relayed by his carpenters to Jervis, his own eye, unassisted, was not slow to register evidence even more lethal — not of honest damage from ocean or enemy, but of dirty work at home, of a kind perfectly back-breaking. 'From the great number of sails which I have observed blown out in this fleet without any cause of stress of weather, accident or mismanagement,' he wrote on December 19th, 1797, 'I have entertained a strong suspicion that some fraud or imposition was practised in the manufacture of the canvas.' — A charming Christmas present for the Commander-in-Chief, the knowledge that his sails were not reliable !

Again, to the roll of ships incapacitated by service or battle must be added the victims of sheer bad luck, and some disasters of this class were major tragedies. 'It is with extreme concern I relate,' writes Jervis heavily, 'that the *Parnassus* transport, with Swiss troops embarked, struck on the rocks called Les Moines and immediately went down, by which 278 souls were lost ; the number saved only seven Swiss, and four of the crew.' And again : 'From the report of five men from the *Courageux*, picked up in her launch, and of several pieces of wreck, there is too much cause to apprehend that she is wrecked, and every soul on board at the time perished.' This blow is so heavy that even Jervis cannot keep the heartsick note out of his voice : 'At any time the loss of such a ship would have been very great, but in the present circumstances of my force, compared with that of the enemy, it is beyond all calculation.' Whatever else was in short supply, there was never any shortage of catastrophes — not so bad as the *Parnassus* and *Courageux*, perhaps, but bad enough. 'The *Gibraltar* struck twice on Cabrite point ; her foremast is carried away by the shock but she does not make water. The *Zealous* struck twice on the reef off Cape Malabite and makes a little water.'

In the wake of and never far behind this story of luck comes the tale of lack — less spectacular than shipwreck but not less erosive to the spirit or less discouraging. A supply of hemp on which Jervis counted has failed him ; in fact, his agent informs him that the Leghorn source of cordage is permanently cut off, and where shall he look ? 'Try Naples', says Jervis, and gives him letters of introduction to the British Ambassador there, Sir William Hamilton — husband of that Emma who will appear later. 'We need a great supply of nails, elm and oak board, lead and leather', he says in another dispatch, which for all his calm and control just skirts the verges of desperation. 'But above all we are in the greatest distress for sewing twine, our only resource now being in drawing threads from our canvas —' some of it, perhaps, from that defective canvas he had noted earlier. By the way, a caulker's report gives an idea of the drain that running repairs imposed on their scant supplies : 'Used on the above service [repairs to nine ships] : Pitch, eleven barrels and an half ; oakum, twenty-three hundredweight.'

A day-to-day struggle even more exhausting, for an item even more essential — food — became increasingly desperate as Napoleon's stranglehold continued to tighten on the kingdoms and other independencies ringing the Mediterranean. A great concern of any naval commander worth his salt was to supply his men, while in port, with fresh meat and vegetables. Jervis, ahead of his time in his ideas of diet and its effects on health, made especially strenuous efforts in this direction, and for his pains was involved in a series of grimy encounters with the crooks who were the local supply agents. For instance, in his continuous attempts to buy live cattle, he started with one Donato Orsi but dropped him on account of a bread contract 'in which he tried to overreach me most grossly' : then when he tried to buy cattle from others he found Orsi constantly bobbing up one step ahead of him, trying to spike his wheels ; 'he used every art [*dirty trick* was in his vocabulary, but not for their Lordships of the Admiralty] to defeat the supply, and tampered with farmers and drovers.' Yet he could also write the Admiralty another sort of letter : 'Mr. Vaughn, Agent Victualler at Gibraltar, continues to furnish His Majesty's squadron with live cattle in good condition, upon such moderate terms as would surprise anyone unacquainted with his probity'. Among his thousand harassing worries Jervis could snatch a moment to pay tribute to an honest supplier ; all his driven, over-busy life he could always find time for appreciation — quick to censure but quicker to praise. Later on, again in connection with the battle for food, it is pleasant to catch another voice, icy as Jervis's but somehow even more compelling and intimidating : Commodore Nelson is astounded to hear that a shipment of bullocks has been prevented from embarking from the port of Genoa, and earnestly hopes, for the sake of the Genoese themselves, that there is some mistake which can be explained to his satisfaction. Since he made no move against the Genoese, it may be conjectured that the bullocks came through in a hurry.

The gloom of the overall picture was not lightened by the evidence of Jervis's proxy eyes — his scouting ships, paid spies and friendly amateurs passing on the result of observation or rumour. Relentlessly their reports and separate testimonies kept pyramiding, all to the same conclusion — that the phenomenon of Bonaparte was no mere flash in the pan, but an enemy of first-rate ability and gigantic resources, and those resources were being continually enlarged as one country after another, swamped by the Napoleonic advance, contributed its quota of men and supplies whether freely or under compulsion. Then there was Napoleon's ally, Spain, whose hostile preparations were not on a less massive scale : 'Admiral Langara with ten sail of the line and Mons. Richey with seven,

left Cadiz Bay the morning of the 1st [August 1796] and
Admiral Solano with eight sail of the line, and having two
thousand troops embarked, was expected to sail the same day.'
An English spy in Barcelona contributed his bit : all along
the coast of Catalonia they were impressing (forcibly enlisting)
men very fast ; reports had it that the French were sending
eight thousand men to occupy Minorca. By December '96
Jervis knew the worst, as far as size went, of the French fleet
ranged against him — eighteen sail of the line, with about
twelve frigates and four or five storeships — and even the
most fleeting and accidental evidence of English eyes continued the tale of the huge power mushrooming all about
them ; on Christmas Eve a lookout 'counted thirty ships
from the masthead. Could perceive plainly from the Deck,
them to be line of battle ships.'

In the face of these gathering warheads, Jervis must have
been stunned by a new misfortune. Not that he was any
stranger to hard luck, but this specific example was unheard-
of, incredible. Desertion : not of one, not of a group, but of
Admiral Man and his whole fleet ; Man, setting out for home
against orders and taking the seven ships of his command
with him. The nature of this catastrophe so affected Jervis
that his most vocal letters on the subject to the Admiralty —
and he was articulate by nature — are somehow unbelieving,
as if he simply could not credit what had happened. At the
same time his comments are remarkably restrained, considering his need of the vanished contingent. Perhaps he blamed
himself for not realizing how near Man had been, for months,
to a nervous breakdown ; the hulking spectre of French and
Spanish war-might, which Jervis faced with equanimity, had
shaken Man to the marrow, so that he simply turned tail.
His welcome in England included degradation from his rank,
and he was ordered to haul down his flag. Complying, he
wrote the Admiralty a humble, heartbroken letter : 'My
flag is struck this day . . . I acted for the best that my judgment with the assistance of respectable officers dictated, but I

have done wrong and I am extremely sorry for it.' Not that Man's humiliation could have been the least comfort to Jervis, who would rather have had his ships.

Here follows, in a word, Jervis's own estimate of his position after his first five months in the Mediterranean : 'The wear, tear and loss of boats is incalculable. We are now in our eighteenth week's cruise, and if the enemy does not give us battle, I MUST OBSTINATELY PERSEVERE IN MAINTAINING THIS POSITION until the armies on both sides go into Winter quarters'. So we see Jervis, having vainly dared the foe to combat with his rickety Fleet, prepared to hang on at all costs with ships weakened and riddled by a thousand deficiencies, in the face of an enemy so potent that Nelson could write him a few months later, 'All is lost in Italy, the Republic of Venice is actually French, and Buonaparte is within 150 miles of Vienna with 150,000 men'. Then, even he yielding for a moment to the general trance of hopelessness : 'THERE SEEMS NO STOPPING THESE EXTRAORDINARY PEOPLE' — a tremendous admission never echoed by Jervis, in public or private letters, for one single instant. He did admit, when Captain Miller shouted for help in blockading Trieste, 'The *Petterel* sloop is the only vessel I can spare, the blockade of Leghorn, attention to the Gulf of Genoa, the island of Corsica and Porte Ferraio, with the protection of trade to and from the Levant, having exhausted all my resources'. For his resources were drained not once but a hundred times over, yet the one thing to be sought vainly, in this fantastic chronicle, is the note of faltering in Jervis's voice. Did he lack masts, pitch, ropes, workmen and a thousand other things ? Never mind : somehow he could report, 'The weather now being favourable for shifting masts, fitting rigging and other equipment, every exertion is being made to get the squadron ready for sea.' Did the command to evacuate Corsica shake him into exclaiming, 'I shall find the utmost difficulty to provide for the embarkation from Corsica, there being no surplus of transports and a very great lack of water-casks, bedding, etc.' ?

Never mind ; somehow Corsica was evacuated. And just as he pulled these particular rabbits from his hat, he produced others by an endless sleight-of-hand, evolving — in a thousand cases of need — something out of nothing.

However, even in that worst period of all, 1796 up to early in 1797, it makes a pleasant change to record the occasional rays of sunshine that filtered in upon the darkness, some from outside sources it is true, but many emanating from that central dynamo of power called John Jervis. Ships under his orders, excluded from port after port, still cruised busily scouting for news of enemy movements, and were not slow to avail themselves of other opportunities. They could do nothing against large concentrations of fighting ships except look them over while keeping well out of reach, but on meeting smaller or weaker craft sailing alone or in twos, they pounced. The result of these pouncings may be seen in Jervis's reports on prizes, the first of which lists *fifty-three* ships taken in the first few months of his command, together with interesting descriptions of their cargoes. 'Corn, wine, Cloath and other Bale Goods. Needles, awls and leather. Brandy, bread. Brass 24-pounders, 13-inch mortars and gun-carriages.' The one dead loss in this collection of Godsends is an unnamed ketch whose sole freight was a hundred Austrian prisoners of war.

Another ray of cheer was the gathering indication that although the Spaniards had an awe-inspiring armada of mighty ships, their discipline and seamanship were such as might not stand up to the shock of battle. At 2 a.m. of a morning late in October, a couple of Jervis's observation ships 'fell in with the Spanish Fleet, amounting to thirty-eight sail'. Enormous, that looming flotilla, a concourse of vast ghosts on the shadowy water. But : 'The wind was variable, the whole fleet seemingly in much confusion'. The wind changed suddenly and began to blow hard, and the Spaniards 'continued in great confusion while in sight. Captain Fremantle informs me', concludes Jervis, with all the professional's contempt for unprofessional performance, 'that their topgallant masts were on deck and the utmost irregularity and disorder appeared in all their manœuvre.' Such news was as good as a present, and not long afterwards we find him writing to thank the Queen of Brazil for another present. 'Her Majesty's splendid gift of refreshment,' he calls it, *refreshment* conjuring up visions of thin sandwiches and ice-cream, but happily the Queen's idea of refreshment was more robust and included 400 bullocks, 100 pigs, 600 chickens, 56 pipes of wine, and hundreds of pounds of chocolate, oranges and refined sugar, Jervis listing all this in his regulation report to the Admiralty.

And talking of presents, another one might be mentioned at this point—a lighter moment in the greyness and harshness of the Mediterranean struggle. Another ruler was involved, a male this time, one of the neutrals to whom Jervis paid as much court as he had time for — the Dey of Algiers. The Dey, it seemed, was bitten by the wish for an 'Englisch-builded Schip', a fighting one of course. His desire was wafted to the ears of Jervis who arranged for one to be presented to him, and Captain Fremantle duly delivered an armed zebec to the Algerian port. The correspondence which followed on the subject of this gift is a rare spectacle, the actual writer being the Dey's agent, Levantine by the sound of his name and the look of his English — butchered and strangely spelt, but somehow delightfully adequate as a medium for conveying the Dey's sentiments. On delivery of the zebec, the Dey (nobody's fool apparently) sent two experts aboard to inspect the offering, First Builder Master Great Bachi, Captain of the Port, and one Ali Rais, who took a desponding view of the zebec and 'who altogether they have said to him, that hi was an ouldest Schip', and only worth breaking up for timber. Their opinion was promptly reported by letter to Captain Fremantle, who took a high and outraged tone ; the Dey's reception of the gift was an insult to his ruler, the King of England. The Dey at once backed down a little

in the acrimony of his complaint, while maintaining un-
impaired his poor opinion of the gift. 'He will conserve the
same friendship with the King of Great Britain but he will
not accept the present, being only fit for timber : and if it is
timber : he has enough in his own territories.' An undoubted
snub ; Fremantle drew himself up even taller and the Dey
shrank into nervousness and mildness, all the same continuing
to refuse the zebec, and with his placating tone the national
honour had to be satisfied. Jervis was satisfied, too, and
wrote to the Admiralty that Fremantle had handled the
situation 'in very fine style indeed'.

Returning to the Queen : Only ten days after her lavish
treat Jervis could notify his superiors of something much
sweeter than refined sugar. He had been wooing Portugal,
with the result that the Portuguese, for mixed motives —
creditable and base and from their desire not to be gulped
down alive by the Napoleonic ogre — were coming in on
the English side. Jervis could count on them for seven ships
of the line carrying seven hundred and eighteen guns altogether, and the seven warships could reinforce him at twenty-
four hours' notice. How desperately Jervis needed this help
was perhaps his own secret ; Portugal could not have known
how badly off he was. But only eighteen days later (January
1797) Admiral William Parker arrived from England with
five sail of the line, and at first glance diagnosed the situation
for bad as bad as could be. So urgent was Jervis's need for the
reinforcement, wrote Parker, that he had procured a Portuguese schooner, which met Parker with his orders long before
he entered the Tagus anchorage. A Sister Anne on the watch-
tower, maritime style ; the lonely ship hovering and waiting,
waiting through darkness and dawns for the sight of Parker's
sails. But Parker brought with him not only ships, but his
own tale of bad luck : the Colossus had lost a mainmast and
its toppling caused other damage so serious 'that it cannot
be repaired at sea', and as for Jervis's own prospects — suppose the Spanish fleet to come out of harbour and force a

battle — they simply could not be worse. Two of the Commander-in-Chief's best ships are useless from the damage they have sustained, writes Parker gloomily, and follows this up with the stark, hopeless assertion : 'He is too weak to do much with the Spanish Fleet if they should put to sea'. This was an expert's verdict on the Fleet that only two weeks later fought and won the battle of Cape St. Vincent.

For a battle must come, everyone knew ; it only waited for the moment that an enemy fleet would come out of its anchorage, for whatever reason, and give the English Fleet a chance to attack. All that mounting rumble and roar of preparation in Spain and France, all that movement of ships and men massing all these months, must reach some climactic point of action before very long. It did, in the shape of orders from France — ostensibly from the Directorate which was still the nominal governing body, but it may be reasonably conjectured that the voice was theirs, but the orders were Napoleon's. The Spanish fleet at Cartagena, they commanded, was to join the French fleet at Brest, so as to escort and protect a French army of invasion on its way to England. But almost a month before, Jervis had sent orders to Parker in which imminent action rings like an alarm-bell : 'Nelson is retreating down the Mediterranean with troopships and storeships. I must be in a position to go speedily to his assistance in case the Spanish fleet attempts to interrupt his passage through the Gut.[1] I shall therefore cruize off Cape St. Vincent. Join me as soon as possible.'

By February 1st, Jervis's source of information told him that the Spaniards had left Cartagena, sailing west on their way to the Straits of Gibraltar. Through these they must pass on their way to the rendezvous at the Northern French port, and Jervis with his insufficient muster was waiting for them to come through the passage. The recent addition of Parker's five ships had brought up his strength by a third, else he would hardly have attempted what he was now daring

[1] The Straits of Gibraltar.

to do — and which, on the face of it, must have seemed a last forlorn hope. Of what was coming through the Straits to confront him he had no exact idea, except that it outnumbered him in some proportion, great but unknown. His own squadron, reclaimed from unseaworthiness — due to his incredible labours over the past year — was mostly in adequate condition, and their crews healthy, disciplined, feverishly interested in prize-money and spoiling for a fight, after the long months of waiting. The total number of his ships was fifteen. Of their fifteen captains Horatio Nelson was one, arriving in the nick of time for the battle — about seventeen hours before.

The seaward coast of Portugal is shaped like one side of a box tilted backward and sticking out into the Atlantic. The southernmost corner of this box, nearly a right angle, is called Cape St. Vincent. Around this corner — so to speak — must come the enemy, and Jervis with his Fleet had been hovering off the Cape long since, with every lookout straining and every ear on the stretch for any sight or sound of the Spanish ships.

Up to February 13th stretched a long blank ; nothing. The night of the 13th fell, bringing with it not only darkness but a shift of wind. Then all at once, upon this changing wind, came sounds, blown-about and ragged as always in the vast reaches of sky and water, but distinct — the minute-guns of the Spanish fleet. Louder and louder through impenetrable blackness they announced the coming of the unknown, until their proximity was signalled at two in the morning, and again at five. Dawn broke, cold, and with poor visibility ; a hazy wall, though not of the densest kind, stood tenuous on the water, reaching as high as the clouds. Through this wall began to appear the Spanish ships one by one, mountains of sail so improbably enormous that they seemed, to one young English signal-lieutenant, like moving headlands.

Jervis was on the quarter-deck of the *Victory*. Captain Hallowell, also there, began to count the enemy fleet. As monster after monster bellied out of the fog, there followed, between the two of them, the familiar conversation :

'There are eight sail of the line, Sir John.'

'Very well, sir.'

'There are twenty sail of the line, Sir John.'

'Very well, sir.'

'There are twenty-five sail of the line, Sir John.'

'Very well, sir.'

'There are twenty-seven sail of the line, Sir John.'

'Enough, sir, no more of that ; if there are fifty sail I will go through them.'

At these words Hallowell administered a concussion to Jervis's back variously described by historians as a punch, a thump or a pat, and bellowed, 'That's right, Sir John, that's right ! And by God ! we'll give them a damned good licking !'

Here, a brief mention of the technics of the sea-fight in Jervis's day is unavoidable. This followed a set, established pattern, hardly ever varied : two enemy fleets lined up opposite and broadside to each other, each ship in a position assigned her beforehand, and known as her 'station'. So important was this station that the majority of courts-martial, after a battle, were held upon captains whose ships had failed to hold their appointed place in the line. Stationed as directed, each ship had an appointed target for cannon-fire — her opposite in the enemy line. Given two vessels of equal size and strength, with good guns and gunners, each had an equal chance of disabling the other or setting it on fire. But this equality of chances also had its drawback, as a naval expert long before Jervis had pointed out : between two fleets evenly matched, no decisive result was possible, and for the sake of this stalemate each side would have spent heavily in blood and suffering, money and exertion.

Jervis, then, faced the Spaniards with his fifteen ships drawn up in line according to custom ; no departure was contemplated, it seemed, from the prescribed order of battle.

But as the enemy fleet appeared in its entirety, in the straggling order that Jervis despised, he saw not only this deficient seamanship, but also the fact that nine ships were sailing well apart from the main body of eighteen. Instantly he drove at the gap between them, to keep them from rejoining each other. This may sound only like commonsense ; in that day, it was an act of the most daring and revolutionary kind, and if the gamble had not come off there would have been no lack of blame — virulent blame — to fall on Jervis ; Admiral Byng had been executed not so very long ago for an honest error of judgment.

Now we have a slight mystery, in the shape of Jervis's regulation report to the Admiralty after the battle (partially quoted) :

'I anxiously awaited the dawn of day when being on the starboard tack, Cape St. Vincent bearing E by N, I had the satisfaction of seeing a number of ships at 49 minutes past ten, weather hazy. H.M.'s squadron under my command, consisting of fifteen ships of the line, happily formed in the most compact order of sailing, in two lines. By carrying a press of sail, I was fortunate in getting in with the enemy's fleet before it had time to connect and form in regular order of battle. Such a moment was not to be lost, and confident in the skill, valour and discipline of the officers and men I had the happiness to command, I FELT MYSELF JUSTIFIED IN DEPARTING FROM THE REGULAR SYSTEM, AND PASSING THROUGH THEIR FLEET IN A LINE, and thereby separated one-third from the main body,' after a partial cannonade. Then he names four captured ships in the margin, first-rates carrying a total of 378 guns. 'The action ceased about five in the afternoon,' he concludes, and appends the usual detailed lists of killed and wounded.

These are Jervis's own words ; the mystery is, that he fails to tell what happened after he cut the Spanish line in two, and which forms the real crux of the tale. The nine enemy ships, separated from the main body of eighteen, began by responding vigorously to attack, and at once the action became hot, with great damage to both sides — yet the state of affairs was such that there was no question of victory, or anything like victory, for either. In fact the nine intercepted ships, through all the hard fighting, were constantly on the alert to rejoin their larger division, and now, by the chances of battle, this is precisely what began to happen. Before them suddenly opened a clear path of water to their parent fleet, without obstacle or impediment. And just as Jervis had seen the gap of severance and hurried towards it, so now the Spaniards saw the gap of reunion and hurried towards that, their need being no less desperate than Jervis's. If the smaller division had succeeded in rejoining the larger, the whole Spanish fleet must almost inevitably have escaped, with all the English effort so far, all that death and damage, spent for nothing.

It was at this instant, seeing the imminent escape of the Spaniards, that Nelson created the spectacular moment of the fight — the high point of the battle of St. Vincent. Four of the enemy ships, bunched together, were leading the rest in their attempted break for the main body. This huddle included the *Most Holy Trinity*, a four-decker reputed to be the largest fighting ship in the world. They were getting away, with no means of stopping them provided by the recognized rules of naval warfare. Again something irregular had to be pulled out of the hat, and Nelson did it. Against orders, or rather without permission, he left his station in the line and threw his ship, the *Captain*, into the path of the oncoming super-monster, the four-decker. At once he was supported by a second ship — the *Culloden*, Captain Troubridge — but the moment of decision, the act, was his and his alone. Jervis, from the *Victory*, watched the two English ships taking on the four first-rates. Few people offered him unsolicited advice, it is reasonable to guess, but Captain Calder beside him was sufficiently appalled at the spectacle to half-ask, half-beg : should not Nelson's ship and its ally be recalled ? 'No,' said Jervis, 'I will not have them recalled. I put my faith in those ships', and signalled the *Excellent* to support Nelson. In the vicious fighting that followed, the sails, masts and wheel of Nelson's *Captain* were so ripped to pieces that she was all but unnavigable.

Then came the second high point, the blazing climax of the drama. Crowding on hard her last vestige of sail to manœuvre, Nelson deliberately rammed his disabled ship into the *San Nicolas*, 'her spritsail yard passing over the enemy's poop and hooking her mizen shrouds', says Colonel Drinkwater, enthusiastically following every move from the *Lively* frigate. Thus immovably entangled with the enemy firstrate, Nelson gave the order to board. Even while he and his men raced over her decks, the *Nicolas* was firing last shots from her lower-deck guns, and her consort the *San Josef*, crowded up against the *Nicolas*, sniped away at the boarding party, or — as Drinkwater says indignantly — 'sorely annoyed with musketry the British aboard the *San Nicolas*.' Having attracted Nelson's attention by this impertinence, the Spaniard paid the penalty. Nelson dashed toward the new opponent, followed by eager men, and a second party from his riddled ship boarded the *San Josef*. Her striking to the victors was a matter of not one shot fired, an officer saying from the quarterdeck that they surrendered, and her captain handing over his sword along with the information that his admiral was dying below. The spectacle ended with the battered *Captain* lashed fast to both her prizes, while the Fleet sailed past the locked group of three, all the ships' companies by Jervis's order lined up ceremonially on decks and masts, going mad with cheering. Then Nelson, filthy-black with smoke, grime and exertion, his uniform tattered like the sails of his ship and his cocked hat shot to fragments, presented himself aboard the *Victory*, where the undemonstrative Jervis fell on his neck.

This is approximately the story of the battle of St. Vincent in amateur's language, and even the rankest of that ilk must see that almost the whole success of the engagement belonged to Nelson. 'Two of the four captured ships were taken solely by him,' says the same eye-witness who was so exasperated by the sniping from the *San Josef*. 'The whole of the British squadron had not hesitated to bestow on him the chief merit of the enemy's defeat.' And while this fever of admiration was at its height — while the whole Navy resounded with his exploit — came the flung bucket of cold water in the shape of Jervis's official dispatch to the Admiralty. He gave no specific credit to Nelson or anyone else ; he named no names ; he made no acknowledgment of the quick thinking, the resource and heroism that had bestowed on his commandership one of the greatest naval victories ever won. Having seen his Admiralty dispatch, we may consider that Drinkwater was not unjust in characterizing it as 'brief and meagre'. 'Not to have Nelson's name even mentioned in this official public dispatch, produced no small degree of surprise among the Commodore's personal friends', he goes on to say, and adds bitterly that such mention is, all too often, the only reward ever enjoyed by those cited. 'No sooner was Jervis's letter published, than Nelson's friends were not backward in expressing their disappointment. They called for a publication of particulars, and before long an attempt was made to gratify their reasonable expectations.' In this manner Drinkwater refers to his pamphlet *The Battle of St. Vincent*, one of several narratives published or unpublished but privately circulated ; one that exists is about fifteen pages long, all written out by hand and anonymous, the author merely signing it, By an Officer of Rank.

Now why, on an occasion so enormously important, did Jervis suppress all mention of the officers who created the victory of St. Vincent, for Nelson was the chief but not the only one — Jervis who in a thousand other dispatches could not point out gallantry in sufficient detail or explicitness, Jervis who was always urging notice and reward for courage or ability in all ranks, highest and lowest ? Jealousy seems out of the question, on the evidence of hundreds of his public or

I

private letters ; a reader may search in vain for the least indication of the jealous temperament, which betrays itself in countless involuntary fashions. His Fleet, by Jervis's orders, had unrestrainedly saluted Nelson's heroism as had Jervis himself, on his own quarter-deck ; all his life his recognition of merit was spontaneous and generous without limit. All these considerations made his departure from custom, on this single occasion, very remarkable, and many people have tried to guess the cause. Drinkwater quotes a contemporary historian [1] in a footnote, whispering as it were in very smallest type : 'It is known [but on what authority ?] that in Jervis's original dispatch he had given Nelson all due praise ; but was prevailed on by Sir Robert Calder, the Captain of the Fleet, to substitute another, on the ground that AS NELSON HAD DISOBEYED THE SIGNAL OF RECALL, any eulogy of his conduct would encourage other officers to do the same.' More mystery ; to what 'signal of recall' does Drinkwater refer ? Jervis turned down Calder's suggestion that such a signal be made, and Drinkwater's own account of the battle fails to mention any. At any rate his quotation ends, 'The surprise is, that a man of Jervis's sagacity should not have detected the lurking jealousy that gave rise to such a recommendation'.

So Calder was jealous, and influenced Jervis ? But it is hard to imagine Jervis submitting his official dispatch to Calder or anyone, either for approval or disapproval, and harder still to imagine Calder having the temerity to suggest to his chief changes or modifications, let alone a suppression so drastic — especially since Calder himself, during the battle, had ordered a premature broadside, and had been told by Jervis in so many words to keep his mouth shut for the rest of the day. The answer must lie buried somewhere — in some intricacy of Jervis's character perhaps, some sudden crotchet of his convictions that made him, for once in his life, do something so completely out of character.

[1] Sir John Barrow, a Secretary to the Admiralty.

In any case, news of the victory burst like salvation over a country long darkened by the most ominous presagings of defeat. Jervis's news came to England on the *Lively* sloop which also carried, as a passenger, our observant Drinkwater. He was sure that news of the victory must have preceded them and they would have a hysterical reception, but no ; 'not a word nor a sign of welcome met our landing'. Then he notice the universal deathly gloom — 'nothing but long faces and desponding looks in all classes' — and was told the reason : on receipt of the news that the Spanish fleet had sailed to join the French fleet, and that their meeting was considered inevitable, the Bank of England had closed that morning, and cash payments were suspended all over the country. It was pleasant to announce that the Spanish Dons would never keep their tryst with the French Citoyennes, Jervis having — by a sort of inverse appropriateness — knocked out their marriage on St. Valentine's day. And quite as important, he had struck a mortal blow at Spain's international prestige and demonstrated her worth as an ally, to France or to anyone else.

In those days the gratitude of the nation was a rich emotional thing, pouring itself out cornucopia-like in royal audiences, stars, ribbons, acclamations, votes of thanks and titles with perpetual incomes attached. Everyone concerned in the battle of St. Vincent did well. Nelson was made a Knight of the Bath, Parker a baronet ; others were knighted or promoted ; all admirals and captains received gold medals specially struck. Jervis, the Commander-in-Chief, was created Earl of St. Vincent, incorporating — by the King's suggestion — the name of his victory in his title. With this came a pension variously reported as two or three thousand pounds a year, the King lamenting the fact that he had no power to extend it beyond the term of Jervis's own lifetime, and hoping that Parliament would see fit to bestow it on the next two heirs to the earldom.

The new title was somehow delayed, its first announcement to Jervis being apparently lost in the mails, but at last the patents arrived.   Up to July 15th, 1797, six months after the battle, he was still signing his letters John Jervis.   On July 16th — for the first time, and then for the rest of his long life — he signed himself

St. Vincent

VII

THE ADMIRAL AND THE FIERY FURNACE

(*Continued*)

THE victory just won lifted the prevailing fogs of anxiety and fear like a gust of sea-wind, once more letting people see the shape of hope and giving the greatest possible boost to the national morale. However, one victory was by no means the answer to the whole situation ; in fact it was but the half-way point, roughly, in the Mediterranean campaign. Spain had been badly hurt in her pride and in her navy, but the greater part of that navy still survived, and in its faltering commandership were a few captains whom even St. Vincent acknowledged as gallant, honest and capable officers.

Moreover, once the actual battle was over, too much of his anxiety and attention were engaged by the blockade of Cadiz — a massive operation, for the port held not only the defeated Spanish ships now engaged in licking their wounds, but other of their squadrons, fresh and undamaged ; it was also full of merchant ships of every description. Yet it is in relation to Cadiz that just one week before the battle of St. Vincent there appeared another of those indications, however uncertain, that the tide had begun to turn — a rumour that his blockaed was as effective as he could wish, and that all was not well in Spain. 'I have every reason to believe,' he wrote on February 7th, 1797, 'that the province of Andalusia is in great want of bread corn,' because its price there was double what it is in Lisbon. Therefore he tightened the blockade, 'and we have sent away many ships loaded with corn from Hamburg and salt provisions from North America' (an interesting sidelight on some specific staples of early American commerce). In the whole business of corking up Cadiz the single purpose of the English was again, of course, to provoke the Spanish fleet into coming out and giving battle. With this object in view two determined attacks on the harbour were made under Nelson's leadership, but the Spaniards were much too prudent to leave their niche of safety.

Likewise, between the detonations from Nelson's bomb-vessels, we can hear other explosions — of rage — and St. Vincent was entirely cognizant of them. In a port jammed with shipping piled-up and immobilized for months, other interests were involved beside the war ; patriotism was all very well, but people were being ruined. 'The merchants are loud in their clamours for the fleet to go out,' St. Vincent wrote at the end of June '97, 'the consequence of which, they flatter themselves, must remove the blockade.' The merchants were quite wrong in their conclusions, for the Earl was not to be budged from his watch-dog stance in the bay's very mouth. 'Nothing short of dire necessity shall remove us from this proud position', he trumpets, and in spite of a serious shortage — 'we are hard run for water' — he calculates that he can keep it up for two months.

The blockade, in fact, dragged on for much longer than two months and petered out into sheer stalemate, and two weeks later St. Vincent was empowering Nelson to try a new project, an attack on Santa Cruz, the Spanish base in the Canary Islands — a story of defeat that belongs mostly in Nelson's chapter but whose ending is partly embodied in St. Vincent's routine Admiralty report of August 16th, '97 : 'I have greatly to lament the heavy loss the country has sustained in the severe wound of Admiral Nelson'. The regular list of killed and wounded puts it more succinctly : 'Rear-Admiral Nelson's right arm shot off'. A bitter pill, and in addition the Santa Cruz episode gave proof that Spain, for all her recent naval catastrophe, was still capable of resistance or — who knew — of future aggression, and that in any case, as an enemy, she was by no means to be counted out. No, the victory of February 14th, tremendous as it was, had not lightened in any considerable degree the burden's weight; it still dug into one man's shoulders as many-pointed, as intolerably crushing, as ever.

All the same, between blasts of continuing activity on the Spanish front, St. Vincent's preoccupations were turning more and more to where, beyond Spain, still loomed the other enemy : the enemy with her bogus cap of liberty perched on her wild locks, terrible in her lustre of unbroken victory, her burnished cuirass of new ideologies and new patriotisms, her superb armies by land and — what touched St. Vincent most nearly — her navy, brought up to scratch in a few years as by a miracle, reflecting in its high standards the efficiency and organizing genius of Napoleon, and as yet barely touched by attack, let alone by defeat. Or to put it another way : the long slow climb of thirteen months toward the battle of St. Vincent was only the preface to another long slow climb of seventeen months toward the battle of the Nile, which did for the French fleet what St. Vincent did for the Spanish, only with a thoroughness that the Spanish escaped. Again, this is mostly Nelson's story. But St. Vincent's energies were now aimed at the supreme objective of combat with the French fleet, and since he realized its quality as much more formidable than the Spanish, he realized also the degree of preparation necessary to meet it. All over again every resource of English minds, bodies and nerves, of materials and ingenuity, would be strained to the uttermost, as though the victory of St. Vincent had never been ; all over again their chief would be exhausted and drained, and by what means he replenished himself no one cared, just so long as he managed it.

For his own situation was unaltered ; his new titles and dignities brought with them no softening of the rigours he had endured as John Jervis, no modification or division of responsibility. Still he was pulled this way and that by a thousand calls for help : General O'Hara, Governor of Gibraltar, hopes to get fresh provisions from Bombay, otherwise he cannot keep his troops well in the summer heats, and asks St. Vincent 'to station a force here sufficient to keep our communications open with the neighbouring ports of Africa', closing with the cheerful news that the enemy have two frigates with gun- and mortar-boats in the port of Algeciras. Still the state of his Fleet kept him balanced on the razor-edge of apprehension ; seven of his ships were in such bad condition, he warned the Admiralty, that by hook or by crook they should be got into an English dockyard before September. Still a thousand un-foreseen contingencies stoned him from day to day : 'An immense number of letters for the seamen of my fleet being detained in the post-office at Lisbon for payment of a very heavy postage charged upon them in addition to what had been paid in England, I trust [for some] speedy redress of this hardship upon the poor fellows.' Nor did he neglect to placard the ships with notices that he was thinking and working for them : 'Men! your letters have been detained on account of an unreasonable high-postage charge. The moment the Commander-in-Chief heard of it he applied warmly to the Admiralty and the Postmaster-General. The moment the letters arrive on board they will be sorted and delivered.' Again with his men in the forefront of his mind he warned his superiors : 'The discontent already shown in this Squadron from the delay in paying for frigates and corvettes captured by it, will not be allayed by this measure [undervaluing two recent prizes] when it is made public.' And yet again he reported to the Admiralty on a different note, but to the same end : 'I submit a plan of the anchorage of this squadron under my command, a copy of which was given to every line-of-battle ship, and the Captains assembled to receive information touch-ing the depth of water, nature of the ground, and precautions necessary to be taken in gales. By this means I hope their Lordships will see that I was attentive to the security of the ships committed to my charge, in an anchorage very unsafe.'

The ships committed to my charge : glorious words that sum up the man and his whole life's aim — his care for his children of the Navy, his incredibly-detailed care by day and night, a thousand evidences of it raying out of him upon men in high places and low, without distinction. And just as no ship's detail could escape him, so no war detail, however mosquito-like, could hope to evade that microscopic eye. A swarm of rowboat privateers had sprung up to sting and harass ; these he dealt with by having them pursued and burnt to the water's edge, while finding time to render a considerable service to a recent enemy. 'A number of American ships being blocked [in Cadiz Bay] by French privateers, with the connivance of the Spanish, Rear-Admiral Nelson detached the *Andromache* to give them convoy, and left them past the Gut in safety yesterday.'

This period, also, was to see his encouragement and patronage of Nelson leading directly to the greatest triple blaze of sea-victory, sea-hero and sea-legend, that the world has ever known. That it could lead, as well, to planting something not far from murder in another man's breast, and that he himself would be the target for this murderous intent, he was not of course to know. But for the moment Nelson was *en route* to England for treatment of his amputation wound, and poorer by his loss St. Vincent, assuredly, must have felt.

Nor could other of his daily conditions give him any feeling of prosperity. Want and shortage had walked as long and intimately at his heels as a couple of spaniels ; no reinforcements, no masts, no stores. Here occurs a variation — a funny domestic note — on the theme of mysterious leakages from ships'-stores of water : 'My own opinion is, that the water was drawn off by the people of the ship, to supply the Women who still infest H.M.'s ships in great numbers and who WILL have water to wash, that they and their reputed husbands may get drunk with the earnings.' This warning to the Women— something unfriendly about that capital — was followed, almost in the same breath, by a deadlier warning to another type of offender. These were prisoners taken by him and released on condition they should not re-enter naval or military service for the duration of the war ; when some of them were found in the crews of ships captured later, he served steely notice on France and Spain, promising 'the most summary execution of every officer and man who falls into my hands, acting in violation of that most sacred of all engagements, the Convention for the release of prisoners of war.' Bad faith always enraged him ; inefficiency always depressed him. 'I regard the vast superiority of the enemy less than I do the bad sailing and working of some of the ships under my command.'

His assorted headaches of the next few days, comprising the court-martial and execution of two homosexuals, the appointing of convoy for a Spanish prize valued at £300,000 and the crucial intelligence that the French squadron had left Toulon and perhaps was approaching him, included something new : a crisis in calamity never before encountered on the Mediterranean station — mutiny. And the mutiny St. Vincent had to face was of a character so special, so unheard-of even, that its beginnings and birth-marks demand a separate mention, however brief.

* * *

On the day of April 16th, 1797 — almost exactly two months after the victory of St. Vincent — an incredible thing happened : a major Fleet division refused, as one man, its admiral's orders to sail. The fleet was the Channel Fleet anchored off Spithead ; its refusal was mutiny, of course, but of a kind never before known or beheld — an organized effort, carefully planned and laid down beforehand, carried out with military efficiency and precision, also without fuss, threats or disorder of any kind. The strike, overdue, was against conditions unchanged literally for over two hundred years : starvation pay, insufficient or non-existent leaves, food that was verminous garbage and lightweight at that, and floggings under which a man's flesh peeled from the bones and blood spurted from his nose and mouth.

Against all this the Fleet spoke out with one voice, and before that voice Lords of Admiralty, Cabinet Ministers, the King himself, bowed down. The highest officers of the land tore backward and forward between Spithead and London trying to palliate the disastrous situation ; all the demands of the mutineers were finally met, including the unlikeliest demand of all — for a universal pardon, since the strikers were not minded to suffer reprisal once the strike was over : they imposed the condition of no beatings, no hangings, no punishments of any kind. And this also was granted because authority was helpless to do otherwise. The King signed a general pardon at five in the evening, and before midnight a hundred copies of it, still damp from the press, were being rushed to Spithead for proclamation throughout the Fleet.

This, then, was the mutiny at Spithead, a mutiny conducted with such dignity and punctilio as to have been graced with the name of 'respectable' ; also, at least in theory, the Spithead mutiny was a success. In both these regards it differed from the Nore mutiny, which took place around the same time and was neither respectable nor successful. The shades of difference between the Spithead and the Nore mutinies were inescapably linked with the current political situation.

All England was suffering what every nation suffers during a war in which it has so far been defeated and from which it expects daily and hourly tidings of new defeat — agonies of insecurity, the queasiness of fear and vanishing national credit. The kingdom was in a ferment ; from every part of it arose the noise and tumult of public meetings calling on the King to dismiss the Ministry. At other meetings, not so public, countless secret societies were agitating for the abolition of the Crown and the setting-up of a republic. Ireland in especial — no friend to England for centuries-old reasons — was working up to open rebellion. The Nore mutiny took place at Sheerness, a dumping-ground for large numbers of Irish naval recruits. The presence of this large Irish element in the ships' companies gave the origins of the mutiny a political flavour which on inspection turns out to be doubtful, or at least intermixed with other origins not in the least political.

The mutiny of the Nore began on a foul old hulk called the *Sandwich*, bursting at the seams with rank filth, disease, stench and suffering. The ship was being used as a receiving-station during this intensive period of Irish naval recruitment ; into her were being crammed the human quarry garnered by this activity — the jails scoured, men forcibly kidnapped or lured into the service by payment of a bounty. Originally designed for a complement of 750 men, the *Sandwich* was now jammed to suffocation with over 1600. Through this mass, in consequence of the atrocious overcrowding, contagious fever, skin infections, diarrhoea and ulcers were running riot. A letter of protest from the ship's doctor, describing his help-lessness in the face of conditions,[1] seems to one reader at least a pattern of controlled despair hard to equal in any professional writing.

When the sense of misery past endurance burst its bounds, the uprising began. Objectionable officers were put off the *Sandwich* by the mutineers, and the mutiny was organized on the lines of the one at Spithead : strict order and discipline, election of delegates, no liquor allowed, respect to officers and carrying out of duty. But the Spithead affair had been a huge demonstration, the gesture of an entire fleet ; at the Nore, where there were only three large ships and the rest convoys or frigates always being moved about, there was no comparable solidarity. The authorities rallied almost at once and cut off the mutineers' food and water by notifying the Navy victuallers. Militia appeared, and the seamen could not go ashore without being arrested. A young man named Richard Parker recently in prison for debt, a former school-master — unstable, unhealthy, unlucky — had allowed himself to be pushed to the forefront of the mutiny into a dangerous prominence from which he, as president of delegates, attempted

[1] Appendix II.

to carry on negotiations. The Spithead ringleaders had more sense ; even to this day, their names remain in darkness. The mutiny broke down, and Parker was hanged. He seems to have been vain, voluble and melodramatic, also a little on the hysterical side, but he was certainly no criminal. His execution inspired George III — still smarting from the humiliation of that general pardon signed under duress — to write to the authorities, urging that the body be hanged in chains on the most conspicuous point of land in sight of the mutinous ships.

It was news of Spithead and the Nore that percolated little by little into St. Vincent's ships, by men newly sent out from England in reinforcements to the Mediterranean Fleet. It is well at this point to remind ourselves of the period's slowness of communication, difficult to take in by the light of present-day tempos. The ships' companies under St. Vincent may be considered as totally ignorant of what had just happened in England. In addition, naval authority had tried to suppress the news by holding up mail, destroying newspapers and so forth. In vain : as well try to suppress the convulsions of an earth-quake. All round the world, wherever there were British ships, ran the seismic shock of events at Spithead and the Nore : by ships' grapevine, by smuggled letters, by whisper-ings ashore and afloat wherever seamen gathered together. Many of these carriers — not all — were Irish. Many of them belonged to a bright-red political club in especially bad repute, called United Irishmen. The news of the second mutiny would carry with it an especial edge of bitterness. For the Spithead mutineers had won, at least in theory, the concessions they set out to obtain, even though their present fear was that the government would try to go back on its promises ; the mutineers of the Nore had nothing to remember but the soreness of defeat and the horror of Parker's death. With that tragedy new and raw in their minds, on top of the old disaffec-tion toward England, it was natural that the Irish among them should form, in the general atmosphere of ferment, the hottest and most emotional centres of inflammation. In other words, one might venture to say that their mutinous activities were not of political inception or origin, but had taken on a political colouring as they went along.

The repercussions of the home mutinies were not slow to burst out, with a sort of smouldering violence, in St. Vincent's squadron. From about the latter end of May '97 the shadow of the gibbet begins to fall across his dispatch-books as ship after ship, sent from England to reinforce his Fleet, arrived at Gibraltar. Trouble had started in so many of them during the voyage that the first request their captains had to make of him was permission for court-martial. Now, one word as to the lifelong position, of the man whose lot it was to set in motion all those mills for grinding out floggings and hangings, on the question of punishment.

St. Vincent's nature was, actually, without one trace of cruelty. Thousands of witnesses to this survive in the shape of his mountainous correspondence, official and unofficial, written to the highest in the kingdom as well as to the poorest and lowest. One may search it in vain for the least trace of that vindictiveness, retaliatory appetite or pleasure in punishment that are the hallmarks of the genuinely cruel temperament. In fact, he seems to have had very little capacity to hate — that is, in the true malignant sense that destroys every other consideration, including judgment ; there is no demonstrable instance that the fever of hatred ever obscured his clarity of mind or made him inaccessible to reason. His letters are also evidence of his readiness to avoid punishment wherever possible, this leniency — it goes without saying — extending itself impartially to all ranks. He punished with impersonal severity, without personal malice, in strict proportion to the offence. The present circumstances, however, were more than a little bit special.

St. Vincent's acquaintance with insubordination in all its countless shadings had begun in his twenty-fifth year, and he was certainly no stranger to mutiny. But this mutiny, at this moment, was a weapon more lethal and that struck at him with more deadliness than he had ever before experienced. Behind him were months of racking strain and exhaustion, of superhuman effort never relaxed ; he could look back upon uncounted outpourings of bravery and sacrifice, upon hundreds of men dead or uselessly drowned in ships foundering on rocks and reefs. And after all that gigantic expenditure of strength and suffering and death, freely given for England's survival, what did he find ranged against him ? A handful of scoundrels (his probable expression) plotting and muttering in the depths of the forecastle, by their presence eating out the comeliness and pride of his shining creation, his ships' discipline, like maggots in a barrel of biscuit. Mutiny in any case was the damnable thing, but mutiny in wartime — mutiny in just this instant, when it might cripple or even destroy the final intent for which he was girding every nerve and every muscle — was a thing utterly beyond the pale, and small wonder that he should turn on it with the concentrated ruthlessness of a man defending his lifework.

I enclose the Minutes and Sentences of a Court-Martial passed upon : with these ominous words begin no fewer than thirty of his letters between May '97 and July '98, giving his dispatch-books a grim appearance, coupled with references even grimmer. For if the ships' crews made him eat the gall of mutiny he was the man to make them eat it again to the last mouthful, and with extra bitterness added. Because not only the man hanged for mutiny tasted death ; all his former companions of the crew shared the meal with him, for St. Vincent had decreed that a mutineer must, in every case, be executed by his own shipmates. From this horror there was no escape — not by any extremity of turns and twists, not by any tactic of prayer, evasion or delay. Around the condemned man must gather, to work his doom upon him, his former cronies of the daily task, the hammock and the mess, all knowing intimately his way of eating and sleeping, his very breathing ; to these men fell the lot of swinging aloft the living weight of one who had been at least a daily associate, perhaps an intimate friend.

And among them must have been those who knew in their secret hearts that they had sympathized or plotted with him and that, but for luck, they would be standing where he now stood, feeling the rope's prickle drop over their heads and settle about their bared necks. This was the sort of thing that pushed men into hysteria or maddened resistance and St. Vincent, well aware of it, stood ready to counter the new threat with a new weapon. Or not new perhaps, but given a new potency under his handling and development of it — the Marines. These forces for land combat, carried on English battleships from 1664, had a long and distinguished history ; now St. Vincent cultivated further their sense of pride and consequence by stepping up and elaborating all their routine ceremonies, until he had made their half-hour morning parade one of the high points of the day, with the band (if there were one) blaring God Save the King in majestic cadence and all on board required to attend and stand bare-headed until the command to shoulder arms. For another sort of occasion, too, the following document illustrates his use of the Marines :

'Every ship of the squadron is to send two boats with an officer in each, and two Marines properly armed, to assemble round H.M.'s ship *Marlborough* at eight oclock tomorrow morning, to attend a Punishment.'

Dread, the capitalized word, casting a colder chill somehow than more specific terms like hanging or flogging.

'The sentence is to be carried into execution by the crew of H.M.'s ship *Marlborough* alone', continues the inexorable voice. 'Whenever there is occasion to inflict Punishment on board any of H.M.'s ships under my command, an officer's guard of Marines [is] to attend with arms and bayonets fixed.'

From such steel-spiked orders — the vast majority of them issued in this fourteen-month period — perhaps derives the legend of St. Vincent as a good deal of history has handed it down to us. A figure harsh and inhuman, dusty and leaden, inaccessible to appeal, repelling approach or interest by its aura of impervious officialdom ; the genial and inveterate giver of dinner-parties afloat and ashore would hardly recognize himself, and not with any degree of pleasure. Those few months out of the seventy-odd years of his career have heavily obscured his ten thousand acts of delicacy and compassion, his anxiety to take the lash out of a rebuke by a favour bestowed in the next breath, his understanding of honest failure and his generous voice raised to protect such failure — and not only for those of his own country by any means, for the following letter was written to the Spanish Minister of War : 'Don José Figueroa, commander of the corvette *San Leon*, was on a very dark night suddenly approached by a squadron of His Majesty's ships. Though he made every effort to escape and stood a chase and cannonade of two and a half hours, he was compelled to surrender to the great superiority of force. I am much struck with the good breeding and intelligence of his mind, and shall be happy to hear that he has not lost ground in Your Excellency's good opinion.'

Meanwhile, the mutiny writhed its way through ship after ship on a scale unsuspected and only defined, at last, in the dying confessions of three men, separately taken down by three different ships' chaplains. 'The mutiny on the *Princess Royal* commenced with the United Irishmen. Beware of them! It was intended to murder officers without exception, to go up the Straits and take the ships from Nelson [that brings a smile, in all the painful chronicle] and go with them to Ireland', declared Michael Connell, while Thomas Bott's confession was much more methodical and detailed, betraying the society's oath, calculating the number of mutineers in one ship at two hundred, implicating fifty men by name but pausing — rather touchingly — to make an exception in favour of one : 'Charles Sedley is only a dupe, for he is a harmless man'. Three wills follow the three confessions, all of one line each and all on this pattern : 'Guthrie to have my Cloathes, my Wife to have my Pay'.

None of this was pleasant or amusing, even if necessary, and St. Vincent must have met the ceaseless applications for

K

court-martial with endurance fraying out thinner and thinner, until at last—

'Why do they send me the mutinous ships ?' he exploded, after months of it. 'Do they think I will be hangman to the Fleet ?' And the cry of revulsion and disgust, so uncharacteristic of the man, gives not only the measure of the devastation in his nervous system, but something else that he had kept to himself — the breakdown of his health under the colossal burden he was carrying.

A major contribution to the things that were driving him frantic must have been that the mutiny deflected, dangerously, the burning-glass of his attention from its concentration on the enemy. Now that he could re-focus it, at length, enormous and menacing shapes met his eye wherever he looked. The French were extorting from the Genoese a great number of vessels and four thousand seamen to man them, for the transport of troops and artillery ; tremendous preparations were afoot in other quarters. But of all this gathering threat, the part most nerve-racking was : against whom was it to be directed ? What point of assault had been chosen, in secret, for this gigantic battering-ram ? Such uncertainty is more oppressive than anything else, as a figure shrouded must always be more disturbing than one disclosed. At least, though, St. Vincent had the consolation of one first-class auxiliary, for Nelson had returned to duty with his stump completely healed. 'The arrival of Admiral Nelson has given me new life,' St. Vincent, jubilant, had written the Admiralty, and within the week had given Nelson his orders :

'You are hereby authorized and directed to proceed with your squadron to ascertain, by every means in your power, the destination of the considerable armaments making at Toulon, Marseilles and Genoa ; which is differently spoken of, such as Sicily or Corfu on one hand, Portugal or Ireland on the other.' Of these four possibilities Ireland, of course, was the worst headache for England ; revolutionary sympathy there was considered quite strong enough for the Irish to embrace not only the French but also their politics. In addition, if the French 'armaments' came out of their various ports and combined, they had of necessity to make for the one exit from the Mediterranean — the Straits of Gibraltar — and Nelson was warned not to let them get there first. 'Take special care not to suffer the Armament to pass the Straits before you', urged St. Vincent's dispatch, and however little Nelson needed any injunction not to let the French beat him to it, the warning reflects the older man's torment and preoccupation over the enigma : who was Bonaparte's next target ? where was it ? what was it ?

The diversity of opinion on this point was tumultuous, fearful and confused and (at this remove of time) amusing as an example of how far wrong authority could be, even the highest authority in the land with the best facilities for getting at the truth. For on September 16th Spencer, First Lord of the Admiralty, wrote discouraging Nelson's proposed Egyptian expedition ; he thought it 'unproductive', also dangerous, to have so large a squadron tied down to a station so remote as Alexandria, and suggested that Nelson could be much more usefully employed in harassing Malta and supporting the Kingdom of Naples — this letter being written, remember, forty-six days after Nelson had annihilated the French fleet at the battle of the Nile.

A first faint gleam of light on the puzzle — a first exciting evidence that at last they were on the trail — came about mid-July, not through scouting ships or spies or other routine channels of information, but through a random incident : a tiny pointing forefinger balanced, tremblingly, on the invisible hair-spring of chance. For it happened that an English ship under Captain Foote captured a French ship called *La Sensible* stuffed with loot from Malta and also with some passengers aboard, and among them was a wealthy civilian named Collot, known to be intimate with Napoleon. This Collot had unfortunately left his trunks unlocked when the *Sensible* surrendered, nor is it remarkable that next time he came to look them over he found necklaces, watch-chains, diamonds and emeralds missing to the tune of £600. He reported his loss to Foote, who not unnaturally wondered why he was carrying such quantities of jewellery with him.

'Why, because it is easy to convert such articles into money in Egypt', Collot answered naïvely, 'or in any other country.' That last sounds like a belated attempt to cover up, and on top of it — 'although', bragged the simple soul — he sounds simple, for all his wealth and presumable business acumen, 'although I have credits to any amount in the Levant'.

Strangely enough the same Captain Foote picked up, from the same source, another piece of gossip that pointed in the same direction. After informing St. Vincent that Napoleon was transporting 40,000 men and 2000 cavalry, he adds a much more interesting item : a Knight of Malta, famous as a draftsman, expert in coins and medals and a professional antiquarian, had just been engaged by Napoleon as part of his expedition, and 'it is the general opinion that they are gone to Alexandria'. Foote concludes handsomely in another letter : from *La Sensible* he has taken — along with some flags — a splendid gilt-and-bronze cannon presented by Louis XIV to the Knights of Malta, and does St. Vincent think the King would like to have them ?

These were among the uncertain traces that led Nelson about two weeks later to Aboukir Bay, when on August 1st, 1798 — following the hunch that Spencer was still distrusting six weeks later — he hunted the French fleet down at last and finished it, with nine ships out of thirteen taken and the two largest consumed in a gigantic inferno, their ironwork going molten in flame, their hulls wasting to skeletons in flame, their masts spiring and roaring upward in flame, their ammunition exploding at last and all rocketing up sky-high, then raining down fragments of ships and fragments of men, all in flame. It was Nelson's victory, but it was St. Vincent who had given him the chance and the means. For this he had battled through four years of grinding adversity, for this he had fought mutiny and brought it to heel, for this he had put power in Nelson's hands — at the cost of drawing rebuke, hatred and attempted revenge on himself. This part of the story belongs in Nelson's chapter. But if Nelson fought the battle of the Nile it was because St. Vincent had put him there to fight it, marking him as the one who could bring the desired end to pass — for there were other men who had prior claim on the command St. Vincent had given him ; there were others who had a better right to it and were not slow to say so.

By September 28th the news had reached home and the streets were seething with hysteria, cheers, strangers embracing ; Spencer the doubter was receiving congratulations on 'the almost incredible victory — the stupendous news of the total destruction of the French naval force at the mouth of the Nile — this grand and magnificent event that has fallen to the lot of Nelson, with his one lame arm and his gallant English spirit — I cannot contain my joy and my joy for you, God bless you ! —'

And meanwhile, what of the real author of the grand and magnificent event ? One has the impression of a chain long-stretched beginning to give link by link, though actually this imminent collapse was anything but sudden and had been heralded, as seen before, by plenty of warning. If St. Vincent's first mention of his health to Spencer had been six months before, we may assume — having now some idea of the man's power of endurance — that he had been ignoring unpleasant symptoms for a long time previously, that only their development into something much more alarming could have pushed him into saying so, and that probably any other commander, in his place, would have retreated to bed long ago. Sick men were on his hands all the time ; he was always demanding for their need what he would not demand for himself. He sends home his Fleet Captain, Calder, whose health has broken down, 'very materially injured by the excessive heats, and I hope that their Lordships will dispense with his further services in this climate'. He sends home his Agent Victualler at Gibraltar, whose health is 'ruined by the climate', and with this same killer, in other directions, he can hardly keep pace. 'The rapid decline of young men in this squadron, whether from ill-treated venereal complaints or the climate, is inconceivable.' All around him they were dropping out and being sent home, but there was no dropping out or home-going for him — although the grinding exactions of his job did drive him, nearly at the end of it, into dwelling a little on its special rigours.

'This service is unlike any other,' he wrote to Spencer. 'We have no relaxation in port, where we never go ; the officers are all kept to their duty ; no rambling about the country ; and when at sea we do not make snug for the night but are working incessantly by the lead to keep our position, insomuch both mind and body are continually upon the stretch.' He might have saved his breath ; their Lordships were very sorry to hear that he was affected harmfully by anxiety and overwork, but they displayed no hurry over providing him with a successor or, indeed, with relief of any sort.

'My health suffers exceedingly from sitting too long at the pen,' he apologized later on to Spencer for sending him a dictated letter, and again : 'A violent inflammation in my eyes and head compels me to make use of the pen of my secretary,' and yet again, to one of his captains, 'You found me bereaved of motion and sense by my deplorable health,' which sounds like a multiple neuritis, also he had begun mentioning his dread of the cold, which he felt excessively in his head ; this sensitiveness to cold on the head would still be with him when he was an old, old man. But for the moment he was a mere youth of sixty-four who in finishing his job had achieved the impossible ; transformed hulks of dubious wood and canvas into a fighting fleet, moulded deficient officers and crews to the shape of his own pride and spirit, reduced the fearsome sick-lists arising from foul ship-board conditions to vanishing-point, learned the lesson, and taught it to other commanders, of how to keep ships at sea longer than ever before while maintaining the health of the crews, and — the culmination — had fought and beaten the cream of Spanish and French sea-power with a handful of ships which his own admirals declared, a few days before the actual battle, were unequal to any such contest. He had achieved not one near-miracle but a series of them and his frame of mind, at this point, must have been Simeon's : Lord, now lettest Thou Thy servant depart in peace.

There was to be no peace, however, for St. Vincent ; his abilities were unique and indispensable and his Lords could not let him depart. They made him hang on for an-other thirteen months, strenuous ones, after he had described himself as being at the end of his rope, beset not by one but a combination of maladies — a sure sign of physical, mental and nervous bankruptcy. From this time on, the sick man's confidential letters pleading with Spencer for a little rest, a little surcease, went beyond urgency and began taking on the sharper and sharper note of a person who knows he cannot last. 'I repeat with utmost anxiety my request that I be allowed to rest for five months ; NO INSTANCE WILL BE FOUND IN THE ANNALS OF NAVAL HISTORY OF A COMMANDER-IN-CHIEF GOING THROUGH THE WORK I HAVE DONE IN DIFFERENT CLIMES DURING THE LAST SEVEN YEARS.' In other words he was well aware of what he had done, and concludes on a note foreign to his voice — of despairing expostulation : 'The machine thus wrought [used] cannot endure forever.' The last two excerpts are from letters written some months later, but they applied with equal force to his extremity in the Mediterranean.

Meanwhile his illness could not deflect his attention from what rowelled him at least equally — the question of his successor. Suppose someone inadequate took his place ? Suppose all he had accomplished in those four years should be imperilled, even lost ? Hardly able to see or move, his anxiety lashed him into long exchanges on this point with the Admiralty.

'The person to succeed me should possess both temper [*i.e.* courage or spirit] and good nerves, or he will be in continual hot water and terrified at this anchorage, which appals many a good fellow under my command. This —' and his conclusion has the dying fall of a final weariness '— this is the best opinion I have to offer.' But almost at once he finds the strength to extort from himself one more effort of judgment. 'Lord Keith has shown great manhood and ability before Cadiz, his position very critical, exposed to a hard gale, an army of superior force to windward of him, and twenty-two ships of the line in Cadiz Bay, ready to profit by any disaster which might befall him.' Keith, in fact, was the next inheritor of the Mediterranean purgatory.

As St. Vincent boarded the ship that would take him home in July '99, turning his back in final departure, his feelings and memories — of a man who has lived through such an experience as the four years of the Mediterranean campaign — are inaccessible to us, only to our conjecture. Among a thousand reflections and lingering worries he may have spared a thought for the nasty pill that his superiors had given him to swallow some months earlier, presumably as a reward for his services : a report brought back to him by one of his young officers that 'their Lordships had come to a resolution not to confirm any more of Lord St. Vincent's appointments'. A small later discovery is an undated list of lieutenants who were made commanders out of St. Vincent's ships during his incumbency ; ten names are in the margin, a number not excessive over a period of four years, but were any of these the dishonoured commissions ? Nothing indicates whether they were or not. In any case the thought may have come to him, accompanied perhaps by an ironic smile : how lucky for their Lordships of the Admiralty, how lucky for England, that they had not been inclined to dishonour or nullify the commission he had given the man who had just won the Battle of the Nile.

VIII

THE ADMIRAL AND NELSON

To divest a great name of its lustre : to imagine it as it was before fame transfigured it, merely one among innumerable others : is perhaps one of the hardest things in the world ; hard to free our minds of hindsight, in this one man's case especially. Our awareness of what he became is too rooted, too immovable, to allow of our visualizing him before the events that made the two commonplace syllables of his name clang on the ear like two strokes of Big Ben.

Yet Horatio Nelson's career, up to his thirty-fifth year, had not been much more remarkable than that of other naval captains with first-class names in their profession for courage and ability. He possessed in a high degree, it is true, that magic of personality that impresses itself without effort ; people of all classes with whom he had exchanged only a few words remembered him all their lives. Still, before his association with St. Vincent, one would hesitate to assign him a decisive margin of reputation — *or* prospects — over such men as Troubridge [1] or Collingwood. It is also true that Fleet gossip accorded him some extra shreds of notoriety ; it was said that he did more or less as he liked under whatever Commander-in-Chief he served, and some of his disgruntled colleagues were not slow to throw the fact in his face. Nelson threw it back again, with indignation apparently genuine. It is possible that he himself did not realize the truth of the insinuation, being what he was — a born crusader of fiery convictions, to whom

---

[1] St. Vincent considered Troubridge the greatest seaman that England ever produced.

the end must forever obscure, or at least partly dissimulate, the means. But if his previous chiefs had pretty much allowed him his head, and if it were not because of pre-eminent rank or reputation, it must have been, again, his personality that secured him this special handling. Above and beyond all this, the essential core of Horatio Nelson was, one might venture to say, single-mindedness — a single purpose and intent beside which all his other attributes faded or became secondary. He was a fighting instrument of matchless power, and the moment he was unused a rust of despondency clouded his steel, manifesting itself in doubts, complaints and general pessimism. (*Lying in port is misery to me; if I ever feel unwell, it is when I have no employment.*) On the other hand, difficult commissions brought him to life with a bang, and the more appalling and impossible they were, the more good they did him; his spirits soared and his health improved.

Jervis arrived to take over the Mediterranean command in 1795. Nelson had already been on the station for two years, as captain of the *Agamemnon*. He had been lucky; battles on sea and land had fallen to his share. He would have been luckier if his part in them had not been clogged and thwarted by his commanding admirals. They, slow-thinking, slow-moving men, were content to call him off after a partial success and sit back, well pleased with the destruction or capture of one ship when all his instincts told him that by following up his advantage he could have accounted for more than one, even crippled a fleet — and Nelson's instincts were often more reliable than other men's considered judgment. Again and again his ardour of the chase was doused just when it was hottest, giving him the deathly knowledge of unique opportunities thrown away, lost forever.

In this period, as well, he came to a full acquaintance with the bitterness of knowing himself slighted and passed over by his superiors, in their reports on actions for whose very inception he had been responsible, to say nothing of their success. 'When I reflect that I was the cause of re-attacking Bastia, after our wise generals gave it over — that it was I who joined the Corsicans and with only my ship's party of Marines, drove the French under the walls of Bastia — yet I am scarcely mentioned. My heart is full when I think of the treatment I have received : every man who had any considerable share in the action has got some place or other — I, only I, am without reward.' In the midst of his resentment, however, he had the consolation of living hard, of being active and used — yet with the prescience of genius that senses its own capacity, he knew he was not being used to the uttermost. The man who was coming to fight the Mediterranean campaign, and who was widely known as a commander who stood no nonsense, was going to change all that. Did some obscure presentiment of this stir in Nelson when he wrote his wife that Jervis's arrival would cause 'great joy to some, and sorrow to others' ?

Jervis's first interview with Nelson was on January 14th, 1795, and next day Nelson spoke of it in a letter to his wife. How we would like detailed descriptions of Jervis, of his surroundings, of Nelson's feelings before, during and after the occasion ; instead, we have a bald, barely-interesting : 'The Admiral is just arrived and as by the death of Lord Hervey the *Zealous* is vacant, as also the *St. George*, the Admiral has offered me the choice of either, but I shall refuse both on many counts.' How even the worst letter-writer could make such hay of the beginning of a friendship that was to be so momentous is hardly conceivable, but there stands the letter. So we, ourselves, must imagine that initial meeting of a ten years' relationship, most likely in the plainly-furnished cabin on Jervis's flagship : the stocky older man advancing, his head characteristically downbent, his blue glance coming up under his heavy eyebrows and nailing the visitor before him, the captain of the *Agamemnon*, slight, high-shouldered, and nearly twenty-five years his junior. There we may leave them for a moment, frozen into their attitudes of mutual assessment, while we glance at another letter of Nelson's to his wife. Apparently he had forgotten his previous mention of the Jervis interview and, on his second try, does a little better.

'Joined Sir John Jervis yesterday and was received not only with the greatest attention but with much apparent friendship. I found the Admiral anxious to know many things which, I was not a little surprised, had not been communicated to him from others in the Fleet. It would appear he was well satisfied with my opinion of what is likely to happen, of the means of prevention, etc.' Then Nelson, with all his unrevealingness of style (until overwhelming emotion loosened his tongue) lets something important be seen. 'HE HAD NO RESERVES WITH ME OF HIS INFORMATION, OPINIONS AND THOUGHTS.' Jervis was a man, one might hazard, not given to sudden confidences, and now Nelson says something equally significant : 'He concluded by asking if I had any objection to serve under him WITH MY FLAG.'

Those last three words were the high, the clinching, point to which everything else in their interview had led up. First, the instant mutual liking ; next, the older man applying to Nelson for inside information that other subordinates had held back, either through ignorance or fear ; after that, the exchange of confidential views and opinions ; and on top of all, the offer of the flag. For the flag meant stepping out of the ranks of the anonymous ; it meant the right to fly a distinguishing pendant unlike any other in the world, which identified its possessor forever ; in a titular sense it meant that Jervis was going to put Nelson forward for promotion to rear-admiral. To make such an offer after the presumable two or three hours of their interview, Jervis must have been tremendously, irresistibly struck — by the impression that of all the officers on his staff, superb seamen some of them, this was the one he was going to depend on in a unique sense. But in whatever form his opinion was cast, his mention of the higher rank is absolute proof that he was prepared to go to all lengths in order to keep Nelson in his service during the Mediterranean command.

Here occurs one of the exasperating discrepancies that rear up like nettles in the path of historical enquiry. According to Nelson's own account of it, and the day-to-day correspondence between the two men in the Mediterranean Dispatches, Jervis had rather more than a decisive hand in Nelson's promotion from captain to rear-admiral. But the Sea-Officers' List — the regular Admiralty record of seniorities and promotions — tells a different story : that Nelson's advancement was a matter of strict routine, accomplished in the ordinary course of seniority. Yet the two aspects of the affair may present not so much a contradiction as an overlapping, explained by Jervis's happening to offer his influence at a time when Nelson's promotion was due in any case. The fact remains that what St. Vincent could do for Nelson, he did do, and at once : he followed up his offer of the flag by making him Commodore, with captains under him. He had not the power to create him admiral, but the commodoreship lay within his gift. A delay of weeks or months — who knew ? — might intervene before the Admiralty moved in the matter of the appointment. St. Vincent's way of combating the discouragement of this waiting period was to raise Nelson's rank so far as he was able, giving him that much incentive to stay in his service during the conduct of the Mediterranean campaign. But whether St. Vincent were actually responsible for the appointment, whether his intervention speeded it up somewhat or had no real effect on it, there is no doubt that his offer — to throw in his weight as Nelson's champion and supporter — was more than welcome.

Nelson's reply to the offer of the flag was characteristic, also funny. An ardent and transparent soul, calculation for his own interest was not really his strong point, yet every person must calculate in the crucial hours of his life and do it as well as he can. So now he told Jervis that he would prefer to go back to England unless his flag came through, and yet if the war went on he would like to serve under Jervis. In other words, 'I will go back to England unless I am promoted, but even if I'm not promoted I will stay with you, anyway'. Nevertheless, departing from the interview, he knew very well that Jervis had committed himself to working for his advancement by every means in his power. Actually it came through in about ten weeks, and not long afterwards he wrote to his wife : 'Sir John Jervis has such an opinion of my conduct THAT HE IS USING EVERY INFLUENCE, PUBLIC AND PRIVATE, FOR MY CONTINUANCE ON THIS STATION'. His next words are rather thrilling, heralding as they do his perception of unguessed power in himself ; of great horizons ahead, curtained as yet by the future. 'I cannot but feel a conscious pride, and that I have abilities.' So out of their first interview, when they were complete strangers to each other, we have something instinctive and profound happening between them : a meeting of minds, a total recognition.

Jervis used the new Commodore hard during the next thirteen months that were carrying the two of them toward the battle of St. Vincent. This is not Nelson's story but the story of his relationship with Jervis, so his services at Genoa, Leghorn, Corsica and Elba must be telescoped to a mere mention. But nine months after that initial conversation Nelson was writing to his wife : 'Sir John Jervis honours me with his confidence, and you know me well enough to be assured THAT IN NO WAY WILL I EVER DESERT HIM'. His first trust and liking for Jervis had deepened into devotion, and the terms on which he had joined his command — their qualified tone, their ifs and buts — had vanished in favour of a complete allegiance. How well Nelson understood too what Jervis was accomplishing under grotesque handicaps is voiced in another letter to Mrs. Nelson : 'At home they know not what this Fleet is capable of performing, anything and everything, and with a Commander-in-Chief fit to lead them to glory.' The letter is dated four months before the battle of St. Vincent, so the perfectly confident tone of the assertion is not a matter of hindsight.

And Jervis's opinion of Nelson ? If only the Admiral's

letters on naval affairs could partake in any least degree of the verve, detail and malice of his youth when describing country dances to his sister — but alas, his pared-down official style reveals no opinion of his but with reservations and keeps us at arm's length, however candidly he may seem to write. In any case, effusiveness was not his way, still less the exalted (though a fleeting note of exaltation was struck from him three times in his life by three people : one a friend, one his wife, and one a Tunisian slave who snatched at freedom by leaping aboard an English ship and wrapping an English flag about his body).[1] Also he totally lacked Nelson's emotional response to people and events, and an immutable law of his nature compelled him to see advantages and disadvantages equally. He was to demonstrate his opinion of Nelson at no very distant date, not by words, but by taking on knowingly a situation that dragged out into a long-term harassment and that might have ended in his own death. But, for the present, the following extracts from five brief letters of the period convey the note of slightly-qualified though mounting appreciation. 'He is a reasonable and disinterested man in money matters — an excellent partisan but does not sufficiently weigh consequences. . . . He will hoist his broad pendant on board a frigate as an established commodore AND I WILL GIVE HIM ALL I HAVE. . . . The Commodore is the best and fittest fellow in the world [to conduct a proposed assault] yet his zeal does now and then (not often) outrun his discretion.' But in the end he comes through whole-heartedly : 'His zeal and activity cannot be exceeded.'

To Nelson, himself, Jervis's letters of similar date reveal his continuing divination of his future value, with their constant assurances, promises and inducements. 'I send commission, trusting that you will serve with me to the end of this war. You mentioned an officer that was useful to you, I therefore have removed him into the *Egmont* with you. When the service you are now upon is over, I shall continue your

[1] Appendix III.

broad pendant until your flag arrives, I hope I shall see it
hoisted e'er long. I probably shall learn what the Board says
of your broad pendant soon,' which will tell them how they
stand, and he hammers it all home with a last conclusive
thump : 'I will not have a third commander under the rank
of admiral unless you are the man'.

But far more eloquent than the flattery of promises is the
flattery of his war directives. Jervis entrusted Nelson with
appalling commissions : he leaned his full weight against him.
For instance, during the first sweep of the French advance :
'You must go over to Bastia immediately and cooperate in
retiring the troops, keeping Leghorn in blockade to prevent a
descent during this most difficult operation'. An eighteenth-
century Dunkirk ? Then about two weeks later : 'The
moment I was assured of your arrival at Bastia I felt perfectly
at ease with respect to the evacuation, etc. I wish you to keep
up the water of the line-of-battle ships, as to the rest you will
do it better than I can direct.' The gigantic sigh of relief for
the rescued English troops can be heard, and with the single
caution on the problem of water he gives Nelson his head,
though another admission is forced from him, heavily and
unwillingly : under the circumstances, 'I fear nothing can be
done for the merchants at Genoa'. For the thunder of war
could never quite drown out those thinner cries — of civilians
whose all was being engulfed, their property and perhaps their
lives, and these distressing pinpoints of sound continued to
pierce the Mediterranean campaign from its beginning to its
end.

Unexpected among the harsh orders of war, rather touching
too, is a commission of a quite different nature, the kind that
a man entrusts only to a close friend. One of St. Vincent's
chronic preoccupations was the delicate health of his wife, and
now it seemed this lady wanted a special dress for the Queen's
anniversary. Therefore the husband obediently begs Nelson
to beg some lady of his acquaintance to buy 'an elegant light
plain velvet, the colour to be a rich blue. It must be of the

Cornelia Knight

Dr. Andrew Baird

Admiral Sir John Orde

Two friends and an enemy

finest kind, otherwise the weight of it will be too much for her to carry. I am totally ignorant of the quantity, but it is only for a robe,' and he goes on to explain for Nelson's benefit that the 'white crape or gauze petticoat' is usually supplied and embroidered by the ladies themselves ; not bad for a tough old sea-dog like St. Vincent. The letter about the velvet is marked 'Secret'.

Four months later the battle of St. Vincent was fought, and Nelson had taken the first giant step from the status of heroic captain to that of captain-hero, whose far-more-select pantheon is inhabited by — what number ? as many as twenty, in the whole history of the world ? And just how soon or how late after the battle did he come to realize that his feat had been scanted and passed over in his superior's official dispatch, just as it had happened to him under other commanders ? The knowledge must have filtered to his ears at some time, especially when Jervis's brevity was being freely criticized and all his friends were up in arms about it. But now Nelson has changed ; far from complaining, he actually repudiates the idea of credit for himself separately : 'I will partake of nothing but what shall include Collingwood and Troubridge. We are the only three ships who made great exertions on that glorious day.' This letter to his brother, about seven weeks after the battle, raises into sharp relief his new grandeur of spirit, as if an inner greatness were keeping pace with the outer.

On the other hand, he took a lively interest in the rewards that were on their way, though he and the other recipients, twenty-two weeks after the battle, still knew of them somehow incompletely : 'None of us have had our proper notification of our honours'. The honours arrived in due course and with them the bills — for expenses contingent on registering Nelson's coat-of-arms and on his nomination and installation as a Knight of the Bath. 'I have had a genealogy from the York genealogist', he informs his wife, adding coldly : 'Enquire who is to pay the fees, for I shall not'. They amounted to £428 : 7 : 6, no trifle. The Admiralty has footed the bill for Jervis's

L

honours, Nelson ends, and he certainly expects them to do as much for him.   (They did.)

The immediate effect on Nelson of the battle seems to have been an exhaustion more or less complete, for in a letter to his wife two weeks later it sounds as if Jervis had been constraining him to take his ease : 'Don't think I am forced to go out, as Sir John Jervis is all kindness to me.' Yet he is restless. 'But I cannot bear an idle life.' Do those last words hint, perhaps, that Jervis had already given him some advance idea of the project that was to lose him his right arm ?

The second effect of the victory appears to have been the expectation of an early peace — by no means confined to Nelson, for a single decisive victory has often brought about a cessation of hostilities.   Contemporary letters show how widely this possibility was being discussed, and Nelson's hints to his wife about an early homecoming grow more frequent if somewhat contradictory : 'My situation with Sir John Jervis is as usual, he will not be very fond to let me go home,' but then again, ten days later : 'Sir John Jervis has promised me a frigate to take my body, and my rags may travel in due time with the *Theseus*'.   But for Nelson there was to be no peace — not for another eight years — and even while he seemed to entertain home-going plans he was simultaneously, and deeply, involved with plans of quite another sort.

Treasure opens the story of the assault on Santa Cruz, a town and harbour on the island of Teneriffe.   With whom the whole thing originated appears — by the light of their correspondence — uncertain ; sometimes Jervis seems responsible for the idea, and sometimes Nelson.   The truth probably is that the initial suggestion came from Jervis, but that Nelson took it up with such fire and enthusiasm that the sponsorship appeared to have passed from Jervis to him.   In any case, the battle of St. Vincent was not six weeks old when Jervis was writing Nelson a thrilling letter.   Two ships laden with gold to the tune of six or seven millions sterling (multiply by fifteen for present-day values) had left Vera Cruz and Havana, bound for Cadiz. Jervis's dispatch to Nelson is dated March 31st, and at that time 'the ships are certainly on their passage, and much agitation is felt in Spain on that account'. The 'much agitation' was well-founded — on the fact that the English still maintained their relentless blockade of Cadiz, stopping every ship coming or going, and certainly the treasure ships could never get through. Therefore — according to Jervis's spies or other sources of information — they intended to make for the harbour of Santa Cruz in Teneriffe and lie up there, hiding from the English until they could deliver the gold into a Spanish port. Spain's need for the money was desperate ; if the English Fleet intercepted or seized the treasure she was bankrupt, and her bankruptcy would not only knock her out of the war but out of her position, centuries old, as a first-rate European power. So now Jervis asked Nelson's opinion and suggestions on the possibility of attacking Santa Cruz, and twelve days later Nelson replied with a long letter.

'It becomes my duty to state all the difficulties, since you have desired me to enter into the subject,' he begins formally, and points out the inconvenience of the anchorage and other disadvantages. Almost at once, however, his cautious judicial tone changes to something quite different. 'But now comes my plan,' he announces breathlessly, 'which could not fail of success.' 'My plan' involved using the garrison of 3700 men at Elba for a surprise attack on Santa Cruz. 'It would do the business in three days, probably much less. I will undertake, with a very small squadron, to do the naval part.' A mounting fever is felt below the surface as the idea takes stronger and stronger hold of him. The town's water supply is easily cut off and, 'in short, the business could not miscarry.' Then Nelson allows himself the luxury — rare with him — of counting chickens prematurely. 'Of the six or seven million pounds sterling,' he calculates rapturously, 'if this sum were thrown into circulation in England, it would ensure an honourable peace.' And ruin Spain, he has pointed out earlier. Then, finally betraying how deeply the idea has entered into him : 'It has long occupied my thoughts'. Another way of saying, perhaps, that he had not stopped thinking about it day or night.

That was April 12th, and by May 6th St. Vincent had begun to back-pedal. The assault was 'no longer the important object it was when Nelson suggested it'. Again a shift of responsibility, with the implication that it was Nelson's. Probably St. Vincent had gone cold on the idea because some intelligence had reached him that made the treasure seem not yet sea-borne or even apocryphal. But early in July his interest revived with a roar, and no wonder, for he had received definite news 'that the *Prince of Asturias*, richly laden, from Manila to Cadiz, is at Santa Cruz'. Once more the project was ablaze ; Nelson's 'favourite design' of attack was to be put into execution. St. Vincent formally ordered him to Teneriffe 'there to make your dispositions for taking the town of Santa Cruz by a sudden and vigorous assault. In case of success you are authorized to lay a heavy contribution on the inhabitants, IF THEY DO NOT PUT YOU IN POSSESSION OF THE WHOLE CARGO OF THE PRINCE OF ASTURIAS. — God bless and prosper you', he adds unofficially. 'I am sure you will deserve success. To mortals is not given the power of commanding it.' Nelson was delirious with joy and began counting chickens again. 'If the treasure fall into our hands,' he chortled, 'the King of Spain will be like Billy Pitt, give nothing but paper.' Writing to Lady Nelson that she would not hear from him for a short time, but not to worry, he sailed blithely for Teneriffe.

The result of the attack, of course, was total and desperate failure ; too many men were killed, some of them very promising. Nelson's right arm was shattered below the shoulder, though he made no mention of it in his official report. 'I am become a burden to my friends and useless to my country,' he despaired, next day, to St. Vincent. 'When I leave your command, I become dead to the world ; I go hence and am no more seen.' He begs for a frigate to convey the remains of his carcass to England, and apologizes for his left-handed writing.

In this bad moment St. Vincent did his best for him, though he himself wanted comfort almost as desperately as Nelson ; part of the price paid for Santa Cruz had shaken him to the marrow. 'I am in such anguish of mind that I cannot enter into details', gasps his first letter to Spencer, an admission of weakness unique in his war correspondence. 'It has been my fate during this war to lose the officers most dear to me ; by that of poor Bowen I am quite unmanned.' Then he rouses from his misery to help the newly-mutilated man who needed his help. 'I grieve for the loss of your arm,' he wrote Nelson. 'I will bow to your stump tomorrow morning, if you will give me leave.' Then he sent off a letter to Lady Nelson. Her husband is wounded but not dangerously ; he promises her his early arrival in England and has the honour to be, with very great respect, her ladyship's faithful and obedient servant. On the same day he made his official report to the Admiralty, from first to last appearing as Nelson's apologist and defender, at least by implication. Although the enterprise has failed, the King's arms have gained added lustre by reason of the gallantry of the officers and men involved. He is sending the disabled Admiral home and 'hopes that he will live to render important services to his country'.

'A left-handed Admiral will never again be considered as useful', again lamented to St. Vincent the man who was yet to win the battles of the Nile, Copenhagen and Trafalgar. But his last communication, before boarding the *Seahorse* that would take him back to England, sounded no note of repining, only of gratitude and love. 'Thank you for your unvaried goodness to me, which I shall never forget.'

After the recent fiasco, among the papers in Nelson's cabin had been found the rough draft of an ultimatum to the Governor of Santa Cruz, for use after the presumed surrender of the island. In it Nelson demanded 'the full and

entire cargo of the *Prince of Asturias'*, otherwise he will destroy
Santa Cruz by bombardment and levy a big contribution on
the populace, and whether the Governor's answer is acceptance
or rejection, Nelson allows him exactly half an hour to make
up his mind. Next day, writing to that same official whom
he had menaced with death and destruction, he is demonstrating how nobly it is possible to eat humble pie. 'I return
Your Excellency sincerest thanks for your humanity in favour
of our wounded men in your power.'

Then, in a postscript, the enterprise of Santa Cruz wheezes
out on a very low, gentle, domestic note : 'I beg Your
Excellency will do me the honour to accept of a cask of English
beer, and a cheese'.

*   *   *

'I am exactly as I left you,' Nelson wrote to St. Vincent
from aboardship, toward the end of August. From his
arrival in London, likewise, he kept his chief posted. 'I had
a miserable passage home and am not the least better, I have
suffered great misery. Lady Nelson sends her love, God
bless you.' The history of his arm picks out like a spotlight
one detail of the suffering, in all its atrocious mass, endured by
the war-wounded of that day. The current practice of surgery,
after an amputation, was to tie off the severed arteries and
muscles by a ligature which remained unchanged until it
sloughed away naturally, but which, while it remained on
the wound, was as fertile a source of infection or gangrene as
any other decayed dressing. The peculiar horror of Nelson's
experience was that his ligature, by some clumsiness in applying it, had fastened itself to a nerve, this point of adhesion
being about an inch and a quarter up the stump. It could
not be detached or pulled loose and took its own time — four
months — to come away of itself ; during that period he
endured excruciating pain and to get any sleep at all had
recourse to the usual sedatives of the day, laudanum and
opium. To less intimate friends he put a good face on the

matter, doughtily assuring the Duke of Clarence, 'Not a scrap of that ardour with which I formerly served our King has been shot away'. To St. Vincent there was no need to pretend he was anything but wretched. 'My poor arm is the same, the ligature fast to the nerve and very painful at times.'

Yet now he shows that he can face the future, if he can depend on his Commander-in-Chief's encouragement. 'The moment I am cured I shall offer myself for service, and IF YOU CONTINUE TO HOLD YOUR OPINION OF ME, I shall press to return with all the zeal, though not the ability, I had formerly. Believe me with greatest affection your most obliged Horatio Nelson.' St. Vincent was constantly in his thoughts and conversation, whatever his company. 'The King asked how your general health was. I told H.M. that considering the great fatigue you was undergoing that your health was tolerable. Sir Gilbert Elliot [1] is a warm admirer of yours, I told him of your goodness to his son.' And in a postscript, an agreeable reminder of the honours that were preparing for St. Vincent : 'I have seen your sword. It is very handsome.'

The arm being healed by January '98, St. Vincent was clamouring to have Nelson back and Nelson was clamouring to rejoin him. 'To you I trust I am going, and every blessing attend you.' The letters of First Lord Spencer officiated between the two like a clergyman's benediction. 'I am very happy to send you Sir Horatio Nelson again. If your Lordship is as desirous to have him with you as he is to be with you, I am sure the arrangement must be perfectly satisfactory.' St. Vincent thanked him resoundingly. 'You could not have gratified me more than in sending him.'

Now, in words from which there was no retreating, he made Nelson the elect. 'YOU, AND YOU ONLY, CAN COMMAND THE IMPORTANT SERVICE IN PREPARATION. You shall have some choice fellows of the inshore squadron.' To Spencer

---

[1] During the Mediterranean campaign, Elliot had said of St. Vincent : 'I cannot but admire the resources he finds continually, where other men would only grumble or despair'.

he defined 'the important service in preparation' for which
Nelson was irrevocably destined. 'I mean to send him to
endeavour to ascertain the real object of the preparations
making by the French, which Captain Day, an intelligent man,
seems positive are intended against Ireland.' Another reminder of the looming enigma that was making English lives
a nightmare, also of how constant and feverish were speculation
on this point, and how far out.

Nelson, on his side, announced his safe arrival to his wife
on May 1st, 1798. 'My dearest Fanny, I joined the Fleet
yesterday.' But his first thought after that was for his chief.
'I found Lord St. Vincent everything I wished him.' He must
mean in spirit, not body, for instantly he adds : 'But I have
my fears he will not be much longer in this command for I
believe he has wrote to be superseded which I am sincerely
sorry for, it will considerably take from my pleasure in serving
here.' Probably St. Vincent's joy at seeing him made him
appear, for the moment, better than he was. Nelson, before
getting down to business, had one sour observation to make on
a person whose name we shall meet again : 'Sir John Orde is
here giving fêtes etc., but I have no time for such things when
we had better be alongside a Spaniard.'

Together once more, the senior and the junior Admirals
threw the combined weight of their skill and energy into
piercing the fog that surrounded the end-purpose of Napoleon's
preparations. For this nerve-racking puzzle, now, over-
shadowed all other issues of the day to a point where the total
English war policy, for the moment, moulded and shaped itself
to the shape of this one single menace. Moreover, the manner
of doing it was put in St. Vincent's hands, and his alone. Should
he keep the full strength of his Fleet where it was, on the
Mediterranean station ? Or should he take the terrible risk
of cutting it in two by detaching a squadron and sending it on
what was possibly a wild-goose chase, in pursuit of a deadly
clever and cunning enemy ? With a number of his best ships
sent away, suppose he were attacked by Spain or France or

both, in the very moment when he had so fatally weakened himself ? Or — ghastly thought — were France's secret tactics designed to decoy him into doing that very thing ? The final decision was a desperate gamble, no less, and it was entirely up to him.

Not being able to see into a man's inmost mind, we are not privileged to know by what reasoning St. Vincent decided to take the risk — of detaching a squadron and sending it away under Nelson, to hunt down Napoleon's fleet. Probably it was a process of slow gravitation, pushed along not only by Nelson, afire for action, but by the stray bits and gleanings we have noted along the way, all of them gathering momentum toward an irresistible conclusion. At any rate, Nelson had his official orders almost from the moment of his arrival : 'On falling in with the said Armament or any part thereof, you are to use your utmost endeavours to take, sink, burn or destroy it' — except that Nelson, at this stage of the game, was as much in the dark as anyone else. 'No one knows to what place the Armament is destined', he was declaring three weeks after his arrival, and went on to offer such unconnected items as he had picked up. Napoleon in person is inspecting the troops embarking from Toulon, but is not going with them, according to the general opinion. 'I have no further particulars to tell you', he wrote next day. 'They order these matters so well in France that all is secret.'

All this was in May, '98. In the first week of June the English Minister of War, Dundas, wrote the First Lord of the Admiralty an astute and remarkable note. 'The suggestion of Egypt being Napoleon's objective may be whimsical [farfetched] but I cannot help having a fancy of my own on that subject.' Three weeks later Nelson — of course with no knowledge of Dundas's guess — was writing St. Vincent a still more remarkable letter. He intended once and for all to go to Alexandria in search of the French fleet, having eliminated, by a process of close reasoning, any other place as their destination. It cannot be Malta ; so powerful a force would be unnecessary. It cannot be Naples or Sicily ; they are presently at peace with France. It cannot be Spain ; the winds are wrong at this season of the year to get a fleet of transports to the westward. Then he brings forward a tremendous reason to support his contention. 'Should the Armament be gone to Alexandria and get there, OUR POSSESSIONS IN INDIA ARE PROBABLY LOST.' He has taken a census of his captains' opinions and Troubridge, greatest of them all, thinks the same thing — steer for Alexandria. Then Nelson goes on to justify himself before the man whose opinion mattered most to him. He is afraid St. Vincent will say, ' "You should not have gone sail a long voyage without more certain information of the enemy's destination." My answer is : who was I to get it from ? To do nothing I felt was disgraceful. Therefore I made use of my understanding, and by it I ought to stand or fall. If I am wrong, I ought for the sake of our country to be superseded.' Then an affirmation, unconditional, of his whole feeling for St. Vincent : 'However erroneous my judgment, I feel conscious of my honest intentions, which I hope will bear me up UNDER THE GREATEST MISFORTUNE THAT COULD HAPPEN TO ME AS AN OFFICER : THAT OF YOUR LORDSHIP'S THINKING ME WRONG.'

Therefore with hopes alternately springing or collapsing he put all his stakes on one number and set sail for Egypt. When late in July — three weeks after his letter to St. Vincent — he wrote again, the occasion marked as low a point of despondency as he would reach.

'I am as completely ignorant of the fleet as the day I left Cape Passant,' he groaned.[1] 'I am sure we are betrayed.' Then he hits at a possible interceptor, but the gesture has the character of despair : 'I expect the French Minister will copy this, therefore I here assure him I will get at the French fleet. God bless you, ever your faithful Horatio Nelson.' And just nine days later, after a month of scanning sea spaces vast and empty, his heart leaped to behold, at anchor in Aboukir Bay,

[1] Appendix IV.

the crowded masts that meant he had run down the elusive enemy at last, Napoleon's fleet. And even after the victory, the nine ships taken and the two burnt, and the blaze of Nelson's reputation tending to obliterate everything and everyone else, it is pleasant to record that there were those who could look behind the façade of glory and recognize whose mind and whose hand had worked ceaselessly at upraising it. The English Ambassador at Naples was a man of undefeatable astuteness and penetration (this was long before the Nelson-Emma affair) and now he wrote to St. Vincent of 'the joy that Lady Hamilton and I felt at the news of the victory gained by our dear friend Sir Horatio Nelson AND THE BRAVE BAND SO WELL CHOSEN BY YOUR LORDSHIP — BY A CHIEF AND A BAND OF HEROES CHOSEN BY YOURSELF AND ALL TRAINED IN YOUR OWN SCHOOL.'

Sir William was more than right ; St. Vincent, backing Nelson to the limit, had surrounded him with the promised 'choice fellows' — Troubridge,[1] Ball, Saumarez, men of unmatched reputation in naval history — and in stripping himself of his strongest captains, perhaps had weakened himself even more dangerously than by the heroic action of dividing his Fleet.

Also, while the autumn air was filled with the thunder of war and the uproar of victory, the air around St. Vincent was filled with other noises far less agreeable — and to him, at any time, particularly uncongenial.

*　　*　　*

The trouble had begun as far back as May, when he had just handed over to Nelson the command of the detached squadron. As a result of this appointment he was having, in short order, unpleasant interviews with two disappointed admirals. The first of these two angry men was Sir William

---

[1] His ship unfortunately grounded on a reef, but he was able to warn two others away from the same danger. 'The leadsmen had just called eleven fathoms when we struck,' he lamented.

Parker, whom we met in the darkest days of the war, coming with his five ships to the aid of Jervis. Now, boiling over on the subject of the detached squadron, he wrote a letter of intense but restrained bitterness to the Admiralty.

'I naturally expected to be sent, but the ships separated without any notice being taken of me, to be under the command of an officer very much my junior. This must necessarily be considered a doubt of my abilities or worse, and I must feel it the most injurious conduct toward me and the most serious attack upon my reputation as an officer.'

The Admiralty's answer evidently failing to satisfy him, he continued bombarding it, in the next three months, with a dozen similar letters. His first indignation had fallen to a broody, dogged note, but he would not give up ; he returned again and again to the charge, demanding his removal from St. Vincent's command. 'This I feel degrading to me.' He would serve anywhere, under anyone, so long as it was not St. Vincent. 'It oppresses me and injures my health.'

The other disappointed candidate was more mettlesome and articulate, and capable of demonstrations far more lethal. As long ago as October 3rd, 1797, eight months previously, a new hand had made its appearance in the dispatch-books — a penmanship fine, spiky and angular—of Admiral Sir John Orde reporting his arrival on the Mediterranean station. Knowing what is to come, one sits up and takes special notice of this scratchy stilted writing, being tempted to read into it a quarrelsome, place-proud martinet ; a fretful stickler and precisionist, whose dignity one would like to see punctured ; the villain of the piece, in fact, obligingly endowed with the proper antagonizing qualities.

How inconvenient to find, therefore, that in defiance of all known canons of fiction, Sir John Orde turns out to be not only a very nice man but a very fine one, who possessed in great degree that candour of soul called uprightness. Taking the rather advanced view for an eighteenth-century admiral, he hated the routine flogging of naval discipline, and if on

assuming command of a ship he found it practised, with a
man regularly appointed to lay on the punishment, he put a
stop to it. He liked to have his ship's company happy and
comfortable and therefore inclined to obey cheerfully ; he
had prided himself that such was the state of affairs in his
present command, the *Princess Royal*, and to find sedition
aboard, during the recent outbreak of mutiny, had given him
the most terrible shock. In fact, he was even easy-going
enough to let some matters slide, for about a month before
the blow-up St. Vincent was penning a daily report to the
Admiralty which, beneath its official surface, carries an under-
tone of disgust. Sir John Orde is here at Gibraltar to water
his four ships, but also to 'extirpate the weevil from the
Hector, she having been long infested, AND THROUGH WANT
OF TIMELY PRECAUTION, it has increased to an incredible degree'.
Far ahead of his day in notions of cleanliness, he hated dirt in
any form, and living dirt like weevils was no joke ; had not
40,764 pounds of bread recently been thrown overboard
from the *Theseus*, unfit for men to eat from the ravages of
'that same destructive insect' ? And perhaps the weevils
were thrown up to Sir John in the day of dissension, who
knows ? But in regard to the present situation — Nelson's
appointment to the detached squadron — we find Orde
writing a letter to the Admiralty, very much in the tone of
Parker's.

'My Lords — Sir Horatio Nelson, a junior officer and just
arrived from England, is detached from the Mediterranean
Fleet with the command of twelve sail of the line. I must not
say I am surprised at this measure, but I cannot conceal from
your Lordships how much I feel hurt.' Still, in conclusion,
he declares his unweakened intention of service to his country,
'however unpleasant it may be rendered, or wounding to
my feelings'. Unpleasant and wounding it certainly was, and
in a degree unknown to anyone but Orde himself. Beneath
the controlled surface of the Admiralty letter, a violent situation was boiling up. Sir John, in fact, was being the recipient

(on the word of an eye-witness) of some uncommonly rough handling.

Here, a mention of some aspects — hitherto inconspicuous, or at least as regards this narrative — of the Commander-in-Chief's temperament. St. Vincent, who had once described himself as not having much patience, was no angel and no professional Father Christmas ; he was an eighteenth-century admiral carrying out a murderous assignment. Without a high tone and a whiplash manner to back it up when necessary, he would not have lasted long at his job. He could be over-bearing and tyrannical ; he could be outrageously harsh and haughty. In the present moment of his command he was face to face with an engulfing peril whose direction and intent no one knew, and he had to deal with it quickly and with the most potent weapon in his reach. Nelson was that weapon. He had divined from the first moment that the frail little man's spirit was cast in the dimension from which come great and heroic feats, and accordingly he had sent him to hunt down the Napoleonic menace. And just at this time — when he was beset by a thousand anxieties, not the least among them his frightfully vulnerable position with his ships cut down to half, his precarious health, the nightmare possibility that Nelson's Egyptian guess might, after all, be wrong — just at this time, here was a subordinate, a meritorious officer but not to be mentioned in the same breath with Nelson, forcing him into a stubborn, reasonable, long-winded correspondence on the subject of seniority and hurt feelings.

It was a moment in which a man might be excused for blowing up, and St. Vincent blew up. The trouble is that letters, the main testimony to this fracas, do not take into account the savage interviews — the head-on personal colli-sions — between the two men. Yet even of these a trace has come down to us, by allusion. Collingwood, another of the matchless galaxy of captains who might be called the St. Vincent school, wrote regularly to his wife and sister. It was just before the Christmas of '98, a season at which one might be more than usually sensitive to the poison of hatred in the air.

'Our station of late has not been very agreeable', he records. 'The disagreement between the Chief and other flag-officers shuts the door to the few comforts to be found there.' No one could escape the unbearable tension and acrimony attendant upon a long-drawn-out and serious quarrel. Collingwood had managed to keep clear of it, but 'I could not help feeling disquietude at the many violences I witnessed. Sir John Orde is proud and carries himself high ; he needed not great sensibility to feel indignities. They were generally gross enough for the roughest minds.'[1] In other words, St. Vincent had exploded at once into unreasonable anger, and once having overstepped, or 'carried his resentment to extremity' — as Collingwood puts it — he had little choice but to go on managing affairs with the same high hand. The alternative was apology, and this he rejected. He had done what the pressure of circumstances dictated, and he saw no need for apology.

Finding St. Vincent much too hot to handle, Sir John withdrew to his flagship and with undampened zeal continued to bombard his chief with letters ; by the end of August they were writing each other two and three times a day. Six months of this may be reduced to dialogue, with explanatory asides.

ORDE : You yourself asked me to serve under you and I was glad to do it. Was it any misconduct of mine that induced your Lordship to give an officer in the Fleet, junior to myself, so important a command as is entrusted to Admiral Nelson, whilst you keep other admirals and me inactive ?

ST. VINCENT : Those who are responsible for measures have the right to appoint the men they prefer to carry them into execution.

ORDE : Pressing considerations have compelled me to

[1] *The Times* of October 5th, 1799, had a reference to 'furious quarrels' on the station over Nelson's appointment, so evidently their existence was public property.

write the enclosed letter to the Admiralty, which I send open
for your perusal.

ST. VINCENT : I have not read your letter, nor shall I.
If you wish to seal it, I will forward it to England in the first
dispatch I send.

ORDE : In view of your Lordship's treatment of me, I
must renounce all claims to your friendship or your favour.
(This letter goes on and on.)

ST. VINCENT : Stop writing me long letters ; you are
hindering me in the performance of my duty.

ORDE : I am an officer acting from a sense of ill-treatment.
I do not apologize for anything I did.

ST. VINCENT : If you continue like this I shall order you
to England, and I shall not wait for the Admiralty to authorize
me to do so.

At this point Orde wrote another letter of protest, not to
the Admiralty Secretary but to the First Lord, Earl Spencer.
'I served him with zeal, fidelity and success. His Lordship,
in return, betrayed and degraded me.' He sent it unsealed to
St. Vincent, as previously, and this time St. Vincent read it.
The dialogue continues.

ST. VINCENT : The moment you communicated to me the
letter you sent to Lord Spencer, I considered it impossible
you should remain an hour longer in the Fleet. You are
hereby required and directed to strike your flag in the *Princess
Royal*, and hoist it in His Majesty's ship the *Blenheim*, which
will anchor near your ship in a few days. I give you twenty-
four hours to get yourself and your possessions aboard her.

ORDE : Although ignorant of the cause and object of my
removal, I will obey orders, and in half the time your Lordship
allows me.

Now St. Vincent, in his turn, wrote the Admiralty :

'Rear Admiral Sir John Orde, having very much annoyed
and interrupted me in the discharge of my duty, by attempts
to force me into a correspondence of a nature highly derogatory
to discipline, I have directed that Admiral to proceed to

His sister Mary

His nephew Henry

His wife Martha

His family

England, as per enclosed order.' His unsleeping sense of justice compelled him to add : 'Sir John Orde is a good officer and could serve to advantage under any other naval commander than myself.'

Orde wrote the Admiralty, too, almost simultaneously. It is his letter that is sensational, in view of the request it contains — in making which he leaves out none of St. Vincent's honours.

'The Right Honourable the Earl of St. Vincent, Knight of the Bath and Commander-in-Chief of His Majesty's ships employed in the Mediterranean : having in my humble opinion acted unbecoming the character of an officer by treating me in a manner unsuitable to my rank, I request their Lordships of the Admiralty to order a Court-Martial to try the said Earl of St. Vincent, for treating me in a manner injurious to my credit and character, and contrary to the practice of the service.' Not a frequent occurrence, one might think — an admiral asking for court-martial on a C.-in-C., a peer and a national hero. Once again Orde wrote St. Vincent, never abandoning (to his great credit) his tone of high and dignified protest, but hitting again at Nelson's appointment. 'I am ordered to quit the Fleet like a culprit and embark on a ship the most inferior, for a service of lowest degree [convoy] in comparison to the most important, entrusted to my junior on the station.'

'If you had kept quiet about the Nelson appointment, as I wished you to do,' St. Vincent hit back, in effect, 'you might eventually have succeeded to the command of the Fleet, as my health will not admit of my continuing in it much longer.' Dangling an inaccessible carrot was not St. Vincent's way, let alone vindictiveness, but by now both men were beside themselves. Orde's precise handwriting had become illegible, he forgot to date his communications out of sheer agitation, and meanwhile St. Vincent was hurling copies of Orde's 'singular letters' at the Admiralty, together with copies of his own replies.

M

Orde now made a serious strategic mistake, though one — in line with his previous very open tactics — perhaps unavoidable. Not only did he notify St. Vincent of his request for the court-martial, but he was fool enough to name two men whom he wished to take with him in the *Blenheim* to testify against St. Vincent when the court-martial should be held.

It was the end ; St. Vincent sat down and fired off four letters, like four bullets. Three of these were to Orde and his witnesses, Captain Draper and Purser Yeo. Their substance follows.

To Orde : I will withhold *no* witnesses that you wish to bring against me, and will do all I can to see that they are in England when the court-martial requires it.

To Captain Draper : Since you are a witness named by Admiral Orde, do you now wish to accompany him in the *Blenheim* and follow his fortunes ?

To Purser Yeo : Send me a letter at once, testifying that on your first application to accompany Admiral Orde to England in order to testify at the court-martial, I gave you every facility for doing so.

The last two letters drew from Draper and Yeo disclaiming squeals, with a rapidity creditable to frightened rabbits. No, no, they protested, his Lordship had misunderstood ; they would not dream of going with Admiral Orde, they wanted to stay with his Lordship, they loved his Lordship dearly.

The fourth letter shot off by the Commander-in-Chief was to the Admiralty, and this one contained the most lethal charge of all. If Orde's request were granted, St. Vincent wrote, he would leave at once for England to stand his trial, since it would be 'highly unbecoming to continue in so important a trust as I now hold' with a prospective court-martial hanging over him. By the dates on all this correspondence, St. Vincent must have passed the whole of September 6th writing long letters relative to the Orde affair, and how he cursed Orde for wasting his time and strength may be imagined.

The sequel followed, but not rapidly. Orde reached England by October and at once submitted to the Admiralty a thirty-seven-page day-to-day journal of his quarrel with St. Vincent ; in it his handwriting looks like an old, old man's, yet in this miserable moment he could find time to express his concern for his former officers and men, lest their attachment to him should injure 'their Fortune and their Prospects'. He also renews his request for the court-martial.

The Admiralty dealt with this in short order, and in what manner may be imagined. St. Vincent was threatening to resign from a command which only he could fill, moreover one under which his admiral, Nelson, and his picked captains had just won the battle of the Nile. Even before Orde had submitted his journal, their refusal was on the way. It stunned him into silence for nearly two weeks. Then, recovering a little, he wrote the Admiralty an affecting letter which for once rouses no feelings of friendship for the Earl. He has received their Lordships' refusal of the court-martial. He continues to dwell with bewilderment and pain (why not?) on his humiliation 'in the eyes of the Fleet'. He bows submissively to their Lordships' decision, while hoping they do not question his motives 'of rescuing my character and professional situation, now cruelly attacked and debased, from shame and ruin'. Then the conclusion, in which one may see his unclouded honour, goodness and dignity. 'The greatest part of my life has been devoted to the service. I hope that I have been no discredit to it. I would wish to die in it, free from blame or any just attaint.'

Here terminates one part of the Orde–St. Vincent affair, but it is only an act that has ended, not the whole play. Orde made some further gestures of self-rehabilitation by publishing the journal of the quarrel he had submitted to the Admiralty, but this did little to ease him. He had declared his submission to the Admiralty, but inwardly the knowledge of injustice ate at him like a live coal. Shamed, rebuffed, brooding on the injury done him until it reached the proportions of monomania, he was waiting for only one thing : St. Vincent's return to England.

The object of his watchfulness, a gravely-sick man, came home in August '99. Orde waited a decent interval — three months — until recovery might be supposed, or a degree of recovery. Then, with a second, he drove out to St. Vincent's country home and sent in a challenge to a duel, demanding satisfaction for the 'deceitful and tyrannical' behaviour he had suffered.

The Times of October 5th, 1799, carried a curious item. Sir John Orde had been arrested at four in the morning at Durant's hotel by special constables Townshend and Sayers. A local J.P. named Ford, tipped off about the challenge and about the rendezvous chosen, had 'intervened to frustrate an intention', *The Times* continues, 'which in every event would have proved fatal to the country.' Townshend hung onto Orde, in spite of outraged protests, until eleven o'clock in the morning. He had wished to send Sayers at once to arrest St. Vincent before he could leave his home, but Orde, greatly a gentleman, objected ; such an invasion before dawn might alarm the delicate and ailing Lady St. Vincent, he pointed out. Still detained by the officers, he capitulated at last and gave bail for keeping the peace. At once Townshend, energetic arm that he was, posted off to the country, found St. Vincent waiting upon the duelling-ground chosen in Brentwood, and arrested him too. In the end the Earl also gave bail to keep the peace, £2000 of his own and £1000 apiece from his two securities, Lords Spencer and Melville.

A comic-opera atmosphere may surround the duel in general, but men have been wounded and killed in duels ; one need look no farther than Castlereagh and Alexander Hamilton. In this case, the secret warning given, the speed with which action was taken, the arrest in the small hours of the morning, the very high bail — all this proves the authorities' cognizance of Orde's intention and of the fact that any encounter between such adversaries must mean one dead man, if not two. In fact, the affair was serious enough to cause the King to intervene in person, and to define the whole situation with the distinguished trenchancy and commonsense that occasionally marked George III. 'Sir John Orde has been so absurd,' he wrote to Spencer, 'as to turn into a personal affront, what was only his commanding officer's employing that discretional power which his station authorized. In my name I expect that Lord St. Vincent will not accept any challenge from Sir John Orde, and that Sir John Orde will not offer any further insult to Lord St. Vincent.'

His Majesty having dropped this crusher on Orde, *The Times*, three days later, dropped another. Orde, it said, may have been disappointed of the command of the detached squadron, but : 'the country was to be congratulated on his disappointment'. Any other appointment than Nelson's must have resulted in detriment, loss and injury to the Kingdom. The article ended with a majestic compliment to Orde on his bravery and high reputation. It was the finisher. Encased in this august commendation like a fly in amber, stuck fast, also, in the displeasure of his Sovereign, he could do nothing but retire from the arena once and for all and hold his peace.

From all this long-gone commotion one fact emerges : St. Vincent broke Sir John Orde's heart. That he did so on no light occasion, but under the driving lash of circumstance, is perhaps the best that can be said for him. In accordance with the iron rule that inexorably imposes ruthless moments on all great careers he, a good man, had mortally hurt another good man ; and he had further unpleasantness to go through, by no means confined to the challenge, for shortly after Orde's arrival in England it was St. Vincent who received the Admiralty's reprimand. In cold, grave, measured tones they pointed out that they had refused Orde's request for the court-martial, it was true, but all the same 'their Lordships can by no means approve of your sending home Sir John Orde ; the reasons given by you do not appear sufficient. They therefore direct that you do not in future send home a Flag Officer without instructions so to do,' and end with another, if tacit, rebuke : they will support him in every *proper* exercise of his authority.

Now it was St. Vincent's turn to protest against injustice, and protest he did, bitterly. 'I submit to the rebuke their Lordships have thought fit to convey to me, but my pride of character is very much wounded by the censure. I deny positively that I ever treated Sir John Orde, or any other officer, improperly, EVEN WHEN THERE WERE MEETINGS AND COMBINATIONS TO RESIST MY REGULATIONS.'

Here is the hidden kernel of much of the bitterness ; Orde had obviously persisted in foregathering with other aggrieved admirals, in defiance of St. Vincent's command not to do so.

'My reputation suffers extreme injury', concludes his blast at his superiors, 'by a sentence passed upon me without my defense being heard.' And his soreness evidently rankled, for months afterwards the incident was still a fertile source — in his dispatches — of oblique references to subordinates who combined against chiefs, along with back-handed slaps at the Admiralty. The whole episode, part of the tragi-comedy of human behaviour, is also a taste of what St. Vincent had to go through because of Nelson's appointment. Incidentally, he had — if he had liked — an easy way out of the whole affair. It is perfectly true that when Nelson, healed, was returning to duty, Lord Spencer had written St. Vincent : 'If you send [out] a detached squadron, I think it almost unnecessary to suggest your putting it under the command of Sir Horatio Nelson.' In view of St. Vincent's estimate of Nelson from the very first, the suggestion was more than 'unnecessary' : it was almost laughably superfluous. Yet St. Vincent could have sheltered behind this virtual order if he had wished, deflecting Orde's anger from himself to Spencer. Obviously, it never occurred to him to do so. By his readiness to try conclusions to the end, in defence of his action, it is clear that he regarded the Nelson appointment from first to last as his responsibility and *his* appointment.

Everyone being impartially chafed all around, in the wake of the Orde affair, St. Vincent could settle down again to getting on with the war. He was also about to assume a rôle he had never filled in his life and never would fill again, the mere thought of which would have made him snort with disgust. The image of the Earl as an unwitting emissary of romance — considering his type — could hardly be funnier. And yet when he ordered Nelson to use Naples as his base, in connection with a stepped-up campaign against Malta and Minorca, he may have supplied a necessary element, hitherto deficient, which added to other elements became one of the great love stories of the world.

IX

THE ADMIRAL AND NELSON
(*Continued*)

NELSON had known Emma Hamilton, wife of the British
Ambassador at Naples, for about five years previously. The
attraction between them, whatever it was — perhaps non-
existent, perhaps latent or dormant — would have continued
in that state, presumably, for lack of mere contact. Nelson's
previous stays at Naples had been few and far between, his
absences had extended over months and years. He had
appeared at the Embassy and been entertained there, accompanied by his loutish stepson. Now, preceded by the glory
of the Nile victory, he burst upon the view of the Hamilton
household in all the dazzle and lustre of a conquering hero.
Emma had already written him hysterical letters of congratu-
lation and worship. To these favourable ingredients for
incubating a passion, St. Vincent added the only one that had
been lacking : nearness — the warmth of propinquity.

The back-drop of this love in its initial stages was a nonstop
burlesque performance at which, if presented on the stage, the
imagination might boggle. Naples, an anachronism, a tiny
independent kingdom yet surviving in the terrible new world
of revolution, presented to the gaping onlooker a jumble of
staggering wealth and staggering poverty, of rococo palaces,
trompe-l'œil paintings of unexampled virtuosity, and sump-
tuous evening parties where orchestras and choruses performed
cantatas composed to order. Any extravagance was counte-
nanced, no one cared about anything ; the good humour and
the vermin, the beauty and the laziness and the hot sun, were

sufficient to the day. Its queen, Marie Caroline, possessed more intellect than her younger sister Marie Antoinette but fewer good looks and less charm ; its king, Ferdinand, a frolicsome baboon of royal Spanish and Austrian ancestry, was given to chasing his courtiers playfully with the contents of a chamber-pot. His chief passion was the daily pursuit and slaughter of such quantities of birds and animals that even his royal visitors, reared in the tradition of the hunt, were slightly stupefied. Outside of this daily obsession he had a fetish for women's fine rounded arms, and his queen always made it a point to ask favours while drawing and moulding a pair of long white gloves onto hers, which were lovely ; Ferdinand, following the process with a smile of vacant pleasure, was likely to grant what she wanted without specially having heard what she had said. But by one of those stubborn paradoxes which reduces so much to illogic, Ferdinand is decidedly more likeable than his wife, superior though she was to him, and by another contradiction he might be a rackety fool, yet had unexpected flashes of dignity, even of commonsense —especially where his own welfare or survival was concerned.

In this *opera-buffa* land, where everything was slightly askew, the British Ambassador was a figure not less out-of-drawing than its king and queen. Sir William Hamilton was thin, elegant and amusing, a man whose gaiety never impaired his intelligence and whose perceptions travelled to the point in a straight line. A born collector and connoisseur, he belonged to the great race of patrician originals such as Charles James Fox and Lords Holland and Egremont, who from their pinnacles of wealth, high birth and considerable physical attractiveness treated the conventions of the day as rubbish and lived to please themselves, especially as regarded women. In accordance with the practices of this caste, Sir William had first educated, then married, an effulgent young prostitute (or nearly) who had been kept by his nephew and who was handed over to Uncle Hamilton, without her consent, in return for uncle's paying nephew's debts.

This is a late day to venture any estimate of one who has been overhauled in minute detail by history and romance, yet the attempt must be made. Emma Hamilton was a tall woman, apparently five foot seven or eight, with strong shoulders and large bones. Even in her early youth innumerable paintings and drawings of her show her as well-covered, and by the time Nelson came to know her the corpulence of her body was attracting general and unfavourable comment, but the glory of her face and head remained such as to strike the beholder with a sense of overpowering beauty, before he recovered enough to become aware of her disadvantages. Emotional, clever and adaptable, like all natural actresses — for she was one, posing hundreds of times before guests in a series of tableaux she called her 'Attitudes' — she had attracted universal admiration as Sir William's ward or protégée and later supported, with similar applause, the rôle of English Ambassadress. Comments of the day on her charming manners are about evenly balanced by comments on her vulgarity, which suggests a familiar pattern — an acquired polish cracking a bit from time to time, and showing what was underneath. She was a tremendous favourite with Queen Marie Caroline, who shared her sister Antoinette's taste for exciting and extraordinary personalities.

Yet her dizzy ascent of the social scale, the glitter and prominence of her position, had no power to change her essential nature from what it had always been. No trace of the rigidity of self-importance can be found in her ; no least touch of pompousness or pretentiousness. Feeling things keenly and instantly, she responded with all the force of an overflowing nature whose springs of kindness, generosity and courage remained, from first to last, perfectly undefiled. Not the least of her attractive traits was her manner toward her husband, often remarked on — affectionate and gay, eloquent of genuine admiration and her desire to be attentive to him. Sir William was sixty-nine when Nelson re-entered her life after the battle of the Nile ; she was thirty-three.

Four days before the New Year of '99, Nelson wrote St. Vincent a six-page letter, detailing most extraordinary doings. The King and Queen of Naples, and the eight royal children, were safely aboard Nelson's flagship, the *Vanguard*. The French were advancing toward Naples daily and there seemed no prospect of stopping them, so the rulers had been advised to flee, which they did — with better luck than their close relations, the King and Queen of France. The escape was carried out at night by Nelson, with three barges, but was mostly engineered by Lady Hamilton, who was also entrusted with the crown and personal jewels of the sovereigns. Probably she supervised the removal of their other effects, as well, into the *Vanguard* and another ship. The value of all this, Nelson calculated, was not less than two and a half million pounds sterling. The royal family was not alone by any means in its desire to quit the scene ; the pell-mell rush to get away from Naples was a horror, people flocking madly to the bay and entreating passage on any kind of sea-going craft, anything at all. Nelson's voice was a clarion-call to safety, notifying British merchants in Naples that they would be received on 'any and every ship' in the squadron, and their property loaded into three English transports. Sir William Hamilton had hired two extra vessels for the émigrés who had fled the Terror in France only to find it catch up with them in Naples, a grisly eighteenth-century Appointment in Samarra.

'Burn all English ships that have to be abandoned in the Bay', Nelson ordered — then, having done all that could be done, set sail for Palermo, another capital of their Sicilian Majesties. It blew harder, he reported, 'than I ever before experienced at sea', but not one of the royal passengers complained. The next day — Christmas Day — Prince Albert, aged six, youngest of the family, died suddenly at seven in the evening. 'In Lady Hamilton's arms', Nelson described the scene, sufficiently upsetting no doubt, but it is plain that the tragedy of the woman holding the dying child was transcended, for him, by his sense of the woman's beauty and heavenly kindness. A good third of the long letter to St. Vincent, in fact, is devoted to Lady Hamilton — how she supplied her own beds and linen for the royal family, cared for them, nursed them, had no sleep for three days, became *their slave*, how much they owed her, how much he himself owed her, and so forth and so on in an admiration without limit. He had seen her in brilliant opulence and in sudden adversity, attending upon the squalid miseries of discomfort at sea ; in both aspects he found her matchless and made no attempt to disguise it.

In the five months of this period (May to September, '99) a number of important things happened to Nelson, all with important effects on his future. First of all St. Vincent's health — half-tottering, half-recovering by fits and starts — had given rise to a tricky situation. Anticipating his complete breakdown, he had handed over his command provisionally : that is to say, he continued in his post as top man and gave orders as usual, but in case of his sudden collapse or departure his successor was ready to step in at a moment's notice. This successor was Admiral Lord Keith as before noted, and one look at his face on canvas — formidable with inner reserves, hooded and withdrawn, saturnine — is sufficient enlightenment as to how much he would have appealed to Nelson, or Nelson to him. The idea of St. Vincent's leaving was nothing new, for Nelson had mentioned it to his wife over a year ago ; but then the threat must have seemed remote, now it was imminent. Frantic at the prospect, he sat down and wrote from Naples with all the urgency of his nature.

'Now, my dear Lord, we have reports that you think of going home, this distresses us most exceedingly. I have more than serious thoughts of going home myself if that event should happen.'

In other words, the thought of serving under anyone but St. Vincent was intolerable to him.

'Do not quit us', his petition goes on. 'If I have any

weight in your friendship let me entreat you to rouse the sleeping lion, GIVE NOT UP A PARTICLE OF YOUR AUTHORITY TO ANYONE, be again our St. Vincent.'

The thought of losing his commander and intimate friend so stayed with him that two days later he sent a further appeal, more urgent than the last.

'My dear Lord, our St. Vincent! what have we suffered in hearing of your illness! Let me entreat you to come to us. If you are sick I will fag for you, our dear Lady Hamilton will nurse you, good Sir William will make you laugh with his inexhaustible wit and pleasantry. Come then to your sincere friends, let us get you well.'

The exhortation was useless ; a month later the Earl had sailed for home. But before this event another thing had happened to Nelson, shattering to the whole tradition and morale of the service which had advanced him to such high rank. In May '99 some fighting had seemed imminent, and he had begged St. Vincent, 'Let me join you. My heart would break to be near my commander-in-chief and not assisting him at such a time.' But only two weeks later, being ordered by Keith to bring ships to the defence of Minorca, he answered first by ignoring the order. Keith wrote a second time, more sharply, and Nelson grudgingly sent three vessels under another commander, arguing that he could not further weaken his squadron at the Neapolitan base, and that between Naples and Minorca, it was better to keep Naples and lose Minorca. Nelson had refused obedience — the unforgivable sin in military and naval worlds — and in a special way : he had shown he would not obey Keith but was ready to obey St. Vincent.

This poses a question, unanswerable but fascinating : if St. Vincent instead of Keith had ordered him from Naples, would he have dared refuse ? Might St. Vincent's authority and influence over Nelson have succeeded in separating him from the enchantress before the attachment between them became unbreakable ? Could St. Vincent's intervention have

cut off at the root one of the famous romances of the world ?
For it was in this period, also, that circumstances threw Nelson
and Emma Hamilton constantly together, and that everything between them — the extravagant mutual admiration
and attraction, the man's romantic temperament and the
woman's lavish nature — trembled over the brink of con-
ventional relationship into what stands, even now, as the
image of a deathless passion.

It was halfway through this period, likewise, that Nelson's
reputation split amoeba-like into two separate halves. That
is to say, his fame was secure with the English man in the
street who, in his millions, was waiting to thunder him a
welcome of love and hero-worship, unflawed by the least
reserve or criticism. But there was also to consider another
aspect of his fame, not among the Nobodies but the Some-
bodies — in other words, his current reputation with his
equals. He was returning to England and so were the Hamil-
tons, Sir William having been recalled as Ambassador ; the
three of them made a four months' journey across Europe
together, staying with or visiting a long line of English people
en route, in residences official or private. And all these people
functioned as telegraph wires leading straight to England,
and the import of the messages they carried was all unfavourable, the combined reportings of onlookers half-scandalized,
half-amused : how she flattered him continually and grossly,
how he ate it up and asked for more, how he babbled to all
and sundry about her angelic qualities, how she sat next to
him at table and cut up his meat, in what poor taste she
dressed and what loud manners she had . . . then the old
husband, tiresome with his perpetual affectation of youthful-
ness while evidently tottering from the fatigues of flight, illness and old age, oblivious to what was going on under his
nose or pretending to be oblivious . . . all this ran ahead of
them and reached London long before they did ; everyone
in the fashionable world was on tiptoe for the advent of the
three-cornered party as for a three-ringed circus. It was all too

delicious, and what would Lady Nelson do when she found out ?

St. Vincent's arrival in London, also, had preceded theirs by a good many months. What he thought of the performance need not be imagined, since his opinion of it is recorded in his letters. A thorough man of the world, he probably subscribed to the man of the world's creed — that anything can be done, given the manner of doing it. Nelson had done everything the wrong way ; the flamboyant advertising of his passion, his continual escort of Emma on occasions public and private, dragging her out onto balconies beside him to share in the applause and cheers — and his former chief viewed the spectacle with contemptuous disgust. Nelson knew he was in a false position, it was evident from his letters, St. Vincent wrote to Evan Nepean at the Admiralty ; he had probably pledged himself to getting Lady Hamilton presented at Court, and was going to get into no end of messes about it. But he had another and much deeper grudge against Nelson ; his reckless behaviour might somehow reflect discredit upon the Navy, an offence compared to which any private peccadillo was a trifle. Nelson had refused obedience to his superior, Keith, no doubt under the demoralizing influence of Emma ; encouraged by her, of what further enormities might he not be capable ? This is the first serious opening of the rift between the two men, though the most threadlike of cracks had foretold it two years before, about midway of their association. Not that St. Vincent — not even he — dared remonstrate with Nelson over his conduct and his bad treatment of his wife, whose only crime was that she was not Lady Hamilton ; but in this moment he would remember that apart from Nelson's professional brilliance he had always distrusted parts of his character, and now had the grim satisfaction of seeing his distrust confirmed.

St. Vincent was fatally right, as usual. The very first night of Nelson's arrival, a member of his party — a Miss Cornelia Knight, whom we shall meet again — was warned away from them by a friend concerned for her reputation. She removed herself from their contamination as precipitately as if they all had smallpox, and took shelter with the Nepeans. Other unpleasant incidents followed, and a couple of weeks later the King himself snubbed Nelson at a levee, asking how he was and then turning his back before England's national hero had a chance to answer.

Before resuming the road of the St. Vincent–Nelson friendship — a road that from here gets rockier with each step — one glance might be taken at St. Vincent's attitude toward the two women in Nelson's life. Of significant contact with them it might be said that he had, virtually, none. Emma he would know chiefly from Nelson's letters, and of course the fame of her spectacular looks and accomplishments extended far beyond the Mediterranean ; travellers came to see her as on a sort of pilgrimage. Any man would be well-disposed toward an unknown lady who was a great beauty and who, as an Ambassadress, had helped toward getting the Fleet victualled and watered by stealth when the Neapolitans did their best to get out of it for fear of antagonizing the French ; in some of his letters to Nelson he had sent messages to her of thanks and affectionate good wishes — expressions largely a matter of convention. Not a matter of convention — far from it — is a later opinion : 'That infernal bitch Lady Hamilton would have made Nelson poison his wife and stab me, his best friend.' This is startling enough — and enough out of character — to compel a pause for examination and wonder. Obviously the remark (made after Nelson's death) was wrung from some moment of anger or pain, and the stabbing part can be taken in the sense of ingratitude or betrayal, but what did he mean by the rest of it ? Emma and Frances Nelson had detested each other at sight and their antipathy is recorded in Emma's letters, but with a cattiness merely silly and with no power of injury behind it ; her talent was for loving, not hating. The charge must be based on some secret conviction of the Earl's — now never to be known — and not on mere violence of abuse, for St. Vincent was not given to abuse nor yet to violence. Moreover, he did not only say it, he wrote it in a letter. And yet only a short time before, taking pity on Emma's frightful financial position after Nelson's death, he could say in another letter, 'Those rapacious Nelsons [1] will strip Lady Hamilton of every feather, and if care is not taken she will be speedily reduced to indigence.' And even later, when Emma's situation was really desperate and her petition to the King had been refused — for £30,000 of their own money that Sir William and she had spent on aiding the Fleet and the escape of the Naples royalties — St. Vincent conceded in a letter to Baird that really she did seem 'entitled to aid from the charitable Naval funds, and you are authorized to make full use of my name in this respect, but,' he adds coldly, 'she should be advised to depend more on her own exertions.' Her own exertions ; of what exertions did he suppose her capable, this former near-goddess used to being lavishly maintained by a succession of men, and now middle-aged, intermittently ill and given to the bottle ? His feeling for her, finally, boils down to pity, but pity without warmth or respect, not unmixed with distaste.

On the other hand, his attitude to the legal wife is neutral in its beginnings, but goes on steadily through concern and kindness to an unmistakable conclusion. Poor Fanny Nelson : from first to last she was the injured party, yet the position of injured party does not of itself guarantee sympathy or liking. In a portrait of her at about twenty-seven, there looks at you out of the canvas a narrow oval face with a long upper lip and a very curious mouth, wide enough to be called coarse if the lips were not so thin ; even at this presumable high point of her youth and bloom, a faint something about her invites from at least one spectator the word *hag-like*. But in a crayon sketch of her made twelve years later the features and expression

---

[1] He was referring to the clergyman brother who succeeded to Nelson's titles, not to Nelson's widow.

N

have quite changed, perhaps because she has grown stouter ; now she seems rather pretty in a middle-aged way, more than anything else inconsequential. Long years of living alone, her husband always at sea, her life passed in restless movement from house to house — other people's houses, never her own — had marked her with the mark of homelessness. And to this eroded woman, out of the lurid Neapolitan scene, had come her husband escorting a married woman some months pregnant by him.

St. Vincent's references to Nelson's widow — colourless to match the colourless Fanny — change in an interesting manner, keeping pace with the change in himself as time and events worked on him. First of all her situation would predispose him in her favour, for his sympathies were always with the underdog. All the same, when writing to his sister, he begins by referring to her as 'a valuable woman'. *Valuable* is one of those lukewarm words straddling two degrees of indifference ; of a person who inspires real warmth, one does not use a term like valuable. 'I was glad to draw the attention of the East India Company to her Ladyship.' So at any rate he liked her well enough to do her a good turn when he could. Then a glimpse much more informative, not only as letting in light on Fanny's circumstances but on his own opinion of her. 'Lady Nelson has added if possible to the lustre of her character by taking Lord and Lady Nelson under her protection, but I trust she will not allow them to sponge on her as was the case with Lady Hamilton, pray read this to her.' Three facts emerge from this one sentence ; if we take 'the lustre of her character' to mean that he had always respected Fanny's un-complaining fortitude under Nelson's cruelty, later references will prove us not very far out. Then the mention of the new Lord Nelson, the country parson who by freak of circum-stance had succeeded to brother Horatio's hard-won honours : apparently Fanny had taken pity on him and his wife, and was introducing them about London to make them less lonely. The allusion to sponging — which for a startled moment gives the impression that Lady Hamilton had sponged on Lady Nelson — means something quite different : that Parson William and wife had sponged extensively on Lady Hamilton, and here was St. Vincent warning Fanny against her in-laws lest they do the same to her. Apparently, with that far-seeing naval eye of his, he knew what went on in both sides of the Nelson ménage, legal and illegal, for all his actual contact with both households was slight or non-existent.

Then in 1807 another reference ; some letters have been requested of him. 'Lady Nelson is welcome to all the correspondence between her late Lord and me.' The greater unseen bulk of this — like the iceberg's below water — may lie in the fact that Pettigrew's *Life of Nelson* had just appeared, a work that infuriated St. Vincent past control. 'I threw away the first volume in disgust — abuse of Lady Nelson — Lady Hamilton furnished the letters and directed the compiler throughout — eternal disgrace on the character of Lord Nelson.' Perhaps Lady Nelson was collecting her husband's letters with the idea of sponsoring a biography to rebut Pettigrew's, authenticated by material from the Nelson family itself. Especially, she wanted to vindicate the character of her son Captain Nisbet, whose unsatisfactory conduct Nelson was always throwing up at her before their break, and here St. Vincent was more than willing to help her : '[I] authorize you to assert in my name that Lord Nelson assured me, that he owed his life to the admirable conduct of his son [stepson] at Teneriffe,' and soon after was enraged into declaring his sentiments full blast : 'I love Lady Nelson dearly and admire her dignified pride and spirit, which I trust will not be subdued by the nefarious conduct of her husband's brother, sisters and their husbands, all of them vile reptiles. Any assistance I can give her, she may command.' This was at the period when Nelson's family were behaving badly over his will.

At the moment, however, Nelson was not in St. Paul's, a shell entombed, but in London and alive — wretchedly and continuously alive — to the threefold difficulties of his position.

For his emotional situation would be bound by its very nature to affect him socially and professionally, and from this corrosion his fellowship with his 'dear Lord' could not be exempt.

Accordingly, the high and glorious compact that had been between St. Vincent and Nelson — the single fusion for the single aim — now entered upon an uneasy stage when it was a friendship, yet no longer a friendship. Between the two of them a surface was maintained, no less anxiously upheld by the one than by the other ; beneath this surface, acerbity and resentment were in constant motion. Oddly enough, it was Nelson who had sounded the first note of covert hostility as long as two years before when he wrote gloomily to his wife, about some slow-forthcoming favour, 'Lord St. Vincent is in no hurry to oblige me *now*, I am got, he fancies, too near him in reputation.' The sudden accusation of jealousy shows an unsuspected aptitude for rancour, an aptitude ably sustained by St. Vincent in a letter of his own, written the very evening the Nelson–Hamilton party arrived in London.

For on this night of November 1800, the old commander, not perfectly restored to health by any means, knew he would be given the command of the Channel Fleet, and knew that the Admiralty would probably give him Nelson as his second in command. And — incredibly — he would rather not have him ; he had found out too much about him. 'He cannot bear confinement to any object ; he is a partizan. [Side-taker.] His ship,' he added, with scorn, 'always in the most dreadful disorder.'

Unfair of St. Vincent, for he knew this to be only half the reality. Perhaps it was true that Nelson was indulgent to his men and that they might be remiss in some formal points of discipline, but when it came to the pinch — and the pinch was the day of battle — they fought for him like demons, and surely St. Vincent knew, none better, that this was the discipline to ensure which all other disciplines had been invented ? 'Although one hundred and thirty-five men short of complement, the fire from Lord Nelson's ship was a perfect hell.'

Testimonies like this show how Nelson's crews, who adored him, worked like men possessed to overcome any deficiency in themselves or their numbers, and it may be doubted that effort so tremendous could have been evoked from them by a less-popular commander.

At any rate, the Admiralty assigned Nelson to the Channel Fleet whether St. Vincent would or no, and willy-nilly he had to make the best of the bargain. England's idol reported to him at his winter quarters, and afterwards he wrote to Nepean, 'Nelson was very low when he came here day before yesterday; appeared and acted as if he had done me an injury and felt apprehensive that I was acquainted with it'. St. Vincent *was* acquainted — well-acquainted — with the sources of Nelson's constraint. 'Poor fellow!' his letter goes on, half-contemptuous, half-pitying. 'He is devoured with vanity, weakness and folly ; was strung with ribbons, medals, etc., and yet pretended that he wished to avoid the honour and ceremonies he everywhere met with on the road.' These are unfriendly words, but no more unfriendly than some sentiments of Nelson's a month later, when St. Vincent had just been created First Lord of the Admiralty. Such a nomination should have been an occasion of genuine pleasure and rejoicing to a dedicated naval man like Nelson, or so the naïve bystander would think. But not by any means : Nelson wrote Emma a glum letter about his reluctance to attend the traditional dinner in honour of the appointment, and thus explained his reasons for going : 'It may be necessary to hold a candle to the Devil'. So St. Vincent was now the devil to the man who owed him his unique reputation, and who now held out to him perforce the guttering candle of insincere congratulations and good wishes ? Such discoveries must be attended by discomfiture and regret, until we remind ourselves that this story is of men, not plaster symbols.

Also, when St. Vincent mentioned Nelson's embarrassed manner toward himself in the letter to Nepean, he was not mistaken. Between the two of them was already, heaven knows, embarrassment enough — of interviews where Nelson was silently aware of St. Vincent's silent disapproval, all this having to be skirted and avoided in their talk — but in addition there existed another miserable constraint to fret and fray their eroded relationship. This was, incredibly enough, the lawsuit that Nelson was bringing at this time against his past and present commander. And its roots, also incredibly, reached longer into the past than one might suspect.

*   *   *

Among the papers found after Nelson's death was a document calculated to administer a slight shock, considering that it was dated October 17th, 1797, when the friendship between Nelson and his chief was at its height. This document was an agreement drawn up by the admirals serving under St. Vincent. There are four signatures, Nelson's among them. In brief, the agreement states that certain prize or freight money, traditionally belonging to them, was being 'arrogated' by the Earl to his own use. To recover this money, the four signatories bound themselves jointly 'to have recourse to the laws of our country, to obtain that justice we are not likely to obtain otherwise', and to deposit one hundred pounds apiece for carrying on the lawsuit.

Whether Nelson was constrained to act with his fellow admirals, or whether he gave his signature willingly, we can never know. It is obvious, though, how nervous he was about the whole thing and how much he hated it. First he looked warily over the phraseology of the agreement, crossing out the word 'arrogates' and substituting 'claims' as less harsh. Then, upon the same document, he jotted down his dubious impressions and comments. 'From inquiry, have my doubts.' The opinion of three lawyers should be taken, he thinks, 'before we involve in law'. His caution is understandable ; upsetting, the thought of being pushed by his peers into a lawsuit against his superior and close friend, especially when there seemed even chances of its being unsuccessful. Did Nelson damp his cosigners' intention, or did his reluctance to come in with them have the same effect ? Whatever the answer, the matter was never acted upon. The agreement, forgotten probably, was left among his papers to gather dust.

There was no hesitation, however, in Nelson's actions and intentions of a later date. His banker and agent, Alexander Davison, was also his great friend, and in May 1800 Nelson was writing him an astounded letter. St. Vincent was claiming a share of Mediterranean prize-money up to November '99, when in actual fact his command had terminated in July, four months previous. During those four months his successor, Keith, was also absent from the Mediterranean in pursuit of the enemy. This left Nelson senior officer on the Mediterranean station, hence its commander-in-chief — a rank which would automatically entitle him to the chief's share of prizes. What was his astonishment, then, to learn of a counter-claim to the same money, and that this claim came from St. Vincent.

'When I laid claim to my right of prize-money as commanding admiral of the Mediterranean Fleet,' he told Davison, aghast, 'I had not an idea of Lord St. Vincent attempting to lay in any claim, to take away my undoubted property.' Then all the affection, candour and naïveté of his heart welled up. 'I am confident the claim will be given up the moment you show his Lordship my manner of thinking. Let my Earl lay his hand on his heart and say whether his Nelson, under all the burden of this command, is not entitled to this pittance of prize-money.' Shocked and hurt as he was, he also felt sure of his ground. 'In no instance before him have admirals claimed to share when they left their command on account of ill-health or otherwise ; in previous similar cases the departing officer did not claim, nor did he have a shadow of claim.'

Talking of prize-money, Nelson himself has left us an interesting table of percentages assigned to the various ranks. Following the Nile victory, he was obliged to burn three French ships on the scene of their capture, as they were so

badly damaged that the cost of repairing and getting them to
England would be far in excess of their value as prizes. All
the same, he hopes that the men who took them will be com-
pensated, and suggests £60,000 as a moderate valuation. He
cannot be accused of having a stake in this estimate, Nelson
explains anxiously, because his share of it can only be £625 ;
whereas if the Admiralty refuses compensation for the burnt
ships, the following officers will have been defrauded of the
following sums :

Commander-in-Chief	. .	£3750
Junior Admirals	. . .	650
Captains	. . . .	1000
Lieutenants	. . .	75
Warrant Officers	. . .	50
Petty Officers .	. . .	11
Seamen ⎫ Marines ⎭	. . . .	2 : 4 : 1

So we see that St. Vincent, who was hundreds of miles
from the scene of battle, would have collected the large sum
of nearly four thousand pounds, and the same applied to any
prize taken by any ship under his command, in waters however
distant from where that command was based.

In the present case, if Nelson expected the Earl to abandon
his claim on presentation of his junior's point of view, he was
badly mistaken. St. Vincent had his own point of view, based
on good technical and personal grounds. The four killing
years of the Mediterranean command had beaten him to the
ground in body, mind and nerves ; if he claimed for the four
months when he was still titular chief, though not actually on
the spot, he felt it no excessive reward for his services. Surely
he was entitled to that much, and in defence of his rights he
was prepared to be as unyielding as Nelson. Their respective
agents invoked the law and the case was set for a hearing in the
Court of Common Pleas. Nelson, in a letter, refers to it as
coming up on May 26th, 1801 ; actually it appears to have been
heard on June 19th, about three weeks later than he thought.

And not the least remarkable feature of the case was the fact that while it was going on — *all* the while it was going on — the two litigants were inescapably bound together by the closest professional ties, St. Vincent as C.-in-C. of the Channel Fleet, and Nelson as directly under his command.

Specifically, Nelson was suing for £20,000 as his share of three prizes, *Courageux* (French) and *Tetis* and *Santa Brigida* (Spanish) taken by the *Alcmene*, Captain Digby commanding. But he was not suing St. Vincent, for so great a man's identity must in the interests of decorum be shrouded ; he was suing one Benjamin Tucker (actually St. Vincent's secretary) as Agent for Mediterranean Prizes, and the plea stated that Tucker had promised to pay this money to Nelson on request. Nevertheless, 'not regarding his several promises made', the plea continues, 'but contriving and fraudulently intending craftily and subtilly to deceive and defraud the said Horatio Lord Nelson in this respect, hath hitherto refused and still doth refuse to pay the said sums of money. Whereupon the said Horatio Lord Nelson saith he hath sustained damage to the value of £20,000 and therefore he brings his suit.'

Clear as crystal for the plaintiff, but the defendant's position is also clear. Digby took the three prizes in September 1799. St. Vincent, it is true, had sailed for England one month before, arriving the middle of August and going to Bath for his health till the end of November. However, he had not yet 'resigned or been superseded or removed from his office', and offered evidence that on October 5th he was still issuing orders as C.-in-C. in the Mediterranean. Since Digby's captures were made during his period of command, he was automatically entitled to his share as Senior Flag Officer. Otherwise prize-money was shared, according to regulations, among the flag officer or officers actually on board at the taking of any prize or 'who should be directing or assisting therein. But that the said Lord Viscount Nelson', the defence points out, 'was not actually on the *Alcmene* at the time of the capture'.

Now Nelson offered *his* evidence ; that by August he, and not St. Vincent, was serving in the Mediterranean as senior commanding officer, and brought forward letters — many letters — from the Admiralty, officially confirming his rank as Senior Flag Officer and issuing orders to him in that capacity. The whole nub of the case rests on the Admiralty's failure to take clear-cut action and retire St. Vincent officially the moment he left the station ; he could prove by good evidence that on the date of the capture he was still C.-in-C. in the Mediterranean, but Nelson could prove by as much evidence, and as good — and from the same sources — that the opposite was true.   The case being heard, the verdict was given against Nelson on February 4th, 1803, 'that the said Horatio Lord Nelson take nothing by his writ against Benjamin Tucker', and that Tucker 'receive from the said Lord Viscount Nelson damages of £500 for his costs and charges'.

If St. Vincent exchanged a tight smile with Tucker on this decision, he smiled too soon.   The suit now moved at dizzy speed, considering the traditional pace of English law. Nelson's agent must have appealed at once, praying that the judgment 'be reversed, annulled and altogether held for nothing', and only one year later the Court of King's Bench did hold it for nothing, the judge's opinion being decisive : that the moment a superior officer left his station, the right of the next flag officer began, and that therefore 'the said Lord Viscount Nelson do receive against the said Benjamin Tucker his damages aforesaid,' and also 'from the said Tucker [in reality from St. Vincent, of course] £334 for his costs and charges and that he have execution thereof and the said Benjamin Mercy+ Mercy CK.'   And with some bored copyist's compression of an ancient formula, the case of Nelson *v*. Tucker ended so far as court proceedings were concerned.

Strange to say, there are accounts of this affair which represent both the Earl and Nelson as not at all interested in the money, but merely as regarding the dispute in the light of a test case, whose outcome they awaited with a calm, theoretical interest. Far from being calm, Nelson, who felt things strongly, was as hot under the collar about it as about anything ever in his life. He was lucky in Davison — a man utterly dedicated to his interests — and in January 1800 was urging him on : 'The Earl being at the head of the Admiralty will, I hope, give a new spur to our just cause. The higher the Earl, the more we must attempt to wrest justice from him, and I hope your courage will not flag. I [will not] give up an inch. Was he forty times as great, I would not suffer him to rob me with impunity.' Nelson's ideas of honesty were Old Testament black-and-white, and the thought of anyone's being considered as above justice, because of rank or wealth, maddened him. A few days later an unpleasant report reached him — that St. Vincent had openly stated Davison's championship of Nelson to be offensive to him. 'Why should it be ?' Nelson demanded angrily in a letter to Emma. 'Mr. Davison wishes that I shall have justice done me, and not be overpowered by weight of interest [influence] and money.'

In this emotional state, and with the thought of the on-coming trial preying on his mind, he sailed to conduct the northern campaign whose climax was the victory of Copen-hagen. When Davison wrote asking for some additional instructions he answered distractedly, 'I will endeavour to collect my ideas on money matters, but everyone pulls at me'. The familiar exhaustion, accompaniment of a major campaign, was prostrating him. A week later (May 12) Davison must have warned him that indications as to the outcome of the suit looked unfavourable. Resignedly Nelson answered, 'If justice is fled from our land, it is useless to torment either myself or you. If it is given against me, I have only to lament that the hand of power has robbed me. If I could have appeared before a jury and told truth, the Earl's cause could not have held water.' And in a couple of weeks, apathetic, he shrugs, 'This day comes on my trial with the great Earl. May the just gain it.' This is the beginning of his ironic references to St. Vincent as 'great'.

And yet — even while Nelson was filling letters to Davison with references to robbery and injustice — his bitter pages were strangely interleaved with other pages to St. Vincent, not bitter at all but full of willing dependence and affection. So were St. Vincent's to him. 'I am glad that in his letters to you he never mentions the subject', Davison had written Nelson, months before, and apparently — even while instructing his agent quite as inflexibly as Nelson — he never did, but more than kept up his end in the interchange of mutual trust and encouragement that went on between the two of them, straight from the heart and obviously sincere. 'Forgive me if I have said too much', Nelson ended a letter on some dissatisfaction of his. 'These are my feelings, which for several years you have allowed me to throw before you.'

Nor was goodwill limited to strictly official matters. 'May this day, which I am told is your birthday,' Nelson wrote him on January 20th, 'come round as often as life is comfortable, and may yours be comfortable for many, many years. . . . It is no compliment, for it is true', he bursts out later, as it were irrepressibly. 'Except for those who have served in your school, I find such a deficiency of resource that even I am astonished. You taught us to keep the seamen healthy without going into port, and to stay at sea for years without a refit.'

Yet, during this unlikely time — curious to say — the two men even made an approach to a more personal intimacy, though indirectly expressed and quickly shied away from, for the custom of the day mostly favoured, for gentlemen, the dignity of reticence. But on leaving for the northern campaign, Nelson had dashed down a short note to his commander. 'Getting under sail. I am always happy when my conduct meets with your approbation, yet I am so circumstanced that probably this expedition will be the last service ever performed by your affectionate friend, Nelson.'

'I was appalled by the last sentence of your letter,' St. Vincent replied, at once. The hint — the more than hint —

that Nelson intended giving up his naval career for the sake of Emma Hamilton struck him into consternation.   True that only lately he had objected to having Nelson under his command, true that he despised and condemned Nelson's recent behaviour, yet when faced by the prospect of his loss, he found he could not bear it.   Once more his sense of Nelson's peerless qualities and value to England was to the fore, and compared to that nothing else mattered.

'Every *public* act of your life has been the subject of my admiration', he went on.   His underlining of the word 'public' was the nearest he dared come to the perilous ground. 'For God's sake, do not allow yourself to be carried away by any sudden impulse.'   The veiled allusion to the love-affair was the first and last he ventured to make.

After Copenhagen Nelson was ill — 'I am tired to death, I cannot exist in this state.   The death of my brother has affected me a good deal ; if I do not get some rest very soon, another will go.   Six sons are gone, out of eight ; but I hope yet to see you, and to cheer up once more.'   St. Vincent was unable to retire him at once, and Nelson raged to Davison, 'Why have I been kept here ?   Was it a matter of indifference to the Admiralty whether I lived or died ?'   But help came the very next day, and he wrote St. Vincent, 'Your kind way of relieving me has really set me up'.   This was June 12th, 1801 ; by July 1st he was sending a note round, 'In the morning I shall do myself the pleasure of assuring you in person how much I am your affectionate Nelson.'

If his proffer of goodwill tried to shake off the constraint of their legal embroilment, St. Vincent still could give him best. 'I have the deepest concern at hearing that your health has suffered', he had written recently, 'for I never saw the man in our profession, except yourself and Troubridge, who possessed the magic art of infusing the same spirit into others'.   Then grandly, withholding nothing — and this being just about the time the lawsuit had started — he gave the full accolade : 'THERE IS BUT ONE NELSON ; that he may long continue the pride of his country is the fervent wish of your truly affectionate St. Vincent'.

Nelson's time was running out ; he had less than four years left. Of that short period he had a whole nineteen months ashore, and his professional ups and downs with his old chief were variegated with plaints about his health '— pains on my stomach, large dinners truly alarm me —' and his financial position. Having long since discovered the drain to which public characters forced to live in a certain style are subject, and feeling the pinch as early as August 1801, he told St. Vincent that he only wanted to get rid of his command, 'in which I am sure of diminishing my little fortune, which at the most does not reach £10,000.' He had no private means and the very large allowance to his wife (a sop to conscience ?) and purchase of a country house for himself and Emma were exhausting his pocket ; he had refused a foreign decoration with a wry, disillusioned, 'These honours are expensive.' The house had cost £9000, and under pressure of this and other obligations he was driven to disposing — or trying to dispose — of various precious stones presented to him by foreign rulers. This time it was not St. Vincent who was trying to rob him, but other people ; England's saviour discovered that the mean-nesses and extortions of commerce had no mind to spare even him, and in a fury he wrote Davison, 'The valuation of the diamonds is shameful ; I would sooner beg, than *give* those fellows my diamonds.'

This was the time when Nelson's emotional climate — hot with a sense of ill-usage, irritated with fatigue and money-worry — was apt to magnify any friction or disagreement out of all proportion. Unhappily, the most exacerbating instance arose between his old commander and himself. If Nelson had a passion in his career more dominant than any other, it was caring for the interests of officers and seamen who had fought beside him or under him. He wanted them to be applauded and rewarded, especially rewarded ; if such acknow-ledgment were slow in coming he fought to secure it and he

would not give up.   At this particular period he was rowelled
by the deficiency of decorations for the victory of Copenhagen.   No medals had been struck ; how could this be ?
With the crusading fervour that was in him he probably
thought and talked about it incessantly and somehow had
got from St. Vincent the positive impression that he would
support such a request.   Accordingly he wrote his old friend
with fullest assurance : would St. Vincent petition the King
to grant special Copenhagen medals ?   And to his stupefaction
St. Vincent would do nothing of the sort, but pointed out
smoothly (he could be smooth as marble or jagged as rough
stone) that it would be improper to petition the King so long
after the battle.

Horrified, Nelson could scarcely find words to convey his
sense of betrayal.   'I was thunderstruck at your Lordship's
telling me you had never given encouragement to the expectation of medals.   I am truly made ill by your letter.   If any
person had told me what you wrote, I would have staked my
head against his assertion.'   Lord Melville tried to soothe him,
pointing out that medals struck in the heat and excitement of
victory were one thing, but medals issued so long after the
event were another and must hurt Danish feelings, just when
England was trying to cultivate Danish goodwill.   In vain :
Nelson was not in the least interested in Danish feelings, only
in getting 'justice for the brave men who fought on that day'.
The upshot of it all was his furious announcement that he
would never wear any of his other medals, until the Copenhagen ones were given.   As for St. Vincent's denying that he
had encouraged the idea : 'Either he or I are liars', he wrote
Davison despairingly, 'and so my affairs stand.'   And what
was the truth ?   Did Nelson hear what he wanted to hear or
did St. Vincent lie to him ?   And why should he, a man as
little given to lying as anyone born ?   Individual opinion, in
this case, can only be satisfied by the individual's own conclusion.

Nelson had a nephew in the Navy, and later on he wrote

St. Vincent : 'It must be my anxious wish to get him employed and with me and promoted.' He certainly made no bones about what he wanted for his relation, and even more striking than his frankness is his tone — of confidence in his right to make such a request, and confidence that it would be complied with. But another time his voice is the voice of a schoolboy : 'We are uncommonly well disposed to give the French a good thrashing and we are keen'. Both letters vary in expression but are one in significance, for they indicate, in spite of everything, an old comfortable familiarity that nothing could really spoil. Far away in London the lawsuit unwound its sluggish coils, but neither of them had the temperament to be forever nursing a money-grudge ; their hundred common aims and objects pushed it into the background, for the war had broken out again in a familiar area and now it was Nelson who was Commander-in-Chief on the Mediterranean station, grappling with the tremendous job St. Vincent had held four years ago. This commission he had received at the hands of St. Vincent, First Lord of the Admiralty ('I shall certainly endeavour to imitate you, when you commanded here with so much advantage to your country'), and who shall say that their differences had power to spoil the pleasure of one in giving, the other in receiving it ? To such a chief Nelson could even admit small physical humiliations. 'I am — don't laugh — dreadfully seasick this day,' he groaned, and the mention of laughter suggests that on occasion St. Vincent may have been heartlessly amused at a constitutional weakness that his junior never got over.

Nelson admitted other things too — this time not to St. Vincent. 'I wish I had a hundred thousand pounds this moment,' he had written at one time to the devoted Davison. He got one-tenth of his wish and over, just six weeks after the seasick letter ; the lawsuit had finally ended in his favour and he found himself richer by £13,000. 'This will put me out of debt,' he wrote Davison, 'and leave my income unclogged,' and one can hear the immense sigh of relief. Yet for him

the elation of victory must have been mixed with the shame
of victory, for certainly St. Vincent was in his mind at this
moment. How would he feel about it ? How would he
take his defeat, a man not accustomed to defeat ? How would
it affect the communication between the two of them ? No
one but the crassest nature could pretend that nothing had
happened, and Nelson, far from being crass, was over-sensitive
to people, atmosphere and states of mind.

   His own state of mind is printed large all over the first
brief note he wrote St. Vincent after hearing of the verdict :
very uncomfortable, formal, disposed to avoid the usual
cordialities that might now be unwelcome — 'The wind is
easterly, and you know that is not to be lost' — and concludes
in haste. Next day, perhaps in an uneasy gesture of holding
out the olive-branch, he writes to say he had promoted a man
whom St. Vincent wanted promoted, and again ends tersely,
'I will say no more : I am sensible of your attention to merit.'
But three weeks later on a notable anniversary, and whatever
his constraints, he had to let his heart speak for him, not his
caution. 'Most cordially do I hail and congratulate you on
the return of St. Valentine ; and may you, my dear Lord,
live in health to receive them for many, many years.' After
good wishes, he ends with a birthday present more welcome
to St. Vincent than any other : 'We have not a sick man in
the Fleet,' and less than a month later was writing his chief
a most remarkable letter — remarkable for its lack of reserves
and surrender of himself (as it were) to St. Vincent, acknow-
ledging unrestrainedly his indebtedness and his need. 'While
I have your support, I can do anything. Take that from me,
and I am nothing. I rely with confidence on you, my dear
Lord, AND THAT ALONE KEEPS ME UP.' Then, exploring a
deeper avenue of confidence, he shares the sad oppression that
weighs him through heavy days and nights : 'My sight is much
fallen off ; I always thought I should be blind.' Then weary,
longing for rest : 'I hope the restless animal, Bonaparte, will
be upset by the French, and then we may have some quiet.'

   o

By October 21st, 1805, the stupid pellet of lead in his lower spine had wiped out, with him, a thousand hopes and plans for happiness. This death evoked an intensity of emotion for which we have records amazingly complete in that they range downward from the highest to the lowest : from the King, who could not speak for five minutes after hearing the news, to Collingwood, 'My friendship for him was unlike anything I have left in the Navy', to the ship's physician who said, 'I am stupid with grief for what I have lost', to the young sailor who wrote home thanking his stars he had never seen Nelson, though serving under him, because, 'God bless you ! chaps that fought like the devil, sit down and cry like a wench', to the Marine who sounded a final note : 'They wanted to take Lord Nelson from us, but we told Captain, as we brought him out we would bring him home ; so it was so, and he was put into a cask of spirits. Your loving brother, James Bagley.'

And yet in this full register of grief one note is curiously missing, and the ear may strain after it and still hear not a sound. St. Vincent was more than usually articulate ; he must have been affected and shocked by Nelson's death and spoken of it at least to his sister Mary, with whom he was in constant touch. One may know he did this, and look and still find nothing. No such letter appears in the immense St. Vincent collection in the British Museum or in his massive group of letters to Dr. Baird, and he was more intimate with his sister and doctor than with any two people on earth. If it exists, then the seeker's resourcefulness was unequal to finding it, or perhaps something lies buried in some muniment-room, attic or trunk. He did write Tucker, 'I was prepared for anything but Nelson's loss,' and besides this there survives one faint, uncertain indication of his feeling, or what might be interpreted as his feeling.

This is the comment of a news-reporter present in the House of Lords on January 28th, 1806, when various memorials were under discussion, Nelson's funeral having taken place just three weeks before. The debate over, St. Vincent was called upon, seemingly as the person there who had been closest to Nelson, hence the one most fit to respond on Nelson's behalf and to speak, as it were, for Nelson himself. He rose; and still we are none the wiser. 'The Earl of St. Vincent said a few words,' states the reporter, 'but in so low a tone we could scarcely catch a word from him.' He had the stentorian voice developed by seamen and was more than used to addressing public gatherings, so his behaviour can hardly be put down to unreadiness of any kind. Perhaps he failed to speak simply because he was unable to speak. At least we are free to think so, even to hope so.

But the empty place unfilled by his voice is as nothing compared to the empty place unfilled by his physical presence on January 9th, 1806, a tremendous day of a whole nation swathed in black and shaken by tolling bells. For St. Vincent was not at Nelson's funeral. And his absence is terrible ; a gap, an aching void. 'Where is he ?' an inner voice keeps demanding. 'Where is he ? what kept him away?' Incredulous, the eye rakes column after column of Mourners, Earls, Admirals, without finding him — although in the Fourth Barge among Four Supporters of the Pall we encounter an old friend, Sir John Orde (but only because the original occupant of the place had been taken suddenly ill). Orde had lately claimed a constant admiration for Nelson, although his attendance would probably have irked the hero, to whom he would never be anything but the man who had opposed his appointment to the detached squadron.

The explanation of St. Vincent's absence may be, after all, simple. We have a clue to it three years later, when he wrote a friend, 'I have declined attending Lord Collingwood's funeral, dreading the icy feel of St. Paul's.' So that was it ; if he dreaded St. Paul's in May, what must it have been in January, with concentrated winter stored in every stone and stealing out to nest in the congregation's bones ? If he had taken his place in the black creeping procession, with its long slow train of barges on the cold river bringing the body from

Greenwich to London and the five-hour ceremony at its end, there would have been another funeral in short order, with the central recipient of honours not Nelson this time but John Jervis, Earl of St. Vincent. One feels that his own inclination might have driven him to attending whatever the risk, so perhaps his wife and physician combined to keep him at home.

This is St. Vincent's book, yet it is hard to leave Nelson ; hard to resist circling his memory a moment more, touching a keepsake here, a relic there. The kind of linen shirt he wore, for instance, elaborately gusseted so that his most sweeping gestures of command could not disturb the ruffles of the attached jabot ; the right sleeve about eight inches long and closed with drawstrings. Or another kind of souvenir, an echo of his indestructibly good and simple heart, from a letter to a genealogist : 'I very much doubt that I have paid for several things you have done for me, therefore I desire you will send me your regular bill, for I suppose you cannot live on air ; and if you are never paid, how is the pot to boil ?' The old unhappy story still darkens the air of the Nelson Ward Room in the Maritime Museum, where up to a few years ago one could pull out drawers and stare at the hard-worn finery, stuck over with rusty spangles, that got Emma Hamilton such a name for bad taste in dress. On one column is a tiny glass case where the material of the death-mask is displayed inside-out, curiously disturbing because the eyes' line of closure is such that they could not be living eyes. And there, on the opposite column, the mask itself ; the features fresh, firm and distinct, but the face become very small in the mysterious contractions of death, scarcely larger than a child's face. A wax effigy of Nelson in the Undercroft at Westminster Abbey has that quality that makes one feel instinctively how excellent is the likeness ; the expression haunting — worn-out and melancholy yet with something in it touchingly youthful, and the handling of the eyes wonderful in that there is no difference in their size or shape, but in one eye there is obviously sight and in the other, none. It seems to have been true that the blind eye only differed from the other in the ragged outline of the pupil, not visible except close up.

This is the story of St. Vincent and Nelson and of their existence so curiously lived on two levels simultaneously — of dissension and agreement, of hostility and concord, all at once. Except that the needle of their friendship, whatever the interim disturbances, swung inevitably back to true ; back to the thing that had been between them from the first, immediate and fundamental and, in spite of everything, imperishable.

A peculiar mortality rests upon Nelson in wax, as it does on all wax mementoes — a reminder of the ruins of time, a dimness and a dust. But mortality, dimness and dust are only for the bickerings between these two, not for the love that impelled Nelson when he wrote, 'We look up to you, we have always found you *our father*,' and his Commander-in-Chief when he wrote, 'God bless you, my dear Lord, be assured that no man loves and esteems you more truly than your very affectionate St. Vincent'.

X

THE ADMIRAL'S HEART

WHAT happens to the man so swallowed up by his profession that almost nothing is left of him for the endearments, graces and attachments that others have been gathering or creating in their season ? What becomes of his personal life ? The answer seems to be, that he must live it where he can — by snatches, in chinks and interstices of time. John Jervis was at sea from the age of fourteen. His absences from England were frequent and long, mostly two to four years ; to get home more often was a rare piece of luck. His capacities leaped to the eye and by their eminence secured him steady employment. No doubt he was glad of it but no doubt, also, he knew that the success of his career was crowding out other things he wanted. There was nothing he could do about it ; it was the price he paid for having ability.

Yet in his earliest boyhood he already had one great friend, his sister Mary Ricketts — to anticipate her married name — and her character is so important to an abnormal experience in both their lives,[1] later on, that it might be as well to essay its description here. Allowing for the difference between the masculine and feminine equations, Mary apparently resembled her brother John as identically as it is possible for a woman to resemble a man. Their attachment was due to this similarity and not to mere relationship, for he had no comparable intimacy with his sister Eliza, whose letters show her as much less remarkable than Mary — all Swynfen's four children wrote enormous letters. Mary, like

[1] Appendix V.

John, was matter-of-fact, methodical, practical and administrative ; like him, as will be seen, she had plenty of courage
and determination. She was affectionate too, addressing her
husband as 'my dearest Life' and being in turn addressed by
two elderly friends (they sound elderly) as 'Madam most
dear to us Both'. All this suggests one of those life-giving
natures whose sweetness and strength are profoundly felt by
a large circle of friends, all these qualities vanishing unrecorded
with the vanishing of their source. Apart from her devotion
to her family and friends her interests were political, rather
an infrequent thing among ladies of the period, and her intelligence was keen but not specially imaginative, at least not
in an extreme or morbid degree. Straightforwardness and
commonsense seem to have been the keystones of her nature.

As for her softest and most emotional side, a curious witness to it survives, and this is her own fault. In Mary's time
it was almost a fashionable exercise for young women expect-
ing a first baby to write long, solemn letters of farewell and
admonition to their relicts and other near connections, these
missives from the tomb to be opened after their deaths, and
in only too-large a proportion of cases their forebodings were
justified. Mary's contribution to this literature is typical in
its length and unnaturally religious tone, but otherwise her
expression of her thoughts was, considering her age and social
position, bold to the point of iconoclasm. 'Bestow not that
regard on a prostitute,' the sheltered young woman exhorts
her husband, 'which was my greatest pride and boast,' and
tells him to subdue his animal nature with charitable works.
'If the expence be not too much,' she adds, with a mixture of
sentiment and economy, 'a monument to be erected ; any
mention of me, let it be plain and modest. I should be happy
to have our love for each other mentioned,' and goes on to
assure him that if he is shedding tears in the reading of this,
it cost her plenty of tears to write it ; here she is guilty of
luxuriating a little. But no sorrowing husband ever read the
letter, for Mary did not die of her first child, nor of her second,

third or fourth. Obviously, though, she could never bear to destroy her lovely composition ; perhaps she kept it hidden away and over the years took it out now and again to admire it and to feel her eyes (not unpleasurably) grow wet, and to this day it exists to betray her as a victim to author's vanity. Other evidence shows that she weathered a great many severe trials, mainly on her own. John in a letter tells her she has had more trouble than any person he has ever known, and laments his inability to give her that help 'which an unbounded affection prompts me to, an affection that can only end with the life of your J. J.' He was ready to love anyone that loved her. 'Captain Drummond, the most married domestic man alive, spoke of you in such terms that I could not help being intimate with him at first sight.'

This was the Mary who was her brother's earliest mainstay, and it may be that the roots of their intimacy were put down during the starving period of the dishonoured cheque and his efforts to repay it. The three-year exile from his own kind had not yet knocked into him that self-sufficiency for which he became noted ; he was still young enough to be lonely, and his contact with her seems literally his one resource. 'Your letter came as a reviving cordial', exclaimed, statelily, the ill-fed boy in his patched and mended clothes ; probably his bones ached at that moment from sleeping on deck. What must she have felt at her inability to send him money, but she could send him love, encouragement — and news ; he was fond of news. The one mystery seems to be how she paid the heavy postage of the time, but perhaps she saved her allowance or her mother gave her the money on the sly ; it would have to be one or the other, with Swynfen as head of the family. But so extreme was John's emotional dependence on her that in 1760, when she had just become Mrs. Ricketts, he wrote, 'I could almost wish you unmarried', fearful that the claims of her new life would diminish or stop their correspondence. He need not have worried ; sixty years later it was still going strong as ever, in all but volume.

A man of Jervis's energy and fire could hardly escape the twenties without being in love, and John, from about twenty-five or earlier, was most certainly in love. He has been described, for some strange reason, as ugly. His many portraits in various mediums prove him anything but ugly ; he was never handsome, but he was attractive as a man need be with his broad shoulders, powerful build, and the vitality that looks at one unchanging out of his changing face, for it did change over the years, considerably — except for his very clear blue eyes. At this point must be interpolated a word as to the sources of information on the girl who attracted him, and the fortunes of their courtship.

There survive massive remains of John's correspondence with his sister throughout the years, scores of letters in excellent preservation, the paper not gone too yellow nor the ink too pale. But a family censorship has been at work, this baleful industry everywhere manifest in parts cut out of the page — words, phrases or whole sentences. This always happens, naturally, just when he is working up to something especially revealing. The same pair of scissors has also mutilated his friskier moments, for enough is left to show that he could be venturesome when he liked, and probably outrageous. These letters reveal his love-affair as through the cracks in a wattled fence, by glimpses here and there — scattered glimpses, yet with a certain continuity.

A second source of information is one of those small, lucky accidents. John's other sister, Eliza, then about twenty, wrote of a country excursion she attempted with a friend. They had entirely misunderstood the remoteness of the neighbourhood where they had arranged to be put down, and once there found themselves in a wilderness miles away from everything. There was no inn, no house or farm where they could seek assistance or information ; the region was served by no stage or carrier's wagon. Staring helplessly about them in the vacuum, no doubt with the feeling that they would be there for the rest of their lives, all at once they beheld the unlikely vision of a carriage being driven rapidly towards them. Eliza, recognizing this heaven-sent apparition, remembered all at once that she had mentioned her idea of this trip to her cousin Martha. It had been very casual, the merest allusion only, but Martha had foreseen the difficulty the two girls would be in, and with no further word of her intentions had sent the family coach into the country to rescue them.

The girl, Martha Parker, was Jervis's first cousin, the daughter of Sir Thomas Parker, First Baron of the Exchequer. Close as was the relationship — Sir Thomas being the brother of Mrs. Swynfen Jervis — her social position was recognizably above that of a solicitor's family, and all allusions to her, in all the Jervis letters, are markedly formal and respectful. In Eliza's letter, for instance, was the carriage sent by cousin Martha ? No such thing ; it was sent by 'Miss Parker', and it is 'Miss Parker's' kindness over which Eliza exclaims in rapture. And by the slight miracle of this letter surviving, a ray of light is shed on what must have been a temperament unusually kind and considerate of others, qualities usually allied with gentleness, and later discovery of John's name for her — 'the gentle Pat' (or Patty) confirms the supposition.

But the third and best witnesses for Martha are two letters she wrote when nineteen years old to Mary Ricketts, which show her simply and solely as a darling. 'Forgive my great neglect in no sooner answering, for no other cause than my dull life. I waited [to write] till there was a ball, in hopes of some scandal, something our sex can enlarge on with peculiar advantage.' She and another girl had gone to a country dance at Chelmsford, but the excursion was a ghastly failure — 'lamentable to the last degree' — partners being so scarce that 'we were both nights exposed to the taunts of our own [sex] who came up to us with the horrid question, "Miss Parker, don't you dance ?"' This question, cooed no doubt too sweetly, seems to have been the partnered girl's standard technique for twisting the knife in the partnerless. So desperate were things at Chelmsford, in fact, that Martha was even willing to fall back on conversation, but alas, 'Mr. Hoare, my former partner on like occasions, constantly retreated as I approached him, fearing I suppose that I might have dancing designs on him, forgetting he was now a married man and out of all danger.' The reference to Mr. Hoare's married state inspires a mettlesome dig, for Mary herself had only recently been married. 'Because you are married you think you can make your jokes of the misses,' says Martha, mock-defiant, and reminds her, 'You was once a miss yourself.'

This was a summer letter, written in August 1760 ; the next — dated three months later, when the winter season was in full swing — indicates more hard luck for Martha, but is a love of a letter nevertheless. 'My dear Mrs. Ricketts' letter was very reviving to the depressed spirits of the unfortunate Miss Parker', she admits dolefully. 'Your short sketch of Bath revived in me a hankering to make one of your party.' For Mary in the rôle of young matron had been junketing in the lovely town whose name was synonymous with the gayest balls and assemblies in England's most fashionable company. The best of reasons, however, were keeping Martha from Bath. 'My purse at present being empty, is proof against all attacks.' So that was that : if a girl had spent her allowance too soon she could sit in the house ; no argument was permitted or — apparently — even thought of. 'How much more meritorious to stay at home than to be racketing about at Bath', she points out virtuously. 'So agreeable to my *sober* disposition, since I am naturally so averse to balls and *finery*.' She must have been fond of pretty clothes, the long-ago girl who goes on to ask an important question, for she has lent a major piece of ammunition to one of the Bath party. 'Has Fanny exhibited in the puckered [pleated?] petticoat, to the captivating of the hearts of hundreds ?' Because if Fanny has knocked over dozens of swains by means of Martha's petticoat, 'tell her that as I had a share in equipping her, I think she ought in justice to let me share some of her conquests'. But if this is too much, Martha is ready with a modified proposal. 'At least she [ought not] to do so much execution at Bath.' For if too many people there have become acquainted with the fascinating petticoat, how can Martha show herself in it elsewhere to any advantage ? Fanny ought to hold back, Martha argues, 'that I at least might have a chance.' She could send a pretty message, too. 'Tell Mrs. Knowles I will write her when I know what part of the world is so happy as to contain her.' All the letters of her earlier life display the same attractive grace, fun and self-raillery, like a constant play of sunlight on a small sparkling fountain, before the attritions of long waiting that stilled her gaiety and changed her to a woman harassed by nerves and semi-chronic invalidism.

The young dancing Martha comes down to us, too, through the letter-dialogue of John and his sister, who wrote to each other constantly about her. The trouble is, that one voice of this dialogue is missing ; Mary kept all his letters, but apparently he kept none of hers. Yet through this one-sided conversation, by statement and inference, may be traced the vicissitudes of his solitary love-affair. Mary was all for his marrying Martha, so much is clear ; she dearly loved her brother and was fond of their cousin, and the match would have been suitable in every way and not without prestige, considering the position of the bride's parents. Besides, she genuinely admired Martha. So did John, once writing to her : 'I agree with everything you say about Miss Parker,' but what did she say ? No letter survives to enlighten us. If his circumstances permitted, he goes on to assure her : 'I would make her the most unreserved proposals.' Circumstances did not permit, but obviously he relied on Mary to keep him informed during his long voyages ; he wanted to know all about Martha and how she fared, well or ill.

The stumbling-block in their situation was, of course, the usual one, and both of them knew and accepted it as insuperable. Marriage in their world was no hot brief episode, but a contract worked out by lawyers, with settlements on both sides secured to prospective children and human foresight providing, as far as possible, against emergencies and sudden disaster. If love and attraction entered into the arrangement, well and good, but matrimonial alliances were primarily designed to promote family solidarity, prosperity and importance, and no intending bride or bridegroom was allowed, for one single moment, to forget it. John was then a jobless naval captain on half-pay. He had no personal fortune, no prospects of inheritance or other private resources. In the circumstances it was unthinkable for him to propose for her, however much both of them desired it.

Barred from direct action where she was concerned, he fell back on indirect, haunting balls and country dances where she was likely to appear and exercising a touching, defensive surveillance over her fortunes of the evening. 'I did not intend dancing if she got a proper partner. Finding nobody took her out I did, and an excellent partner she is if she would take a little compassion on a man, she showed none to me and fairly danced me down.' John being danced off his feet by Martha is an attractive picture, the more so because he distrusted his performance on a ballroom floor. Yet he kept turning up at countless parties, communicating to his sister his impressions not only of one girl, but of the occasion in general. Mary was panting for news of this kind, for marriage and the arrival of a family were pinning her to a tiny, lonely hamlet called Hinton Ampner — to say nothing of other troubles, such as her gradual discovery that there was something extremely odd about the big old country house that she and her husband had rented to live in. John's long letters about normal things must have come to her, in this shivery period, with an extra quality of relief. 'I danced once, then prudently sat down', he reported to her, but his bright amused glance never sat down ; it moved ceaselessly over the assembly, pinning this creature and that for his sister's edification, and one creature in particular. 'Miss Parker was alarmed in her minuet, she near dropped down [had she an awkward partner ?] while Mrs. Parker moved ungracefully but confidently as possible, it was one of her unfortunate-looking-shape nights, you know she appears differently. Have you ever noticed', he continues with animation, having warmed up to a gentle glow of malice — and then the blank patch stares from the closely-written page, giving a view of nothing.

The most flourishing period of this attachment was apparently between 1763–72 ; flourishing, that is, in the sense that both John and Martha hoped vaguely for some great good luck that must come to save them from an endless Sahara of waiting. Or perhaps she hoped, and he found himself unable to make her look reality in the eye. It took her, at least, five years to believe that nothing was going to happen, for during that interval she permitted his attentions — significantly, for a rigid etiquette governed such things. Presumably, also, she discouraged other suitors, for we hear of no definite attempt at other marriage arrangements until John's reawakening career removed him from her horizon.

For — cruelly and ironically — this period of courtship coincided with one of his two prolonged experiences of having few jobs or being out of work altogether. The current war had just been concluded by treaty at Paris, and the prospect of a long peace meant to John what it meant then and means now to any professional military or naval man — a full stop to his career if not its virtual end, and in fact he was not to have a ship for another six years. For once in his life he could see Martha and be with her ; he had the time, but he had no money. 'My clothes are all in tatters,' he wrote his sister in '65. 'Too shabby to go among genteel people.' No rosy report, and he knew, and said as much to Mary, that if a suitable match were offered to Martha she must accept ; a naval captain on half-pay, with no prospects, could hardly expect her to pass her whole youth waiting for him.

And yet indications float to the surface again and again that — against all commonsense — he kept on trying. The

family name for Uncle Parker was 'the Chief', and John wrote
Mary from London, 'The Chief comes to town tomorrow,
when I shall sound him touching—' and then the hiatus,
unfailing, gapes in the middle of the page. But for once the
rest of the letter explains the state of affairs, almost beyond
doubt. 'I was in Bedford Row last night, Miss Parker ruddy
and extremely desirable. I presented her the bracelet but doubt
whether she will have courage to wear [some words blotted
out] painting so much uncovered.' Even in a mutilated
sentence, his offer of the bracelet and the acceptance of it by
Martha — an unmarried woman of good social position —
seem fairly indicative. The 'painting so much uncovered'
could only have been a miniature of himself in an open setting,
and with reason might he doubt that she would have the nerve
to wear an object so self-committing.

The interview with the Chief never sees the light of day
again. If it took place, John did not then propose formally for
Martha's hand ; a subsequent letter makes that much unmis-
takably clear, so was he, perhaps, gently discouraged from
coming to the point ? For a declaration of some sort must
have been his intention. In any case he had rather a brilliant
bit of luck just then, after six years of idleness ; he was com-
missioned in '69 to the *Alarm* frigate, not only as her commander but as a sort of chaperon to the Duke of Gloucester,
the King's youngest brother, who was being sent abroad for
his health. Yet even this responsibility was not enough to
displace the thought of Martha ; he was deeper in than he
knew. 'It is wonderful how much Miss Parker possesses me,
I never confined my ideas to one of your sex so long before.'
This much he admitted to Mary on October 2nd, 1770.

Within the next few days he had a letter from his sister
conveying news of first importance, that shook him from head
to foot. Martha's mother was ill and losing ground slowly ;
in Mary's opinion she could not recover. On her death,
Martha would inherit a fortune, and however Miss Parker
plain had been neglected by suitors, Miss Parker the heiress

could not fail to have them in droves. Now John was terrified
— not that she might marry someone else, but that she might
take a man who wanted her for her money. The thought of
so arid a fate for his Martha made him desperate, yet what —
at that distance — could he do ? Nevertheless, he had to do
something and his pen, half-distracted, canvasses ways and
means. 'Having married her in contemplation, I wish to
anticipate the man or men who would seek her on such principles.' Then, for one moment, he makes a full stop before
the everlasting, major impediment. 'The disparity of fortune
is at present great.' And yet he is driven to action, for if Lady
Parker 'should depart before I have an opportunity to make
proposals to Miss Parker, the rapacious disposition of mankind'
will leave Martha exposed to men whose interest in her is
purely mercenary. Suppose he got someone to propose for
him ? It must be someone who has no personal interest in the
affair, hence Mary cannot serve him. 'Situated as I am, my
passion (for it amounts to that) can only be made known by a
third person.' He suggests a Mrs. Grant, in whom he must
have had extraordinary confidence, then justifies himself
almost humbly. 'One happiness I can without vanity insure
her, that no man is more sensible of her worth or will treat her
with truer affection and tenderness.' His conclusion is apologetic, downhearted and — rarer still for him — almost abject.
'I have troubled you a good deal on this subject, but it has such
hold of me, nothing but my duty as an officer takes place of it.'
From the date of this letter — October 9th, 1770 — the
picture clouds over again for two years, but to a broken thread
of visibility it is possible to attach, here and there, reasonable
suppositions. First of all, Lady Parker recovered at least
partially, so that the crisis John wished to avert no longer
threatened Martha. He also continued writing to her and
sending her little presents, some customs-evading trifles among
them, which he instructed her to distribute ; she was not to
suppose the lot was for her, he informed her genially, adding
that her father's name was a good one to smuggle under. All

St. Vincent in his retirement

this, hardly possible if her parents had insisted on a complete break, suggests that Mrs. Grant did speak to the Parkers and that Martha's desire for even a long-term betrothal was strong enough to extort from them, for the time being, a qualified consent. But they could not have been very happy about it ; the position of her father's daughter should have enabled Martha to look higher than a poverty-stricken cousin, on whom she had already wasted six of her most attractive and engaging years, and who still could not offer definite marriage. Then suppose, after all the waiting, the engagement fell through ? The Parkers wanted something more for Martha than her surviving them as a wealthy spinster.

It took a further two years to justify their misgivings, to cure Martha of her hope, and to make John acknowledge, at last, the death-knell of his. Another peace-treaty was ratified, and in the withered, resigned tone of a man who has beaten the bounds of a problem a thousand times, only to end up short against the same obstacle, he wrote Mary : 'All present view of advancing my fortune being blasted by the Convention, let all which has passed concerning Miss Parker be buried in oblivion, my reflection having convinced me of the absurdity of such an attempt in the situation I now am'. Then, in the final discouragement of a man not only emotionally but professionally adrift, 'I do not yet know what is to become of the *Alarm* and me'. But finality is seldom clean-cut ; there yet remained various ends to be tied up. 'I enclose a bill of lading for two little boxes of Essence for toilettes, packed up in a deal case and addressed to Miss Parker. They cannot be got from the ship without the bill of lading.' Urgently and in a good deal of detail he asks Mary to send for them, and concludes, 'Dispose of them how you please'. Trifling matter as this was, it stayed on his mind for months. He was acutely worried that by some mischance they would reach Martha, small painful reminders of something she would rather forget.

Now, separate and far apart, John and Martha entered

P

upon the winter of their discontent, Martha of course getting
the worst of it. By now she had missed her market, as the
cruel saying is, and her parents became energetic at once in
trying to salvage a bad situation and arrange for her some
sort of marriage. Hopes of a brilliant or important match
had long since been given up ; anything would do that presented the bare bones of respectability or acceptableness. How
Martha responded to these attempts is a sealed book, so that
no one can lay at her door with definiteness the undoubted
fact that nothing went smoothly. Her nerves and general
health were eroded by this time and there are indications
that she was losing her looks ; a disappointed woman no
longer in her first youth might offer, in any case, little stimulus
to courtship.

While all this was going on, Mary was keeping John fully
informed as to details of Martha's unhappiness, and receiving
indications that he was in no flourishing state himself. How
can she look at this one, his letters fulminate at this time,
how can she consider that one ! For two of the suitors were
known to him, and his comments paint them as sufficiently
dire. One of them, he concedes acidly, is indeed a *good* young
man, but something more than goodness would be pleasant,
such as attractiveness. 'That the Chief and her [Lady Parker]
should ever consent to a match so inferior is indeed a matter
of astonishment.' And what will become of Patty in the
dullness to which they are willing to consign her ? 'I cannot
conceive of so great a transition from the genteel, easy,
pleasant way she now lives in, to that of an insipid round of
uninteresting events in a neighbourhood she has not the
least esteem for.' And can Martha herself feel any degree of
pleasure in the prospect ? 'How does Miss Patty bear the
unexpected start ?' [new development ?] Then he betrays
himself still more by reversing his stand on an old matter.
Previously his only concern had been to prevent his present
of perfume from reaching Martha ; now he tells Mary,
'Should the boxes of Essence come safe, present one to Miss

Parker'. Consciously or unconsciously he wanted Martha to be reminded of him, in this moment when she was under pressure to accept an undesirable husband.

No marriage came off, however, as a result of the elder Parkers' efforts. Whether their daughter or the suitors backed out is not revealed, but clearly the situation emphasized Martha's despondent state of mind. 'I feel for her exceedingly,' John groaned in response to some upsetting report from Mary. 'At this present moment I would marry her.' He was far away and helpless, and shortly afterwards was out of a job again.

Returned to London, however, he continued to see Martha from time to time. Improbable that he called on her — he could not stand very high in the good graces of Uncle and Aunt Parker, who might with reason lay Martha's unmarried state at his door — but he must have encountered her about town ; they knew practically everyone in common.

These random contacts took place from July to October 1772. By then John had had enough of the London round, which in any case was hard on a half-pay captain's pocket. A fluent command of French was requisite for a man still hopeful of a career in the world theatre, and living in France was cheap ; he would take a trip there to perfect his command of the language. His farewells in England, however, were not entirely lighthearted. 'Here I am, my dearest sister [Calais] attempting French to every person I meet, male and female, principally the latter, as usual. Not a word of this to the gentle Pat, from whom I parted like a shabby rascal, as I always have felt myself with her.' This seems to indicate no complaint, no reproach on Martha's part ; she would still like him to speak if he could.

This shadow notwithstanding, he enjoyed himself in France, jotting down in his diary — for a man whose accomplishments were pure nineteenth century — some strange sights out of an olden time, out of fairy-tales almost. 'Amiens, a large old town — saw the curious hydraulic machine which

throws up the water 82 feet to supply the town. Saw the
Prince of Condé, his son and retinue go out a hunting attended
by twelve grooms in jack-boots with two led horses each.
The Prince a handsome man of 36, his son a fine lad of 16 who
is already married and has a son. Saw the King and Royal
Family at table. The Seine covered with old barges for the
washerwomen. The villages a chaos of dung and dirt, no
wonder they are devoured with vermin in the summer heats —
the peasants wretched, scarce a healthy man unless in the army,
or a lackey. Waited on my banker in boots and travelling
dress.' Thus attired, he got rather a cool reception. In consequence, 'Always go to your Banker well-drest and in your
carriage,' he advised his diary.

His letters to Mary, of course, rattled away on themes quite
different. 'To be virtuous is here the most contemptible of
characters. This, as a batchelor, one might find convenient,
but the indelicacies of the French women are too bad to relate,
at least in a letter.' This is characteristic Jervis, early, middle
and late ; he had a strong stomach for anything but grossness.
'The only merit they have', he continues, of the reprobated
French girls, 'is being elegantly clean *where covered up.*' He
might have anticipated the ribald query such a statement would
prompt.

But as usual his travelling years as far as Russia and Sweden
(1772–75) failed to take him far from the thought of Martha.
'I feel very sensibly [keenly] Miss Parker's situation and wish
most ardently to be in a state of independence which would
allow me to offer myself to her. Till then I am prevented by a
conflict of passions to advance one step. Any attempt in my
present situation would certainly be fruitless and subject me to
many mortifying circumstances.' The earlier, lost interview
with Uncle Parker, whatever its character, must have served as
a warning.

In '75 the drums of war began to sound again, and John's
career woke up. First the outbreak of the American Revolution, then France coming in as an American ally and declaring

war on England, meant that a naval man might take new hope for his future. And, in fact, the hope, so long elusive and so waited for, materialized in his capture of the French ship-of-the-line *Pégase*, 74 guns. Only recently he had supplicated Mary, as his one prop, 'It will be a charity to write me'. How badly he needed her letters he made no effort to disguise : 'Never let a post pass without writing, my dear sister'. It was also precisely at this time that he betrayed the first rankling of disappointment by growling, 'I hear of marriages everywhere, universal bankruptcy must next ensue', when in point of fact he wanted nothing so much as to get married himself.

Now, however, happiness was not so remote. The *Pégase* was a sensational victory, and on all sides Jervis's professional superiors and equals acclaimed him. 'My pen is not equal to the good conduct, bravery and discipline of Captain Jervis, his officers and seamen. Is it not surprising that he should take a ship of equal force without losing a man ?' For actually Jervis, who got two black eyes from a splinter striking the top of his nose, seems to have been the major shipboard casualty. He looked as if he had been in a fist-fight, he reassured Mary ; his eyesight was in no danger, and he needed it to cope with the congratulations that came rolling in like a tide. These included a blessing from the Quaker, James Fox, in beautiful calm handwriting : 'May thy life be long preserved, happy and honourable to thyself.'

He returned to London as after other wars, but the man who came back this time was Captain Sir John Jervis, trailing about him the glories of the *Pégase* — not only in the shape of a knighthood, but of prize-money in noticeable sums. And of all the praises that rang about him, who shall say that the most joyful in his ears was not sounded by a brief note, 'Congratulations on the deserved honours you have acquired,' signed, Thomas Parker, the man he had not dared ask for his daughter's hand ?

Now that he could present himself in a character other than a shabby half-pay captain fearful of a rebuff, things moved more smoothly but still not quickly. On Christmas Day, 1782, he wrote Mary that Martha looked better than he had seen her for a long time and they would be married as soon as possible, but that 'her confinement has been terrible'. The illness was serious enough to postpone their wedding to the summer of '83, nor can even so constant an affection be made to sound, at this late day in their lives, romantic. Twenty years of waiting had lost them the high and hopeful moments of love — youth, ardour, fun, the prospect of children — but their waitings were not in any sense to be compared. His left him free to range the world in the exercise of a profession full of action, variety and command ; hers to wither on the vine at home and to lose her health. If Martha put him through the hoop during the latter years of their married life, one spectator at least was not without a mean satisfaction and a feeling that she was getting a little of her own back. Nor was her vigorous temperament ever quelled ; as long as she was identifiably Martha Parker she remained a person of strong feelings, and up to an advanced age was ferociously jealous of 'my admiral', as she called him.

A third resident in John's heart — a collective resident — was Mary's family of two sons and two daughters. He loved them all dearly, the girls figuring in all his letters as 'loves' and 'doves' : the eldest son, Henry, was his nearest approach to having a son of his own. He was completely at Mary's service in his desire to help her children, yet when she approached him on the subject of having Henry join his ship as a midshipman, she learned that where her brother's profession was concerned, not even she must expect to be handled with kid gloves. In a stiff, cold letter he agreed that certainly he could get Henry entered in his ship, but that if either of them counted on the family connection doing them any good, they were very much mistaken. Ties of blood were less than nothing to him in such a case, he warned her, except that he would expect more from a relation than from a stranger, and that in fact he would throw out an unsatisfactory nephew rather faster than a boy who was no kin to him at all. Obviously — and deliberately — he was trying to make the prospect as forbidding as possible, and if Henry were that easily discouraged it was all the better.

Henry was not discouraged, however, and joined the *Foudroyant* as a mid, and a few months later Jervis was making Mary's heart glad : 'Henry's conduct is above praise, I never saw such a boy in my life. His sense, judgment and propriety of behaviour in the relation he bears to me is not to be described, and his carriage and appearance of health are improved immeasurably. He is active, properly inquisitive, and much more laborious and persevering than I had thought him capable of.' The genuineness of his uncle's delight may be measured against the yardstick of his first harshness. Nor was Jervis any wet-nurse, yet he managed to keep an eye out for Henry's general welfare. 'He does not much relish the salt junk [pork] of which I shall not allow him to eat to the prejudice of his health. The great joy of his heart seems to be in visiting other ships and going on any service in boats.'

Yet Jervis's love for this attractive nephew turned — by a cruel irony of fate — into a trap that closed on him and from which there was no extricating himself. The earldom, viscounty and other honours he received after the battle of St. Vincent could not descend in his own line since he had, in the classic phrase, no heirs of his body. This being the case, he held the titles with a 'remainder' to the males in his sister's line — that is, express permission for Henry to succeed as earl and viscount after St. Vincent's death. The danger of the 'remainder' device lay in the fact that once the title and the moneys or properties that went with it were transferred to a secondary line, there they had to stay ; however bad the arrangement proved to be in the end, they could not be withdrawn and bestowed a second time.

So it turned out in Henry's case. Who could have foreseen that at thirty-seven, a promising naval captain, he would be drowned ? Yet this is the blow that fell on Mary Ricketts

and her brother, and as Henry had left two daughters but no
son his death meant that the title descended to Edward, Mary's
second boy. Edward, as it happened, had married a girl whom
all his family loathed to an extraordinary degree, and since
they were pleasant and reasonable people, there must have
been something to justify their attitude ; St. Vincent's mildest
name for her was 'vicious', and her oldest son was apparently
an exact replica of his mother. St. Vincent had loved Henry
devotedly ; he hated his great-nephew with equal devotion,
yet it was to this great-nephew that his titles would eventually
come — and not the titles only but the handsome pension
that went with them, and however St. Vincent writhed at the
thought there was absolutely nothing he could do about it.
In his rage he struck out about him right and left, not sparing
even Mary : 'Your miscreant grandson is about to complete
his ruin by marrying the illegitimate daughter of a swindler.
He had the impertinence to propose that I make him an
annual allowance of £500, when I assured him that he would
never receive a farthing from Your affectionate brother, St.
Vincent.'

In a sort of family scrapbook there survives an odd memorial to Henry, a water-colour sketch in which he is represented
as a midshipman, leaning against the tomb that commemorates
him as a grown man. The little boy, his brown hair neatly
brushed and his blue jacket unbuttoned, smiles pleasantly at
you out of the drawing ; in his left hand he holds a sailor's
dirk and his right arm rests on top of an ivy-grown stone that
reads :

> To The Memory of Captain William Henry Jervis [1]
> Unfortunately Drowned.
> Cut off from Nature's and from Glory's Course,
> Which Never Mortal was so Fond to Run.

Behind him is the calmest blue sea and on it — far, far out
— a three-masted ship in full sail.

* * *

[1] Both Mary's sons took the name of Jervis.

The frame that held the long latter period of St. Vincent's life, with its affections of family and friendship, was Rochetts, his house in Essex. And there it still stands, a reminder of how well a man could do himself then on two or three thousand a year ; a vast dark rectangle unadorned except for a sort of massive grey marble hoop set above french doors at the narrow end of the oblong. Enormous stretches of park surround it ; a few minutes' distant is a high-speed motorway, but here everything is silent, remote, withdrawn, and over the whole a thin silvery patina of mist on this chilly day. After all these years the sense of St. Vincent's ownership is still so strong that a hesitancy dogs one's footsteps, a continual waiting for him to appear. Everything must be much as he knew it, except perhaps the trees are fewer. The gate-keeper's beehive lodge is still intact, and just outside the entrance are the stumps of two monster oaks at least four feet across, and the disappearance of this towering, living portal of green is a great loss. The Earl mentioned it fondly more than once, and the sight of him standing beneath it, one day, caused Miss Knight to smite her lyre and write a poem. He also added a stone tower to one end of the house, they tell you, so that he could climb to its top and have a view of the sea. But the tower was considered ugly by succeeding owners, who pulled it down, and in any case the Earl was hardly fit, for many years before his death, to do much climbing. He loved Rochetts and was always anxious to return to it — 'to its calm shades', he said once, source of the surmise that there may have been more trees — and since he was master of that house, certain things about it may be taken for granted. He hated cold, so it was warm ; he hated dead air, so it was well-ventilated ; he hated dirt and disorder, so it was beautifully kept inside and out. Even as a very young man on a country visit he had written to Mary, 'Our bedrooms here are nasty because of a sluttish chamber-maid they brought with them from London,' so presumably nothing slack ever got a foothold at Rochetts. The house had been the home of Martha's parents at one time, so that its face had for them a double familiarity, an extra affection and repose. Bills survive that testify to the lavishness of its furnishings and equipment and also to the scale of the catering : every delicacy, chocolate and truffles ; and the guest had his choice of three kinds of tea.   And — like solidified echoes of a great career — the house was full of extraordinary souvenirs, freedoms of cities enclosed in magnificent boxes of native woods set in gold, the sword that was the gift of the City of London, the bâton presented him by William IV and described by Miss Brenton : 'Covered with true blue velvet and studded with gold lions all around, a wreath of oak leaves and acorns in dead gold around each end, another wreath immediately above of the thistle and shamrock blended, the top furnished with a beautiful George and dragon'.   More stirring even than these was the great hall full of torn and battered trophies of naval warfare ; the fragment of a mainmast, flags brought to him by seamen like Captain Palmer whose greatest pride was their association with the old commander :

The Last Tricolor
Won
By the Naval Flag of Great Britain
The Colors of L'Etoile, captured March 27,
1814, most respectfully dedicated to John,
Earl of St. Vincent ; the Offering of a
grateful pupil to an illustrious master.

On all sides things like these reminded you that you were in the house of a man who had had a life not given to one in a million.

In this pleasant temple of well-earned repose and good living, company came and went incessantly, and planted rock-like in the ebb and flow were a few old friends, intimates of the family for many, many years, for the Earl did not only attach people to himself in lifelong friendship, he reciprocated with lifelong fidelity ; he never wearied of those he loved through seeing them too often or knowing them too well. First of all, perhaps, came Dr. Baird.   Second came Benjamin Tucker, the first sight of his name in the Mediterranean dispatch-books heralding a long connection full of things known, but also not known. In 1799 St. Vincent notified his superiors that 'an Agent Victualler is indispensably necessary to supply the Mediterranean Fleet', and that he had appointed Tucker, son of a purser already known to him. In about five minutes by the clock, Tucker seems to have made himself indispensable to the great man, who wrote the Admiralty in so many words that 'I cannot possibly go on without Mr. Tucker.' Why Tucker is so essential the Earl fails to say, merely adding, 'He is to follow me home as soon as he brings up his cash accounts.' Therefore, when St. Vincent left for England to recover his health, he had in his entourage not one person — Baird — but two, who were inseparably attached to him till the day of his death. Apparently he had scented in Tucker the same satellite-like predisposition as in Baird, and apparently also he welcomed this characteristic in a man who was sufficiently useful, rather than finding it burdensome.

At this point, with a quality of shock, comes a sudden realization : in five years of turning over letters from St. Vincent's enormous circle of friends and acquaintants, there is found not one single reference to Tucker.[1] No one, male or female, describes him ; no one speaks of him in terms either of like or dislike, although the Earl had him constantly at Rochetts on business and as a guest ; apparently no one thought him important enough to mention. This theory is at least plausible in the light of future developments, and upholds an additional surmise that Tucker may have been, in the Earl's pleasant household, the core of a smouldering jealousy, all the worse for having to be kept under, and bursting from conceal-ment only when death had withdrawn the restraint of St. Vincent's presence. Through his connection with the Earl, the inconspicuous secretary associated constantly with gentle-folk though not one of them, nursing who knows what obscure

---

[1] Brenton's *Life of St. Vincent* has — strangely enough, in view of future developments — a pleasant paragraph about him (p. 385). According to this he was talented, well educated and had 'intelligent black eyes'.

resentments — not against the prime favourite Baird, as might
be assumed, but against someone else. Baird, in any case,
was Tucker's family physician, and there are references to
a daughter of abnormal size, perhaps from some glandular
irregularity, who needed constant attention. 'I tremble for
Rachel Tucker', St. Vincent had written Baird at one time.
'The load of flesh she carries has always seemed to me a hotbed
of disease.' The effluvium of this pathological grossness,
joined to the quite unconnected fact that Tucker allowed himself to be used as a cat's-paw in the Nelson lawsuit — a rôle
which a man of sensitive honour, however devoted to the
Earl, must have refused — conveys to one beholder at least a
vague atmosphere of inferior stock and inferior standards, or
at least succeeding events do not altogether give the lie to such
a conclusion. Nevertheless, Tucker functioned for the last
twenty-five years of St. Vincent's life as his confidential secretary and business agent, and there is no doubt that St. Vincent
was deeply attached to him. Otherwise it is difficult to pin
Tucker for a prolonged scrutiny ; the flare of hatred that
lights him up for an instant is quickly snuffed out, and again
he slips back into the shadow.

More attractive — or the most attractive fixtures of St.
Vincent's household, rather — were a constellation of maiden
ladies ; they moved about a good deal on visits of their own,
but the Earl seemed to make a point of having at least two in
residence, as company for Lady St. Vincent. Of course, not
all of them emerge in equal relief ; the two most distinct, Miss
Knight and Miss Brenton, came from naval families, while
Miss Rainsford was either a sister or daughter of General
Rainsford in London, at whose house Lady St. Vincent often
stayed when she came up to town on her own ; her husband,
when writing to the General, would thank him for his kindness
to 'my dame'. Miss Knight, easily the most remarkable of the
galaxy, was an admiral's daughter, widely travelled, had lived
in the best society of Paris, Rome and Naples, known Nelson
and Emma from the early days of their acquaintance, and taken

a walk with them which served her as the theme of some verses. She wrote verse all the time, in fact, though all the other ladies could toss off a spirited jingle at need and the Earl himself could write rhymes with the best of them. But Ellis Cornelia Knight was really a distinguished woman and in social demand, always being invited away from Rochetts, and the frequency of her departures failed to reconcile the Earl to them in any noticeable degree. He called her 'our incomparable friend' and delighted in her conversation, and St. Vincent was not the man to be impressed by mere facility of talk.

Elizabeth Brenton was different, her qualities less mental and decorative perhaps, but more utilitarian in a household increasingly plagued by illness and shaken by the unreasonableness, the crises and the storms, of sick nerves. These she withstood with unfailing patience and good humour, and the impression she gives is of one of those cheerful dependable household friends whose presence is such a Godsend in times of trouble and gloom. She was a sister of Admiral Sir Jahleel Brenton and also of the naval historian Captain Edward Brenton, and by the light of a future collision it is her link with Edward that fixes her, perhaps, a little more clearly in the memory. But in any case she and Miss Knight as principal figures, and other ladies from time to time, were kindly lights in the vast house inhabited by an old husband and wife in failing health ; and when at last the Earl was alone, their presence meant that he need not sit down to his table solitary, but always had to keep him company the pleasant, well-bred, conversable women whom he mentioned in letters as 'my demoiselles', 'my spinsters', or — when mischievously inclined — 'my nymphs'.

St. Vincent's life, from 1808 on, when he still had fifteen years to go, is simple, yet not simple. His official status was retired, which meant that he no longer sat in a central seat of power ; he could no longer make or break a man's career, hang him at the yardarm or let him off from hanging. But from his active days he retained literally thousands of contacts to make things lively, and he also went up to London to take his seat in the House of Lords so long as his health permitted, making an extra effort to be present when questions arose of special interest to him. He might not be at the hub of affairs any longer, but he had his sources of information and knew pretty well everything that went on, and was able in private letters to register his opinion of individuals and corporate bodies with a hornet-like drive and sting denied him in his high official days. Other excitements were not lacking either, for Miss Knight's eminent qualities led the Prince Regent to ask if she would accept the post of Lady-Companion to his daughter, the Princess Charlotte, which she did, so that the Earl's household enjoyed all the scandal of inmost Court circles at first-hand and red-hot — Charlotte's skirmishes and collisions with her father, his unceasing harassment of her, his attempts to marry off the tempestuous, generous, warm-hearted creature against her will — for he hated her popularity which was always rubbing into him the fact of his own unpopularity ; and worst of all through his maltreatment of her he was striking, knowingly or unknowingly, at her mother.

'I saw Miss Knight for half an hour last night, in very good looks but full of anxiety about her Princess, who report says is to be betrothed at Brighton. I do not like the manner of this proceeding.' Neither did Charlotte like it, for the latest candidate being thrust upon her was the Prince of Orange, a runt and ugly into the bargain, whom the robust handsome girl had despised at sight. St. Vincent was well-acquainted with the Regent, whose qualities in a private individual he would have damned up hill and down, yet perhaps it was not merely the aura of kingship that made him indulgent. The two men confronting each other is a picture of grotesque contrasts — the superb old commander with contours of body, mind and spirit beaten hard by a thousand ordeals and disciplines, and the great human puffball, shapeless and swollen from its constant diet of gluttony, cherry brandy, promiscuity and betrayal. The truth is that St.

Vincent found out at first-hand an exasperating fact — that it is easy to despise the Regent but hard to dislike him. 'By far the most entertaining person I ever met,' he had to admit, succumbing to the quicksilver flash and superb manner that had dazzled so many people, and after an hour and a quarter of his company had nothing unkind to say, outside of some mild criticism of his sovereign's way of life. 'The excessive heat of the rooms he lives in plays the devil with his nerves, and I have preached to him in vain.'

Excitements of the great world like these, and a constant round of visiting friends and relations, lapped the quiet shores of the Earl's country domain. His house, nevertheless, was darkened by a shadow fought off for a long time but inexorably creeping onward, that began to exhibit him in the character of a great man trapped and hedged about by a thousand domestic fetters, some merely irksome, some painfully ludicrous. The shadow, of course, was the fate that was overtaking Martha, her health never very good at any time, though there had been intervals when St. Vincent could write to Baird, 'My lady is pure well', 'pure' in this sense being a country term used jocularly by city people. Little by little, though, his letters mirror her illness and the manner in which she met illness ; she fought it hard, she was alert, exacting and determined to have her own way. Illusions appeared, more serious and unpredictable as she grew older, and harder and harder to handle. 'Our dear Martha goes on improving, she willingly submits to any restraint we think proper to impose,' St. Vincent could write Mary earlier, but for one such entry there are dozens to show that she was high-strung and anything but amenable. 'If I could get her into the air, which never circulates around her', he exclaimed once, on a note of futility. 'Her nerves are shaken to a greater degree than I ever saw before. Of course she sees everything on the wrong side and is very irritable. Don't mention this in your letters to her', he cautions hastily, sounding frightened, and in fact the great Earl and warrior lived in a constant state of intimidation and propitiation and sometimes owed it to chance that he was restored to his wife's good graces. He had taken a trip in 1806, for example, and on his return found himself in hot water : why had he not written? He had written, protested the Earl, he had written often. Very strange, sniffed his lady ; she had had no letters. But later he told Mary, 'Martha has lately received a number of letters from me in a lump, which frequently happens when writing from abroad. This seems —' here a sigh of relief — 'to have dissipated her suspicions of neglect.'

But later the word for him was badgered — badgered to a point where he was unable to call his soul his own, though his manner of imparting this has no complaint in it, only concern and endurance. 'I am so constantly in requisition, Lady St. Vincent sending for me almost every moment,' he wrote in 1811, 'that I must soon give up all correspondence.' In other words he could not count on ten consecutive minutes for his own affairs, Miss Brenton recording for Mary one detail of his servitude : 'Your dear brother is in constant attendance at her meals, which she will not touch unless he is present.' Miss Brenton herself was not to escape from the experience without a few scars, either. In the summer of 1811 Martha was better, but : 'Unfortunately as she gains strength her suspicions and fancies increase, this between us — Miss Brenton has a sad time of it.' For Martha had fastened onto the idea that her husband and her companion were profiting by her confinement to her room to carry on a flirtation downstairs, the companion's appearance being greeted by volleys of digs and spiteful hints, and Miss Brenton took it all like an angel. 'Miss Brenton bears all the innuendos with wonderful good humour and is very pleasant and cheerful,' St. Vincent records with pathetic gratitude, for apparently there were as few then as now who could take this sort of thing as a steady diet. But the random shafts and violences of a failing mind could not last forever ; the muffling curtain dropped lower and lower. A first and a second stroke took

St. Vincent in old age

from her, successively, her power of speech and her faculties, and with these words of her husband : 'My last bulletin — all hope of mental recovery is at an end', she passes from our sight.

On a January day that was bitterly cold but sunny and beautiful, the last of Martha was escorted by a nephew to the lovely lonely country church, St. Peter's in Caverswall, Staffordshire. 'The evening is favourable to the last earthly scene of my virtuous partner in this life', St. Vincent wrote, and the phrase somehow chills as anticipating Chantrey's sculpture and turning Martha into stone too soon. Yet this was not his fault ; creeping time that blurs all had blurred the image of the ruddy desirable girl who had danced her John to a standstill, and the image of an old woman lying speechless and mindless, with a hushed household waiting for her and their release, had blurred it further. Only later did her husband remember the gentle Pat, when in a letter he apologized brokenly for not being able to give sufficient consideration to some problem, as he was 'so unhinged' by his wife's death. An order for 'a ream of black-edged paper of the best quality, a pound of black sealing-wax, a box of black wafers' recalls the chill, but a little later he was pitiably upset because her will was to be read that evening. Yet one aftermath of this event made him pluck up sufficiently to open a new door for himself, since a discovery of his, among Martha's belongings, was a small medicine-chest. It gave him an idea, and he sent it to Baird in London. 'Please fill this,' he said in effect, 'with remedies such as a person like myself, not a doctor, can give to the village people when they are ill but not seriously ill. I am tired of seeing them cheated and victimized by harpies of the so-called doctor tribe.'

For this was the great preoccupation of his days, as age and uncertain health cut him off from other interests : the care of people helpless, piteously bewildered and poor and adrift, whose predicament was no fault of their own. His regular outlay in this direction was enormous : 'The air is very

Q

piercing, and instead of a Christmas bounty in money, Miss
Brenton is distributing blankets, woollen stockings and flannel
for underclothing to the poor, according to their separate
wants or choice, which with their supply of soup weekly and
of fuel annually will, I hope, administer to their comfort'.
But his care went beyond lord-of-the-manor benefactions,
however extensive, and took on the far weightier burden of
securing a lifelong provision to those who were facing the
almshouse, for upon his door beat a ceaseless tattoo of appeals,
entreaties, cries for help from old seamen of every rank and
their families ; wherever he turned he was confronted with
their perplexities and miseries, and in all the massive record
of his daily correspondence — copied in duplicate and pasted
up in journals — there is not one single refusal on the score of
his own age and ill-health. He tried to do something for all
of them, taxing and ransacking his own resources, and when
these failed he wrote begging letters far and wide, a task as
disagreeable and exhausting as any on earth. Usually, too,
he got part or all of what he was after : 'I think old Goddard
will be relieved, and he and his old woman pass the remainder
of their days in comfort'. But Goddard or his counterpart
was forever on his doorstep, and with failing sight and stiffen-
ing hands (*I never yet have forsaken any man who served well
under me*) he wrote, wrote, wrote on behalf of one or the
other who had turned to him as a final hope on earth.

An interest less taxing and far more amusing was Captain
Edward Brenton, a visitor to Rochetts since 1813. The
captain was brother to Miss Elizabeth, an experienced naval
man and a professional writer ; he is responsible for some
lurid and discredited stories about Emma Hamilton at the
scene of the Jacobin executions at Naples, yet out of his style
in his *Life of St. Vincent* distils an agreeable personality, reasonable and direct. He was then working on his naval history,
and as his friendship with St. Vincent progressed the Earl
did something kind and generous for him ; he gave Brenton
the run of the muniment-room at Rochetts and told him he

could copy, for publication, any public or private letter from certain important documents. This permission included Miss Brenton, who was allowed access to the same records at any time, in case her brother needed copies of anything while in London.

Of course Brenton was delighted, as no writer could fail to be at so sizeable an advantage, but in the midst of his pleasure he retained an extraordinary degree of forethought. 'I lost not a moment in procuring a letter-book', and would Lord St. Vincent, 'write in it, with his own hand, that I had his permission to undertake this work?' The Earl agreed 'with great satisfaction' and wrote on the first page, 'Captain Edward Brenton has permission to make such extracts or copies from my letter- and order-books while commander-in-chief in the Mediterranean and Channel Fleets, as he may conceive useful to him. 16 May, 1817. [Signed] St. Vincent.'

When Brenton had the remarkable astuteness to obtain this specific permission, he could not see in what good stead it would stand him. Or — could he ? Perhaps he had already taken the measure of the Earl's inner circle ; perhaps, in case trouble should arise later, he had a fair idea of the direction from which it would come. In the meantime here he was, a gentleman quite at home in the library and muniment-room at Rochetts, and Tucker, perhaps not quite a gentleman, watching his familiar comings and goings with green eyes.

Another piece of luck St. Vincent decidedly had in his old age : in 1816 he could write, 'Thanks, my dear sister, for your 81st good wish', for the friend of his first days survived until his last days. He and Mary still wrote to each other not less than once or twice a week, apparently never retailing complaints or symptoms, and at the age of eighty-five he recommended a maid to her and, if you please, in verse.

> The bearer, M. Jarvis, is civil and trusty,
> She never as yet has made gadding her trade ;
> She suffers no music, no books to get dusty ;
> I think she will make you a nice parlour-maid.

But Mary's muse, at eighty-three, was more than equal
to pointing out where her brother's judgment had gone
wrong :

> My Lord, I'm obliged for the character sent,
> And am heartily glad with the maid you're content ;
> But you are not aware what a *creature* she is,
> So horribly pert, so addicted to Quiz! [1]
> And if my advice, noble brother, you'd follow,
> You'll send her a-packing, with a whoop
> and a hollow.

Their early communications, however — the big sheets
closely covered with firm handwriting — had dwindled little
by little to tiny notepaper bearing a few lines, shakier all the
time, more and more spidery and trembling, and at last they
had to dictate what they wished to say to each other : the
long, long correspondence drawing to a close. Yet even so
there were notes of comfort, as when on a July evening St.
Vincent told her, 'Elizabeth and Mary, my constant companions, desire I will add their duty and love'. Earlier in the
letter he had said, 'Dr. Baird is sitting by my side'.

Which brings us again to Baird — and to the part he
played in the last twenty-odd years of St. Vincent's life. Evidence in plenty supports the conclusion that in importance and
affection he came second only to Mary, for, like Mary, he
religiously saved every word the Earl ever wrote him, down
to scraps of paper with jottings or reminders. And there they
all are in the National Maritime Museum, three red-leather
folders bulging with no fewer than seven or eight hundred
letters, and though again the dialogue is one-sided — it is only
St. Vincent's voice that we hear — they testify very remarkably
and impressively to the unrestricted confidence that can exist
between two men.

In the first place, Baird was St. Vincent's main link, in his
retirement, with what was going on in various Admiralty
departments. Ironically, the investigation of 1805 touched off

[1] Sardonic back-chat.

by St. Vincent — in which the doctor himself had given important evidence — was the beginning of Baird's downfall. Or 'downfall' is perhaps too drastic a word ; yet the modernity that St. Vincent channelled into naval affairs led to a scrutiny of the existing medical set-up, and to a consequent decision to overhaul and change completely the system in which Baird — backed to the limit by the Earl's prestige and authority — held so commanding a position. But the Earl was no longer a First Lord or any Lord at all of the Admiralty, and when the armour of his protection fell away from his friend and physician Baird found himself exposed, almost at once, to attack from those not inclined to regard his appointment as irrevocable or heaven-sent — which in turn sheds a certain amount of light on Baird's temperament and professional attitudes.

St. Vincent's retirement was, to Baird, a double calamity ; a loss not only of support but of control. For the Earl in his days of power was able to manage Baird exactly as one manages an impetuous horse, now holding him back, now soothing and gentling him, now giving him his head. Once this restraint was withdrawn, however — once his advice was no longer official, only unofficial — Baird charged ahead blindly, crashing into this one and that one and creating opposition and hatred in all directions. As a superior, apparently, he was rigid, demanding and high-handed. If he had been so not for his own glory, but for the sake of medical perfection, he did not for that reason raise up any fewer enemies. Too many of his subordinate colleagues had smarted under his criticism and caustic reprimands. Now they turned on him together, their attack spearheaded by a Dr. Harness, who was bold and pertinacious and who challenged, totally, Baird's right to regard naval medicine as being under his domination. He had no mean opponent ; Baird was also a good hater, tenacious, conscious of his ability and integrity and fighting hard for his position. The affair developed into a long-term quarrel of virulent animosities, of claims and counter-claims, with ultimate hearings in the House of Commons.

All this failed to strip Baird of his position immediately, but its long-range effect was to surround him with an aura of dictatorship and general inability to get along with people. The Admiralty made a note of everything, and the Admiralty had a long memory. In 1822 a drastic shake-up and reorganization of Navy medicine placed central powers of control in the newly constituted Victualling Board. At once Baird submitted his qualifications for an appointment to this body. By way of reply he received, from the First Lord, a crusher. Baird was not to be considered for the Victualling Board, wrote Lord Melville, for his presence upon it would prevent transactions from being carried on 'with that cordiality and desire of mutual cooperation which the Government have a right to expect'. The solace he offered was not of much comfort, perhaps, to Baird's lacerated spirit. 'I agree entirely with Lord St. Vincent that you have a claim to the most liberal allowance, on your retirement, which the Admiralty have it in their power to grant.' Then, on the neck of the old doctor's pride, he dropped the lethal hatchet : 'It is intended to abolish the office which you now hold'.

All this and more is mirrored in St. Vincent's hundreds of answers to Baird's discontents, discouragements and apprehensions. Unable to take his part actively during the endless feud with Harness and other doctors, the Earl rallied to his side with inexhaustible moral and oral support ; he has written Lord Melville 'to show that to *you*, not to Dr. Harness, the public is indebted for the system which has preserved the health of our ships' crews' : he assures him that the Cabinet 'is well aware of the difficulty of your office, and the enormous and malignant attacks THE STRICT PERFORMANCE OF YOUR DUTY SUBJECTS YOU TO' : he helps Baird abuse his opponents, 'the imbeciles of the Sick and Wounded Board', and applauds Baird's occasional victories : 'I feasted on your triumph over the serpents at Portsmouth'. All the same he was aware of the doctor's failings : 'I advise you to be extremely guarded in your conversation'. Later he cautions him with even more

emphasis : 'My advice is, that you keep quiet ; never com-
mit yourself by writing letters hastily ; take special care to
keep within your instructions,' — for even he had once rebuked
Baird for his "intemperate zeal" — 'avoid argument with
people who have the entrée at the Admiralty.' Then he sums
it all up : 'You have only to preserve your temper.'

In the painful days when Baird felt himself being shouldered
out of his high position, St. Vincent's sympathy was ever-
ready : 'To exclude you would be a monstrous injustice'.
But when the blow fell, his concern had in it overtones of
resignation : 'I am more shocked than surprised at the brutality
with which you have been treated,' and later on the resignation deepens to a point where he says a surprising and uncharacteristic thing. 'The best counsel I can give you is ;
compose your mind and think as little as possible of the past,
present and future.' A novel text for St. Vincent, who had
never practised or preached submission. When he wrote it,
he was eighty-three. It had taken a long, long time to wear
him down to the point where he could advise : Don't think,
merely accept.

If Baird unloaded his troubles wholesale on St. Vincent,
the process was not one-sided ; St. Vincent in return confided
the state of his health in equal detail and continuity. The
discomforts great and small that attend old age and the failing
human mechanism, all these were poured into Baird's end-
lessly-attentive and endlessly-concerned ear. He wanted to
know everything so that he could relieve his friend, and St.
Vincent obliged with the most uninhibited and intelligent
chronicle of his various torments : his painful legs, the loss
of power in his hands, and most of all the malign visitant in
his chest that all Baird's resources could not dislodge, the
cough that racked him day and night and whose mention, in
letter after letter, one comes to dread. 'It was kind of you
to send the medicine, as you were prevented giving us the
pleasure of your company, which', he adds wistfully, 'I had
counted on.' But he could always count on Baird's help if

not his presence. 'Happily the pill composes me at night, otherwise I should be worn down.' Some of his treatment was self-prescribed : 'Poached eggs and spinnage has been my food the last two days and it agrees with me'. But on the heels of the poached eggs, up speaks the old seaman : 'Work is being suspended on the breakwater at Plymouth in order to keep up our enormous standing army, the greatest of all evils that can befall this country'.

For his health concerned him only so far as it forced itself upon his attention ; a thousand other things interested him more, and he was as keen for personal, professional and political gossip as most people, if they would admit it. And Baird the faithful supplied it, painting in vivid colours not only his departmental rows, but the whole London scene, and plenty was going on. The incredible show in the House of Lords, for example, where daily appeared a stout painted woman contesting the divorce action her husband was bringing against her ; a little crazy from her racketing, wandering, outcast life, and perfectly brazen in her craziness, Caroline Queen of England sat listening to the testimony of low servants brought over from obscure French and Italian inns to bear witness to her activities, nocturnal and otherwise. 'I am told the Queen was in high spirits on Saturday', St. Vincent comments wonderingly. 'Not a little extraordinary, after the filthy evidence the chambermaid of the inn at Iscia gave the day before.' Perhaps Baird went up to the visitors' gallery, as it appears in the painting of the trial, and with other men leaned far over the railing to stare down at the pilloried creature below.

Baird knew the Duke of Wellington too, and St. Vincent had some pungent things to say of his family : 'The Wellesleys, all-powerful, are such a grasping tribe' that all of them, he thinks, will get State jobs. Baird's reporting must have been lively, for St. Vincent could never get enough of it : 'Very interesting, and I will thank you to continue.' He and his sister are greatly interested in the divorce action, and would be grateful for London newspapers. The two men had fallen also into a comfortable city habit : 'I hope you will continue to dine with me in Mortimer Street, where we can talk over, at our leisure, men and things.' The doctor's visits to Rochetts were no less important to him : 'Your approach has given me fresh life and spirits'. Nor did he make any secret of the fact that his need for Baird's presence, at times, was great : 'I never feel so comfortable as when you are alongside. You will be doubly welcome on Saturday, for this house will be very forlorn after parting with our pleasant guests'. Very occasionally their rôles were reversed, and it was the Earl who prescribed (not without impatience) : 'For God's sake banish these chimeras and rush into society, which you are formed for. — Your declining to mix with the world is not good policy,' he exhorted vigorously on another occasion. 'I am sure it is bad.' So it seems that Baird wearied him with his everlasting embroilments and dejections, but there are good reasons why no utterance of Baird's survives to prove it. No less than four times over a short interval St. Vincent assured him, 'Your budget, in conformity with directions, is committed to the flames', proving Baird's almost-morbid anxiety to have his letters destroyed as soon as read.

And interspersed with more important subjects were endless reports on local doings : 'A young sucking parson made his appearance today [Sunday] : Jack Martin is supposed to be on his beam ends'. An unnamed acquaintance is about to marry unsuitably : 'He must have a good gulp to swallow the stain and vulgarity annexed to the young lady'. A neighbour, Morgan, is ill with what he calls rheumatic fever ; St. Vincent calls it an overloaded stomach. Another neighbour has given them some uncommonly high venison 'on the occasion of his son's being diapered', and the Douglases contemplate bringing a libel action against someone, but : 'Who are *they* to sue, he is an intemperate man'. Then a second ecclesiastical bulletin : 'The archdeacon is getting worserer and worserer'. With a few strong strokes, also, he could sketch more subtle

aspects of temperament.   Of a certain judge :   'He showed
more courage than belongs in his character.'   Of a certain
Duke :   'He is a stupid drunken hospitable fox-hunter.'   Of
Wolfe, dead for so many years :   'Fascinating in his manners,
a great actor, very ambitious, and could see into every man's
breast.'   Vivid jottings like these are spatters of light and shade
on a thousand people, customs and events long-lost.   St.
Vincent's vocabulary, in fact, grew younger as he grew older :
'Your brother medicos are bloody dogs, and if you had not
arrived, would have sent half the Johnnys in the *Maida* to
Kingdom Come.'   Vigorous expression, however, was nothing
new with him ;   years before, the hearty indecency of his language regarding a dishonest provisions contractor is such as to
put it permanently beyond the bounds of quotation.

From 1818 his clear decisive handwriting began to vary a
good deal, its fluctuations seeming to keep pace with every
setback in his health.   Concurrently, in this his eighty-third
year, came a change in his temperament.   Hardness faded from
his face and only benignity was left ;   one day, to Baird, he
made a tremendous admission :   'We expect too much of
men.'   Incompetence had always brought out the worst in
him, but now he said of James, a servant, 'He has never yet
carried a message or an answer correctly,' yet there is no mention of sacking James.   The Admiral had begun to put up with
things, to make allowance for stupidity and shortcomings.
Never for impertinence, though ;   his new mildness never
extended to that, as people found out quickly.   People like the
Beecheys, for example ;   and the affair was doubly unfortunate
because Sir William Beechey, of all painters, had been most
brilliantly successful in his portraits of the Earl ;   not a canvas
but reveals some striking aspect of the man, even the very
formal presentation ones in which a personality less distinct
might be swamped by the massive robes of his Order with its
plumes and ribbons, its velvet train and gold tassels.   St.
Vincent was devoted to the Beecheys and had presented them
with expensive table-silver, but now all at once he sent Baird

on an urgent and surprising commission. Sir William has used 'language' : Lady Beechey, rallying to her spouse, has sent an 'incomprehensible' message, and the sooner he is clear of them the better. Will Baird be kind enough to go at once and get some pictures belonging to the Earl out of their hands, without seeming to know that anything is wrong ? Two months elapse, and in the interval it becomes evident that Baird, for once in his life acting the part of pacifier rather than irritant, has somehow patched up their differences and they are again on speaking terms. But St. Vincent has lost his enthusiasm for the Beecheys : 'I have not yet forgotten the puppyish reply of Sir William or the impertinent message of her Ladyship' — friendship apparently being, in its response to mishandling, as precarious a thing as love.

The hated great-nephew is another disturbance that threads its way in and out of the correspondence. Now he is trying to pump Baird about the Earl's intentions : St. Vincent, exclaiming at 'the swindler's impudence', allows himself some bitter, futile reflections on 'my hard-earned title which must fall to his son, with the annuity annexed to it ; but', he adds fiercely, 'I have taken care that he shall not squander my property.' No good whatever is to be expected of him. 'It is evident that he will not succeed in the Army.' His wife is no better, St. Vincent's mildest word for the two of them being, 'that vile fellow and his tortuous rib'.

Reminders more painful even than these, however, upset him from time to time. Old ghosts walked ; old wounds re-opened. Emma Hamilton was thirty-two years younger than St. Vincent, and it was not to be expected that she should disappear with Nelson's disappearance. From time to time the unfortunate woman broke surface, thrust up from below by her desperate need for money. Then in her extremity she would sell whatever she had to sell, tangible things if she had them and if not, intangible — intimate recollections of Nelson, unveilings of scandal long hidden. Things like this roused the Earl to fury. 'What a diabolical bitch Lady Hamilton must be to expose the weakness of Lord Nelson ; what a horrid scene she has laid open to pick up a few pounds, God help her!' And with each of her reappearances, other angers came to life in him ; it cannot be denied that on a day in October he snarled, in response to a question of Baird's, some old and some new nonsense, 'Lord Nelson's sole merit was animal courage, his private character most disgraceful in every sense of the word'. Only the hurt inflicted by a loved person festers on and on, unhealing and unforgiven.

He could forgive though, with zest, newspaper reports of his death. 'I am not surprised that the Runners in London had kilt me dead, I shall not die the sooner ; I am getting up my health, my legs are fine as a deer's, and', he brags, 'my spirits have never failed, Ever your most hale St. Vincent.' The most hale was right in saying that his spirit had never hauled down its flag, but his body forced from him sadder and sadder admissions. 'I feel very strongly the kind interest you take in my health, which is indeed precarious. Thank you', he adds touchingly, 'for the means you are taking to keep me warm.' The delicacy that was his forbade him to take even long-standing love or kindness for granted ; his gratitude was a fountain ever-springing. So was his optimism. 'A change of atmosphere has produced the most salutary effects on my carcass, and after a night of sound rest I feel deadly lively, as they say in Hampshire.'

One thing he never let be halted by his unsatisfactory health : the procession of relatives and friends that poured in and out of Rochetts for lunch, dinner or week-ends. And crowded however it might be, he could always crowd in one more. 'Come down on Saturday ; we will lodge you in your own room and Jervis Tucker on a sopha,' and he wonders anxiously if Miss Knight will mind being given 'a small room with no dressing-room'. At the same time, his preoccupation with small pleasures near at hand never dimmed the old sea-dog's long-range vision for things not so pleasant, such as the ruin of his whole life's work. 'I have observed the decline of

discipline in the Navy with great pain', the spectacle forcing
from him an even worse admission, 'and I know not the man
who is capable of restoring it'.   For the day of the giants was
passing, the great sea-captains of St. Vincent's school, and their
like has never again appeared in naval history.   At about this
time he offered the downcast Baird another disheartening
nugget : 'Anything in the way of reforming abuses will only
create bitter enemies to yourself.'   He could also add : 'Any
administration that I have ever seen, abhors investigation,'
and certainly he of all people knew what he was talking
about.

Sombre conclusions notwithstanding, he enjoyed life, his
most brilliant latter sally being — at eighty-five — to rent a
house in France.   Hither he and all his household travelled,
'the water so smooth a birch canoe could have made it, and
even Miss Knight [presumably a poor sailor] laughed and
quaffed all the way.'   While in France he visited the Toulon
dockyards by invitation ; refused a salute of cannon on entering its gates ; made a complete conquest of Mme Missiessy,
wife of the commanding admiral, and on his return home was
in such a hurry to get on to English soil that he tripped and
fell.   'I am much shaken,' he admitted to Baird, 'and will
thank you to keep everyone away.'

Such an injunction from him was equivalent to another
man's death-rattle, but shortly afterward, 'I was glad to hear
of the gay doings at Rochetts', wrote a neighbour, so again he
was going on as usual, only more so.   'A sad gloomy day', he
noted once, and produced his remedy : 'nothing for it but
to make good cheer'.   Not many years before, Collingwood
had said that St. Vincent, on his retirement, had no friends.
At about this time Baird, having missed his travelling connections, walked eighteen miles to get to the man who had
no friends.   On another occasion, 'I was seized with a chilli-
ness and other deathlike symptoms, but by the kind and unceasing effort of Miss Brenton and my two nieces in chafing
me incessantly, circulation was restored and I passed a tolerable

night.' The love and concern that sprang to his relief in his mortal need could not have been so ready if he had not done so much for people. And by help of that love, friendship and good cheer which it was his gift to evoke he fought off the enemy for whom — at last — even Baird was no match, and whose coming he watched with much less concern than those about him. Long ago he had said to Mary, in a marvelling voice, 'Our brother has the greatest fear of death I ever saw in any man of good understanding.'

William Boxall was St. Vincent's valet — another figure who would be lost to us if Edward Brenton had not described his beefy, well-fed look, his neat brown livery and brown top-hat with a silver band around it, his sitting stately and imperturbable on the dickey of their travelling carriage abroad, with the gaping French peasants taking him for St. Vincent. Now, on a March morning in 1823, Baird received from this same William Boxall a letter of ominous import.

'Lord St. Vincent has past a very bad night he got very little sleep and cought very much and he his very week this morning and I think it my duty to inform you of it. I did not attemp to get him up till twelve oclock thinking he would get sleep which his Lordship did and he feels but little refresht.'

It was about a week later that Elizabeth Brenton, sitting beside the Admiral's bed, heard him groan half-audibly. At once she rose and approached, soft-footed and soft-voiced, to bend over him and ask, 'Are you in pain ?'

'Not pain,' he said, then after a moment murmured, 'only weariness.'

And he had a right to his weariness, for he had come a long journey.

XI

A FAREWELL FOR THE ADMIRAL

THE stone vault standing in the ancient churchyard about twenty feet from St. Michael's is grown up all around with long coarse grass, tussocky and bumpy. Of a Doric plainness, it has a central portion with a pitched roof and two wings, dark-grey or blackened with age here and there ; the pediment is badly chipped and eaten away, but the rest of it stands solid and foursquare, constructed for eternity. Than this mausoleum nothing could be more sealed, anonymous and neglected. A small tablet inset above the door is just big enough to have contained the name JERVIS and perhaps a date, but is weather-worn to a blankness as complete as if no word had ever been cut into it. With even his name hidden from us, as so much history has hidden from us the real John Jervis, here he lies to all knowledge quite alone, for Martha, that vigorous being whom we do not really know, evinced even in death an un-expected departure from custom ; she wished to be buried with her parents. Accordingly she at Caverswall, six miles off, and he, here at Stone, sleep apart.

With a kind new friend, the Rector of St. Michael's, we stand and stare at the door, apparently once painted brown or black but now bleached grey-white, its surface hackled with splinters and studded thick with rusty nail-heads. Two key-holes a yard apart keep this portal, but no one knows where the keys are, no one knows who has them or ever did have them. Exactly into the left-hand corner of the door a young tree has rooted itself, forced the wood a couple of inches open and cracked the stone door-frame ; a hand and wrist could easily be inserted into the tomb, but memories of M. R. James's ghost stories inhibit this experiment.

Into the church now, a handsome lofty rectangle not so ancient as expected, built in fact about 1760, its whole body filled with Georgian box-pews, and galleries running along each side. The Admiral's memorial, a huge tablet crowded with tiny lettering and surmounted by the Chantrey bust, is high up on the left-hand side as one enters ; standing below it and peering up, a fine view is obtained of the Admiral's chin and the tip of a projecting nose.

Consequently, up a flight of stone steps and into the gallery, which brings him in profile to within a yard or so, and a little below eye-level. The bust shares with some other works of art the exasperating quality of appearing lethally dull at sight but magnificent when photographed. Behind him Chantrey has massed the instruments and accessories that paint the stormy canvas of his career : his speaking-trumpet, an anchor, flags, cannon and cannonballs. But the spacious life passed in a world of far horizons and spread sails and (in the superb sea-language of his day) 'a press of wind blowing fresh' is not to be captured or conveyed by one stone slab, even one as lengthy as this. After the recapitulation of his honours : JOHN JERVIS, EARL OF ST. VINCENT, VISCOUNT ST. VINCENT, BARON JERVIS OF MEAFORD, KNIGHT GRAND CROSS OF THE ORDER OF THE BATH, FIELD MARSHALL, ADMIRAL OF THE FLEET, it goes on to say, in part :

THE GRATITUDE OF THE NATION WAS EXPRESSED
BY VOTES OF BOTH HOUSES OF PARLIAMENT
AND THE CORPORATION OF LIVERPOOL
PRESENTED HIM WITH THEIR FREEDOM
NOW THE JOYFUL ACCLAMATIONS OF HIS COUNTRYMEN
RECEIVED THEIR TRIUMPHANT SANCTION FROM THE ACT
OF AN APPROVING SOVEREIGN
BY WHOM HE WAS PROMOTED TO THE DIGNITY
OF EARL AND VISCOUNT
BY THE TITLE OF THE NAME OF THE PLACE
WHICH FORMED THE SCENE OF HIS GLORY, etc. etc.

The finished oratorical legend keeps its secret — of how many, many versions preceded it, before it was finally handed over to the mason's mallet and chisel. Because a number of these rough drafts are still extant (some on mourning paper) : suggestions for the final epitaph with words crossed out again and again ; then other words weighed, considered, finally rejected and a fresh attempt made. This is one of the first real memorials to him — not the completed stone, but the endless trouble taken by those who loved him and who wanted as much justice done him as possible. The execution of a monument was a long business, the commissioning of the sculptor and so forth, but as late as February 1825 his friends were still corresponding with each other and exchanging copies of the final inscription, meticulously, minutely corrected. With unsleeping vigilance they stood guard over his honour and repute, with unabating anxiety they continued to do for him what they could. They wanted their tribute to be worthy of him ; they wanted him to have the farewell he deserved.

And yet — with all deference to their effort and devotion — the inscription fails to impress as being this ultimate and desired objective. The sounding trumpet of marble is at once too assured and too familiar ; other men have been honoured in this same funereal strophe of the stately and the stereotyped blended. Or at least one ungrateful viewer was unable to suppress the thought : he deserved better than that. A man like John Jervis, Earl of St. Vincent, should have for his Godspeed something more distinct, something belonging to himself alone. The thought takes hold strongly in the silent church, before the Admiral in marble. He knows the place of this true leave-taking, but he will not say where ; we must find it ourselves. To stand before him, we have come a hundred and fifty miles from London. We must take the way back, retracing our steps to explore other places ; to see if there may not exist, in some corner of the United Kingdom, a better farewell for the Admiral.

R

Hardly to be found, is this farewell, in the flood of eulogy that burst out after his death from newspapers, from Parliament, from sources official and unofficial ; emotion true and false, roaring along in a concourse of rounded periods and Latin quotations. 'The intelligence reached the Admiralty on Friday morning. His Lordship was in his eighty-ninth year.' His achievements were re-stated. 'But for that victory [battle of St. Vincent] a French army would have been thrown into Ireland. The discipline which he infused into the naval service contributed to subsequent triumphs, which conferred immortality on Nelson.' The cortège had enormous space in all the public prints, as if grief could somehow be stated in terms of funerary dimension and the extra volume of massed brass bands. Later on a memorial to him was erected by public subscription.

It is the search for this memorial that brings us, at the moment, to a cathedral aisle. Outside the February day drizzles and darkens, overhead looms the vast arching dimness of St. Paul's. The first verger encountered and asked with utmost confidence for the St. Vincent memorial has never heard the name. Equally baffled are his fellow-vergers. On conference among them St. Vincent continues unknown, yet a faint rumour arises that he may be in the North Transept, or in the crypt. The crypt wins, so through a low doorway and down a winding stone stair, collecting two other vergers *en route* ; past subterranean ranks of heroic dead, past Wellington's huge marble catafalque, past the grim thunderous splendours of Wellington's funeral car with its black-and-gilt and wheels in openwork carving, the vergers' gowns bustle on ahead, stopping time and again to scan urns, pedestals, plaques . . . no St. Vincent. Upstairs again by a different flight of marble steps ; more conferences, more head-shakings. No one has ever heard of St. Vincent. Down to the crypt again, the vergers stumped and the first one angry. 'Now I'm determined I'll find him,' he says, squaring his jaw. Photographer's flashlights pierce the gloom ahead, and he stops before a man superintending the work to ask for St. Vincent. The man is stumped likewise, but no less kind than the vergers and no less willing to take trouble. Now into a silent back-of-scenes land, long corridors smelling of stone-dust and chill, areas piled with the aftermath of bombing — 'Mind the planks' — and from a cubbyhole he produces a gentleman who nods, consults a complicated register, and announces that St. Vincent is Number Sixty. Inside a bright tiny office they begin turning over a stack of monster blue-prints, some half the size of tablecloths, and after a long time our new friend emerges with one of these.

'War damage,' he says quietly, and begins the march toward a damaged St. Vincent, through endless dusky reaches with one bare bulb at intervals, through a vast masons' shop piled with blocks of stone and marble, past effigies rearing up in semi-darkness, waiting for arms and noses to be replaced . . . no St. Vincent. Now our guide stops, really at a loss ; glances about, shaking his head. 'I don't know', he murmurs to himself vaguely, steps at random into a sort of tiny bay or jog containing in its gloom one solitary statue, and with an air of last resorts kneels down, peers at an inscription. . . .

'Here he is.'

Here he is indeed, St. Vincent ; double life-size, a standing figure in coat and knee-breeches, a cloak falling from the right shoulder and half concealing a telescope, whose end he rests on a coil of rope beside him. The statue is a heroic-size bore, quenching interest immediately with its sanctimonious face, slight simper and head drooped at a pensive, meaningless angle. Brenton, who hated it, said it had nothing in it of the Admiral, which is easy to believe. This is not the look with which Jervis sized up the Spanish fleet emerging ship by ship through the mists off Cape St. Vincent (*If there are fifty sail, I shall go through them*) : this is not the steely Commander-in-Chief who drove straight for his objectives, trampling down opposition and knocking aside inessentials as if they did not exist. Below the marble feet is a plain tablet with lettering once filled in with black, but now grey and dim : JOHN, EARL OF ST. VINCENT, AS A TESTIMONY OF HIS DISTINGUISHED EMINENCE IN THE NAVAL SERVICE OF HIS COUNTRY AND AS A PARTICULAR MEMORIAL OF THE GLORIOUS AND IMPORTANT NAVAL VICTORY GAINED OVER THE SPANISH FLEET. Across the whole inscription, making it further illegible, runs the splintery crack of German provenance. So here he stands in the most lost of all lost corners of the crypt ; the repairs he needs are slight, he must wait his turn after those more seriously damaged. Wellington's glories are full in view on first entrance into the crypt, yet St. Vincent did as much for England as Wellington ; he gave it a hundred things there has been no time or space to mention — breakwaters, lighthouses, charts filled with safety instead of death-traps of mistakes, in addition to his greatest gift of all to his country — Nelson. No, the dusty forgotten admiral in the dusty forgotten corner is no more that high farewell we have come to seek than the nameless mausoleum at Stone ; again we must go farther and look elsewhere.

'The awful event that has deprived us of our best friend —' these words, from a letter Elizabeth Brenton wrote her brother, are touched with the real pain of bereavement. St. Vincent was nearly ninety, yet no one who knew him was ready to let him go. 'I had the comfort of being with him near four hours during the day,' and she had comfort, too, that he went 'apparently with little pain'. Genuine grief is the best of memorials always, yet even grief like Miss Brenton's falls short of being what we are looking for ; even her love and regret are not the farewell he deserved.

No more was the row that burst out with indecent promptness after his death, when Tucker darted from ambush and fell upon Brenton, and the lightning speed of his pounce suggests how long he had waited to make it. As an executor he demanded certain papers alleged to have been removed by stealth from Rochetts, and threatened an injunction if the documents were not restored. Nevertheless, 'I replied that I would not give them up,' says Brenton, knowing solid ground to be under his feet. The injunction was served on him promptly, and — whether by accident or manipulation — his case came up late on Friday afternoon, and he was ordered to put in his answer on Monday morning. 'An unfair advantage,' Brenton describes this manœuvre, not without reason, but since his counsel were also friends willing to give up their week-end, he was enabled on Monday morning 'to face my enemies, with my affidavits fully prepared'.

Tucker now unveiled the whole of his accusation, which must have come as a shock to all the Brentons. In it he stated that Brenton and Miss Elizabeth Brenton 'surreptitiously or by other unfair means, obtained access to the muniment-room at Rochetts, and copied letters without permission'. For Tucker to bring this charge against Brenton believing in the truth of his charge is perhaps admissible, but for the meanness of implicating Miss Brenton there are no words — the kind pleasant woman who had been the faithful friend of both St. Vincents, who had served and comforted their last moments, and who now was made to look as if she had connived with her brother to lay hands on the property of a senile employer. The great age of St. Vincent gave a plausible colouring to this interpretation ; not everyone was to know how clear-minded he had been, up to the very last.

Tucker having revealed his damaging and offensive charge, it was Brenton's turn to uncover his big gun. His counsel offered in evidence the original notebook containing 'the express written permission of Lord St. Vincent to make copies and extracts'. At a single blow the ground was cut out from under the feet of Tucker and Co., or in Brenton's words, 'they were utterly confounded', which is not remarkable. The sworn statements of Miss Brenton 'further refuted the execu- tors' assertions as to the clandestine copying, and,' continues Brenton, 'my brother, Admiral Sir Jahleel Brenton, deposed that Lord St. Vincent had given me leave to copy his letters,' *specifically* with publication in view. In fact, 'if he had thought

I would not publish them,' the Earl had told Admiral Brenton,
'I should not have had such permission at all.' By this time
the opposing camp, knocked out in the first round, was in
total confusion. 'Lord Giffard told them they had not a leg
to stand on, and the sooner they got out of court the better.
They in consequence prayed to have their bill dismissed with
costs. Thus my Chancery suit which began on Friday,' concludes Brenton, 'ended on the following Thursday, without
costing me a sixpence.' The picture of Tucker having to pay
Brenton's counsel is attractive, but the case did not really end
on Thursday; weeks later Brenton was still being put to the
annoyance of having to write self-justifying letters to the
press : 'In your paper [the *Morning Chronicle*] there is an
imputation that I had "contrived" to obtain access to Lord
St. Vincent's private correspondence. The executors of the
Earl who brought the same charge were compelled to retreat
with precipitation' — and so forth, demonstrating that such
affairs, in spite of all proof of innocence, never pass without
leaving their poisonous residue of doubt. 'Yes, I know
Brenton and his sister were exonerated, but all the same do
you think, *perhaps*. . . .?'

Of such a farewell, on Tucker's part, the Earl might well
have taken a dim view ; certainly he would have been better
pleased with that of Miss Knight. Cornelia Knight's unsparing
output of verse has been mentioned, and the opacity of her
product is such as to repel the most determined reader, but the
present case was different. She had loved the old man and his
wife, and for twenty-four years their house had been her home
whenever she cared to use it as such ; she must have felt not
only grief, but the same cold shiver of eviction that Dr.
Johnson felt when the Thrale household and haven was lost
to him forever. Her emotions were stirred to the depths,
this churning-up process resulting — as frequently happens
— in a degree of expression above her usual level ; certainly her goodbye to St. Vincent seems the best thing she
ever did. The original can still be seen, dated three days after

his death and written on yellowed paper with a quarter-inch mourning border.

> Great, good and wise, farewell!
> Thy course is run.
> Serene and splendid
> Shone thy setting sun—

after which she touches on his kindness : 'The sick were comforted, the poor were fed' — then goes on, much more significantly, to describe what he meant to those who knew him.

> Let realms and seas thy naval glories tell,
> Historians on thy skill and valour dwell ;
> But let thy friends in silent sorrow mourn
> Those social hours that never shall return,
> That warm benevolence, that converse sweet,
> And all that vivified this calm retreat!

In other words : 'Let strangers praise you for what reasons they please, but only your friends know what they have lost.' Bravo, Miss Knight, and certainly one might be inclined to accept her regret as a final and adequate commemoration, or at least to rate it far above the run of similar offerings. But a stubborn dissatisfaction persists : Miss Knight's poem is nearer the mark, but does not quite transfix its centre. Not yet have we discovered his true farewell ; even than this, he deserved better.

And strangely enough, it may be that the wheel has come full circle ; that what we are seeking may be found in the place where the earliest chapter of John Jervis's sea-story began — at the Greenwich Royal Hospital. For it chanced that His Majesty George IV was to embark on his yacht, which was anchored at Greenwich, and it also chanced that a short time before he had sent St. Vincent a bâton, in purple velvet and gold, as Admiral of the Fleet, a title then conferred on only one man. The Earl was eighty-eight at the time, beset by a host of maladies, but nothing could weaken his resolve to thank the King in person. The yacht's point of anchorage made this unexpectedly convenient even for an aged Admiral, since apartments for his use had been permanently reserved in the Hospital for many years past. Accordingly Baird, Tucker and Boxall convoyed him to Greenwich, and he slept there the night of August 9th, 1822.

It also happened that, among the pensioners, were four ancient mariners who had served under St. Vincent. The news that he would be at Greenwich — actually near them and among them — galvanized these old tars with excitement and a high resolve. They would see him once more ; once more they would tender, with full ceremony, their duty and respect to one who had been their leader and their father and one of the greatest seamen of all time.

A warm bed is especially dear to old bones, to old aches and pains and the depletion of sands running out. All such items these four old men could claim in extra degree, since probably some of them were wounded, perhaps crippled, but it made no difference. All they knew was that St. Vincent would rise at his usual ghastly hour, somewhere between 2 and 4 a.m. They had no idea how long they would have to wait, but they were determined to be ready for him, and they waited. Anyone who has felt the night-chill of Greenwich — the river-damp that lays a stranglehold on the throat and extorts a cough from deep in the lungs — can only hope they had a crumb of fire to warm their vigil.

At length, in the pre-dawn of pale summer nights, there was a stirring at the end of some long corridor, a small glimmer of candles or a lantern in the gloom, and on the stone floor the sound of several persons approaching — steps of younger men accommodating themselves to the slower, infirm walker in their midst.

The four old sailors rose and stood at attention, and by now St. Vincent, dim-sighted as he was, had come near enough to see them. In this moment, and who can blame him, his

voice failed as when he had been called on to speak too soon
after Nelson's death. Overwhelmed, he muttered something
under his breath, only this time, by luck, there were those
near enough to hear his salute and thanks — his hail and
farewell — to his remnant of ship's-company : 'We were
smart fellows, in our day.'

No more was said, no more needed to be said. Silently
the four old men fell in, two before him, two behind, marching in decrepit similitude of a brisk unison step. And in this
manner, escorted by this ghostly guard of honour, the old
Admiral went down to his barge on the river for the last
time.

FROM SWYNFEN'S SOLICITORSHIP

CASE

Examinations of William Willson, Robert Ross and Thomas Scudamore, Marines on Board His Majesties Ship Margate, Transmitted by Captain Parker, Commander of said Ship :

Willson : *Between Christmas and New Year's day 1748 I heard two of the people discoursing about desertions, and that there was an Act of Grace forgiving all offenses. John Roberts answered he knew that, otherwise he would not go home. I replied, What the devil are you afraid of? Is it for desertion? He replied, No, it's for killing my own sister. Yes, by God, I killed her between Woolwich and Deptford on account of one Dick Wiles that I caught laying with her, and my brother who was with me shott her, and I cut off her head and left the country 14 or 15 years ago, I was then about 11 or 12 years old.*

Robert Ross : *John Roberts said, he cut her head from her body. I answered, It's a hell of a Jobb. He replied it was so.*

Swynfen's opinion on the eleven-year-old avenger of the family honour : *In this case it will be proper to have Roberts and the several persons who heard his confession of the murder taken before a Justice of the Peace in order to have their examinations taken, and as they appear Roberts will be committed or dyscharged. If committed he may be removed into the county where the murder was committed, in order to take his trial there.*

TO CAPTAIN MOSSE, COMMANDER OF
H.M.'S SHIP *SANDWICH*

March 22, 1797

Sir,

The infection which has existed for some time in H.M. ship *Sandwich*, having of late become more virulent, and resisted the methods taken to check it, which is solely owing to the ship being so crowded, I beg leave to acquaint you that it is absolutely necessary to reduce the numbers of men already on board. The men are in general very dirty, almost naked, and in general without beds.

I feel myself peculiarly called upon to point out the little avail of prescribing medicines to men who are bare of necessities and compelled to mix with the throng by laying on the decks. The number of sores, scalds and other unavoidable accidents often degenerate into bad ulcers which cannot be cured on board, owing sometimes to their bad habits, but often to the foul air they breathe between decks ; beside being frequently trod on in the night from their crowded state.

Sir, it is my professional opinion that there is no effective remedy but by reducing the number that have been kept for months on the *Sandwich*, for sickness and contagion cannot be prevented where 15 or 16 hundred men are confined in the small compass of a ship, many of whom are filthy in their dispositions. The air is so impregnated with human effluvia that contagious fevers must be the consequence.

Bad fortune has often placed me in a situation where I could not practise my profession agreeable to its principles or my own conscience, but I was never in a situation so replete with anxiety than now, as surgeon of the *Sandwich*. I have only to add that the whole of the evil originated in the ship being so crowded, and these men permitted to remain on board to the very great detriment, both physically and morally, of His Majesty's service. I am, Sir,

Your most obedient and humble servant,

JOHN SNIPE.

THE RUNAWAY SLAVE

SLAVERY was an old-established custom in African principalities of minor potentates, emirs and deys, and the slaves, whatever their degree of intelligence, had learned one thing : that English ships anchored frequently in their ports, and that if by any means they could set foot in one of them they were, from that moment, free. The lesson was so well learned and had sunk in so deeply that every year more and more slaves leaped from moles or breakwaters and swam out toward the ships at anchor, from which they were never turned away. Or if they were hauled out of the water by sailors manning a rowboat or launch attached to the larger craft, the practical result as far as they were concerned was the same.

These attempts became so frequent and such numbers of slaves succeeded in this aquatic bid for liberty, in spite of guards on the mole shooting all around them, that H.M.'s government received a combined protest from Algerian and Tunisian slave-owners. Mostly they were noble or wealthy or both and could not be ignored, and as a result of their representations the Admiralty issued to commanders of ships anchoring in African ports a veiled but unmistakable order ; they were somehow to discourage these desperate dashes for freedom by not pulling the slave out of the water, or by any other means prevent him from achieving the crucial objective — actually setting foot in the ship.

Now Jervis was conspicuously iron-clad in his devotion to discipline as the backbone of all naval practice and had even adopted for his own the slogan of a Spanish admiral : Obedience, obedience, obedience. Therefore it was more unthinkable for him than for another to question, let alone reject, the commands of his superiors. In the present case, however, the Admiralty orders made him see red, and he retorted with the following letter, dated June 1798, about a slave who years ago had jumped from the mole into the *Alarm*'s launch, flung his arms about the flag-staff and managed to entangle himself in the folds of the flag : 'He was forced out by the guard on the mole, though he had wrapped the Pendant about his waist. I demanded of the Doge and Senate that the Slave should be brought on board immediately, with the part of the torn Pendant which the Slave carried off with him, and an apology made on the Quarter-deck to the King's Colours. When this was performed I asked the slave what were his sensations when the guard tore him from the Pendant staff ; his reply was, he felt no dread, for he knew that the touch of the Royal Colours gave him freedom.

'From the days of Blake to this hour,' concludes in thunder his blast and rebuke to their Lordships of the Admiralty, 'it has been the pride and glory of His Majesty's Navy to give freedom to slaves, wherever it carried the British flag, and God forbid that such a maxim should fade under me.'

FRIGATES

FRIGATES were the smaller faster craft employed for observation and scouting duty, carrying intelligence, etc., in contrast to the large line-of-battle ships designed for one purpose only — combat. Frigates were also a peculiarly sore spot in the Mediterranean campaign, throughout which Jervis's dispatches constantly bewail, from his first arrival on the station, the shortage of these indispensable ships. To cite the merest few from literally a hundred complaints on this score to the Admiralty :

April 2nd, '98 : He is so continually called on for convoy that this service dangerously reduces the number of his frigates on duty. And again : 'I am extremely distressed for frigates and cutters to keep up extensive communications and to perform other important services'.

The above were general symptoms of his distress. Later he sounds a note of specific warning much more acute, also much more ominous.

May 10th, '98 : 'I beg leave to call your attention to the deficiency of frigates ; less than twenty additional will not be sufficient for the extensive prospective operations.' (The hunt for Napoleon's Armament.)

His plaints were echoed in fullest volume by Nelson during the nerve-racking pursuit : 'July 20th, '98 : [to Sir William Hamilton] I cannot find, or learn beyond vague conjecture, where the French fleet are gone to : all my ill-fortune has proceeded from want of frigates.'

The point is mentioned only to illustrate again the fact that St. Vincent has been held accountable for not supplying Nelson with enough ships of this class.

THE ADMIRAL AND THE GHOST

MARY JERVIS, John's sister, married a man named William Henry Ricketts. This young man's father, who owned extensive property in the West Indies, had been in the habit of sending his son there on long business trips, as his representative. The fact of William Henry's having a nearly-new wife and a brand-new son made no difference; his father continued sending him to the West Indies all the same. It was during one of his long absences from home, in 1765, that the ghost-story began.

Not long before, he and Mary had rented a house in a tiny, remote hamlet called Hinton Ampner. It was a large house, requiring a number of servants, and the Ricketts employed eight. The story of what happened there from 1765 to 1771 can be read in the Manuscript Room of the British Museum. Mary Ricketts, when the trouble began, kept a day-to-day journal of the disturbances. This original and perhaps only copy is bound up by itself, with one or two other pertinent documents included. Mary's detailed, factual and calm (all things considered) recital is perhaps the most extended and authentic account of such occurrences that exists, outside of the account of the Wesley poltergeist. She was, as has been mentioned, a sensible, competent and dependable woman; her mind was orderly and anything but credulous. If anyone, after reading the journal through, can suspect her of having falsified or exaggerated these events over a period of six years, or kept them up for the sake of a cumbersome and pointless hoax, he or she is welcome to do so.

Even before the Ricketts family moved into Hinton Ampner House, some odd stories were fluttering about. The previous tenants had moved out and one Joseph, a groom, had been left there alone as a caretaker. 'Being in bed in the attic, he saw a man in a drab coat with his hands behind his back in the manner his late master held them, looking steadfastly upon him.' Stuff like this failed to impress the Ricketts ; it was how village people talked, and no educated person would be put off any intention of his by such nonsense ; the Ricketts moved in as planned. Some time later William left for Jamaica and would be gone for months, and here the story opens.

Mary begins it, in her methodical way, by listing the names of her eight servants and placing against each name a character sketch in two or three words, such as 'Of reputable parents and virtuous principles' ; 'quiet and regular' ; 'of strict integrity'. She does this, she explains, 'in order to prove the improbability that a set of ignorant country people should league to carry on a diabolical scheme imputed to them so injuriously, and which in truth was far beyond the art and reach of man to compass'. So the first explanation and easiest way out had been — of course — to blame it on the servants, presumably because the experience began with three testimonies by servants.

On a hot, bright summer evening the nurse was sitting in the nursery with the baby Henry, then about eight months old. A door directly opposite the woman opened into Mary's bedroom. She 'plainly saw,' as she afterwards related, 'a gentleman in a drab-colour'd suit of clothes' walk into the room. 'She was no way surprised at the time,' until a housemaid came in on the man's heels, and no one was in the room. Then the nursemaid was frightened, 'as she was thoroughly assured she could no way be deceived, the light being sufficient to distinguish any object clearly.'

The following autumn a man-servant 'crossing the great hall to go to bed, he saw at the other end a man in a drab-coloured coat whom he concluded to be the butler, who wore such coloured clothes, he being lately come and his livery not made.' As with the nursemaid, it never occurred to him to be frightened until he got upstairs to the sleeping-quarters and found the butler and other men-servants in bed.

So much for stories at second-hand : now for Mary's direct experiences. Her bedroom opened on one side into the nursery, on the other into a small lobby or vestibule to the bedroom proper. This had no windows, only a second door to the hall. When she went to bed she not only locked this hall door but also her bedroom door, thus making of the lobby a small sealed enclosure with two

S

locked doors and no other openings of any kind. The door into
the nursery, where the nursemaid slept with the baby, Mary always
left open.

'Some time after Mr. Ricketts had left me,' she begins, 'I heard
the noise of someone walking in the room within.' The room
within was the lobby. Not frightened at this stage, she made it
her business to get up and search the lobby and her room, without
finding anything.

'In the summer of 1770 one night,' Mary continues, 'I had been
in bed half an hour, thoroughly awake and without the least terror
or apprehension on my spirits. I plainly heard the footsteps of a
man, with plodding step, walking toward the foot of my bed.'
This time she shot out of bed and into the nursery, where a rushlight
was burning. She and the maid came back and searched : nothing.
'This alarm perplexed me more than any one preceding, being
within my own room, as distinct as ever I heard, myself perfectly
awake and collected.'

Now the sounds began to increase in character and variety :
'One night I heard three distinct and violent knocks as given with a
club, or something very ponderous, against a door below stairs',
and for a long time after 'I was frequently sensible of a hollow
murmur that seemed to possess the whole house, it was independent
of wind, being equally heard on the calmest nights, and a sound I
had never been accustomed to hear.' And it is true that a house has
its own habitual intonations, like those of a person's voice, and any
real departure from the norm is instantly noticeable.

Four weeks later 'I waked between one and two oclock' by
her watch, lying on a bedside table under a rushlight. 'I lay
thoroughly awake some time, and then heard one or more persons
walking to and fro in the lobby adjoining. I got out of bed and
listened at the door for twenty minutes, in which time I distinctly
heard them walking.' She woke the nursemaid and they ventured
into the lobby, whose door they found shut and locked 'as it was
every night'.

'I stood in the middle of the room pondering with much
astonishment', she continues, 'when suddenly the door into my
bedroom sounded as if ployed to and fro by a person standing
behind it. This was more than I could bear—' and she stirred up
all the men-servants, who found doors and windows locked and

bolts shot, as usual. The night of May 7th the noises were so loud
and continuous 'I could not sleep, apprehending it the prelude to
some greater noise.' In the night chill of the house, in the deep
country silence, the frightened woman got up and stood at the
lobby door a half-hour, when suddenly 'the great hall door directly
underneath was clapped to with the utmost violence, so as to shake
my room perceivably.'

Now Mary resorted to another expedient: she had a maid
sleep in the same room with her, and both women heard the same
disturbances. 'I could not discover the least appearance of trick',
reaffirms Mary. 'On the contrary, I became convinced it was
beyond the power of any mortal agent to perform. After mid-
summer the noises became every night more intolerable and were
heard till after broad day in the morning.'

Now they mounted to a nerve-shrinking climax:

'I could frequently distinguish articulate sounds, and usually a
shrill female voice would begin, then two others with deeper and
warlike [quarrelsome? hostile?] tone seemed to join in, yet tho'
this discourse sounded as if close to me, I never could distinguish
words.'

Horrid, that malign conversation at her very elbow, loud yet
incomprehensible gibberish. 'Walking, talking, opening and clap-
ping of doors was repeated every night', she continues, then notes
that her brother's ship had anchored at Portsmouth and he had
spent a few days with her and apparently noticed nothing, and she
hated to burden his brief visit with a recital of her own worries,
especially of so incredible a nature: 'So great was my reluctance
to relate anything beyond the bounds of probability that I could not
bring myself to disclose my situation to the friendly brother who
could most essentially serve and comfort me.'

But the very night that John had gone back to Portsmouth,
'I heard with infinite astonishment, the most loud deep tremendous
noise which seemed to rush and fall with infinite velocity and force
on the lobby floor adjoining my bedroom. I started up and called
to Goden [the nursemaid] Good God! did you hear that noise!'
Goden had, and was half-dead with fright. 'Just at that instant we
heard a shrill and dreadful shriek repeated three or four times,
growing fainter and descending until it seemed to sink into the
earth.'

Hannah Streeter, a friend of Mary's who was also sleeping next door in the nursery, 'was so appalled that she lay for two hours almost deprived of sense and motion'. This lady had been merrily derisive of Mary's tale of disturbances and 'had rashly expressed a desire to hear more of them'. Hannah had invited something, and it came. 'From then on until she quitted the house there was scarce a night that she did not hear some person walk toward her door and push against it, as though attempting to force it open.' This horror was the last straw, added to which broken rest and getting in and out of bed at all hours of the night had induced in Mary 'a slow fever and deep cough ; my health was impaired but my resolution firm.' It could be John Jervis himself speaking ; Mary, in fact, decided she had no choice but to tell the whole affair to her brother, whom she expected soon on a second visit.

'The next week I was comforted by the arrival of my brother.' One can believe it, a sturdy, sensible, no-nonsense man like John. At the breakfast table, after his first night in her house, she approached the matter indirectly by regretting that the servants had been noisy last night. Jervis said he had not heard them ; this inequality of hearing extra-normal disturbances appears also in the Wesley journal of phenomena. Then, falteringly, she went on to say that she was going to tax his powers of credulity and that he must trust her. 'He replied it was scarce possible to doubt anything I might say.' This argues well for John's confidence in her. 'I began my narrative, to which he attended with utmost astonishment.' One might think so, and in the meantime a neighbour, Captain Luttrell, had come over for breakfast and eagerly offered to help investigate the causes of the disturbance.

That night Jervis and his hard-bitten sailor servant, John Bolton, checked the door and window fastenings of every room in the house, 'particularly those on the first and second story, examining every place of concealment'. Then he went to bed in Mary's bedroom ; Luttrell and Bolton sat up in another room. Mary went to bed in a third room, with Goden the maid for company. 'So soon as I lay down, I heard a rustling as of a person close to the door.' Almost simultaneously she heard Luttrell, rooms away, call, 'Who goes there ?' The same sound, presumably, was approaching the room where he was, and almost at the same moment she heard Jervis shout, from her bedroom, 'Look against my door!'

'He had heard,' says Mary, 'the continuance of the same noise reaching his door, as if someone were walking from room to room.'

The night-vigil yielded nothing more conclusive, except that now the antics went on in broad daylight, 'doors opened and slammed violently to'. John had seen and heard more than enough to convince him, but he had no advice to offer Mary except his opinion that she should move elsewhere as soon as possible. Then his leave was over and he had to go, but the experience remained on his mind ; his letters of this period never stop asking about the trouble and reiterating his conviction that she should get herself and her family out of the house. Mary's final experiences included 'a very extraordinary effect I had frequently observed on a favourite cat that was usually in the parlour with me, and when sitting on table or chair with accustomed unconcern, she would suddenly slink down with the greatest terror, conceal herself under my chair and put her head close to my feet'. Very uncatlike behaviour, one would think. 'In a short space of time she would come forth quite unconcerned.'

The Ricketts family had no desire to undertake the burden and expense of moving house, but at last, after six years of disturbances, were literally driven to it. After they left, the hullaballoo burst out unrestrained and became so violent and so continuous that people passing the house heard it at any hour and stopped to listen, and villagers opined gravely that 'they' were having a rare ol' time in thurr. The agent who managed the property for the owners was infuriated, finding himself unable to rent the house or even engage a caretaker for it. Desperately factual, he clung with a death-grip to the theory of malicious mischief involving a number of local confederates, and in his attempts to apprehend them wrote out, and had fastened up in all the churches, the Notice of Reward that forms the end-papers of this book.

Many years later Martha, Lady St. Vincent, visited Hinton Ampner. In her tiny precise handwriting she described its lonely situation, 'the most retired hamlet one can imagine', but the house had had to be pulled down long since ; they showed her the site. That the owners should have been compelled to a step so drastic testifies to the gravity of the disturbances, for the house was a valuable property ; enormous, as is shown by a neat ground-plan drawn by Mary and included with the story of the haunting.

A last echo of the affair reaches us forty-seven years later, at St. Vincent's breakfast-table at Rochetts, where the subject came up — as such things do again and again, sources of interest and speculation never exhausted. Mary Ricketts happened to be present, and one guest suggested that the noise was of smugglers, an idea that she indignantly repelled. Another guest went on to hint that the whole story had been exaggerated, and gave the Countess (Martha) as the source of this statement. 'The Countess', Mary returned with asperity, 'could have told you no such thing.'

It was left for St. Vincent himself to put a final — and characteristic — period to this tabletalk ; a stubborn old resident of Hinton Ampner had evolved his own idiotic explanation and stuck to it doggedly over the years, and now St. Vincent remembered and offered it.

'A neighbouring clergyman said it was the commerce of the sexes.'

The Earl said this very, very seriously ; it is left for us to imagine the accompanying twinkle.

All the same it is curious that John Jervis and Mary Ricketts, considering their types, should have had an encounter with a genuine ghost.

BIBLIOGRAPHY

Manuscript Sources

Minutes of the Directors of Greenwich Royal Hospital, 1747–60, Admiralty 67-19.   Public Record Office.

Admiralty Solicitors' Dockets, Admiralty 1-3676.   Public Record Office.

Mediterranean Dispatch Books, 1795–99.   Public Record Office.

Admiralty 1-395
396
397
398
399
400

Wages Book of Sloops and Frigates, Admiralty 33-399.   Public Record Office.

Common Pleas, Geo. III, 65-67 : 43 Geo. III, No. 802. Public Record Office.

King's Bench 122 : Membrane 2074.   Public Record Office.

High Court of Admiralty Docket : 3688.   Public Record Office.

St. Vincent Papers.   British Museum MS. Room.

29,910
29,911
29,912
29,914
29,915
29,916
29,917
29,918
29,920
30,003 (The proposal by proxy, p. 213)
30,006
30,010
30,011 (Hinton Ampner Haunting)
30,012
31,193

The Nepean File. National Maritime Museum.

Letters of the Earl of St. Vincent to Dr. Andrew Baird. National Maritime Museum.

Miscellaneous uncatalogued documents left by Tucker in 1825, comprising hundreds of items : letters (mostly copies), household bills, and an extensive handwritten memorandum on Baird. Admiralty Library.

Notes on Scurvy and Typhus, lent by General Sir William MacArthur, D.S.O., R.A.M.C.

PRINTED SOURCES

A Social History of the Navy. Michael Lewis.

The Bourbons of Naples. Harold Acton.

The Nelson Collection at Lloyd's. Warren Dawson.

Collingwood's Letters and Dispatches. Navy Record Society.

Nelson's Letters to His Wife. Navy Record Society.

St. Vincent's Letters 1801–5. Navy Record Society.

Letters of English Seamen. Navy Record Society.

Nelson's Letters and Dispatches. Nicholas.

Nelson's Letters and Dispatches. Laughton.

Nelson. Carola Oman.

Nelson's Captains. Ludovic Kennedy.

The Durable Monument. Admiral Sir William James.

Old Oak. Admiral Sir William James.

Memoirs of the Earl of St. Vincent. Tucker.

Life of Earl St. Vincent. Brenton.

The Battle of St. Vincent. Drinkwater.

The Floating Republic. Mainwaring and Dobree.

The Naval Mutinies of 1797. Conrad Gill.

House of Commons Naval Enquiry. Public Record Office.

The Expedition to Cartagena. Smollett.

Pamphlet on Victualling, DA 102. Admiralty Library.

London *Times,* Oct. 5th, 1799. Central Reference Library, Westminster.

London *Times,* Oct. 8th, 1799. Central Reference Library, Westminster.

Glasgow *Courier* ; undated excerpt, copied in a contemporary hand and lent by Sir Simon Campbell-Orde.

Mariner's Mirror, vol. 39, pp. 306–7 (1953).

INDEX

PRINTED BY R. & R. CLARK, LTD., EDINBURGH

Whareas some evil dispose

severel Months past freequ

in the mantion house occup

ffenton ampner. This is

or persons will Discover th

to me such person or pers

of Fifty Guineas. to be

offenders. or if any person

Will Discover his or her

therein such person Shall

the Same Reward. to be paid